THE SPIRIT-FILLED BELIEVER'S TOPICAL BIBLE

Reference Edition

W0010628

Harrison House
Tulsa, Oklahoma

Unless otherwise indicated, all Scripture quotations are taken from the *King James Version* of the Bible.

The following prayers are taken from *Prayers That Avail Much®* *Volume 1*, Copyright © 1989 by Word Ministries, Inc., Atlanta, Georgia: "Prayer for Salvation," "Spirit-Controlled Life," "Prayer for Health and Healing," "Prayer To Watch What You Say," and "Prayer for Prosperity."

The following prayers are taken from *Prayers that Avail Much®*, *Volume 2*, Copyright © 1988, 1991 by Word Ministries, Inc., Atlanta, Georgia: "Commitment To Put on the Armor of God," "Praise," "Prayer for Commitment To Pray," "Prayer for Being Equipped for Success," and "Prayer for Hedge of Protection."

Old Testament Hebrew research provided by David Michael. New Testament Greek research provided by Dick Mills.

3rd Printing
Over 28,000 in Print

The Spirit-Filled Believer's Topical Bible Reference Edition
ISBN 1-57794-350-3
Copyright © 1992 by Harrison House
P. O. Box 35035
Tulsa, Oklahoma 74153

Presented to

_____

By

_____

Date

_____

Occasion

_____

Contents

PART I

How To Study the Bible

THE INSPIRED WORD OF GOD

Nautical charts are used by sailors and maps are used by road travelers as their guidebooks and keys to their final destinations. Christians have a map and guidebook that is far superior to any other in the world—the Bible. This book is not just a great piece of literature; it is the main ingredient to a successful Christian life. The Bible should be read daily, consulted constantly and studied carefully. The Scriptures are the inspired Word of God. Second Timothy 3:16,17 says:

All scripture is given by inspiration of God, and is profitable for doctrine, for reproof, for correction, for instruction in righteousness: That the man of God may be perfect, throughly furnished unto all good works.

It is obvious from this passage that the Lord gave us His Word for specific reasons: to confirm our beliefs, to set spiritual and moral guidelines, to give

11

us godly inspiration and wisdom for our daily living, and to instruct us in the ways of our Father. We cannot draw these things from the Word of God without daily study.

Principles of Bible Study

There are many ways to study the Bible, each with its own merit. Below are a few principles that will help you study earnestly.

1. *Always have the right attitude toward studying your Bible.* Approach your daily study with an open heart and mind. Be ready to accept what the Lord has to show you.

2. *Realize that studying your Bible isn't always easy.* Sometimes reading and studying is hard work. Make yourself be consistent and faithful to daily study, and be a diligent student of God's Word. A systematic approach to Bible study can help you overcome difficult periods in your study times.

3. *Keep a record of what you have learned.* Write down what the Lord reveals to you during your study times. This will help you put your new wisdom to practice and provide a permanent record for you to refer to when you need it.

4. *Share with others what you have learned.* Often, if you are willing, the Lord will show you a problem's solution that someone else can use, too. His wisdom is too wonderful to be kept hidden. Encourage someone else by sharing with him how your study time has strengthened you.

5. *Your study time is meant to add to worship and teaching services, not replace them.* This is your private, personal time for you to learn what your Father has in store for you, but it is meant to augment your fellowship at church and other meetings with believers. Your personal study time is not meant to be your only source of fellowship with the Lord.

6. *Find a consistent time and place to study.* For example, you might start with ten to fifteen minutes a day with an eventual goal of thirty minutes. Many people prefer to study in the mornings so that they can be receptive to God and His wisdom throughout the day. The key is to find what works for you.

7. *Be in an attitude of prayer while you read.* Ask the Holy Spirit to be your guide through the Scriptures. The Holy Spirit was given to help

you grow in relationship with the Father, and that includes Bible study!

If you are just beginning to study, here are some methods to help you start on a lifetime adventure of reading and studying the most exciting Book ever written—your Bible.

METHODS OF BIBLE STUDY

Suggested study tools:

—*The Word Study Bible*

—A Bible concordance, such as *Strong's*[1]

—A Bible dictionary

—An expository dictionary, such as *Vine's*[2]

• Daily Devotionals

Think of your Bible as a workbook to be studied until the pages are worn out. This workbook is for you to mark in, draw from, and glean great wisdom from. As you read a passage of Scripture, ask the Holy Spirit what the Father has for you, what truth you are to learn this day.

Mark the passage if the Holy Spirit reveals something meaningful to you. This allows you to remember how you have grown spiritually when you read this passage again in the future. It will stand as a memorial to the Father's faithfulness to you. You may want to mark the passages in different colors in correlation with the symbols used in *The Word Study Bible*.

For example, establish that as you read, you will mark all passages with the symbol for the Holy Spirit (the dove) with a yellow pen. If the Lord reveals new truth to you about the Holy Spirit, mark the verse you were reading that led to the new truth. This will help you record what you have learned from the Holy Spirit through the entire Bible.

The daily devotional is the building block upon which all other methods of Bible study begin. To neglect a devotional time with your Bible is to undercut all other study efforts. Besides, it is your chance for God to reveal His Word to you personally!

• Word Studies

Sometimes you may routinely read a passage and think you understand it, but the Bible tells us that there are "mysteries hidden" deep within the Word. That is why it is valuable to do word studies. This means studying different key words in a passage, for example, *love* or *discipline*. You can look these words up in a dictionary, or Bible dictionary, or find their original meaning in the Greek and/or Hebrew by using a *Strong's Exhaustive Concordance* or similar study tool. Then examine how the words are used in other verses in the Bible.

—Does the word meaning vary from book to book, Old Testament to New Testament?

—Does the word mean more than what we assume it means?

—How does it apply to life today?

• Topical Studies

When you want to learn more about what the Bible says about a given subject, such as healing, then do a topical study. Use the "Topical Concordance" and look up the verses which contain the theme that you are interested in studying. After you look them up, write these verses out in a notebook leaving space between each one. As you go back to study the verses, be sure to read them in the context of the chapter and book in which they are written.

• Character Studies

What made the great men and women of old memorable? How did they develop their faith in God?

One way to understand the godly characters of the Bible and what motivated them is to do a character study. For example, you can study the life of Moses. Follow his life from birth to death in the Old Testament noting the things he did and how he responded to the people around him. Ask questions about his life:

—What gave him the strength to handle persecution the way he did?

—Why did he find favor in God's sight?

• Book Studies

For a change from topical or character studies, you may want to study one complete book at a time. Every book in the Bible is valuable and has a different purpose. Start with a book that will interest you. Ask these questions:

—Who wrote the book?

—Why was it written?

—When was it written?

—To whom was it written?

—What is the key verse?

—What are the key thoughts?

—What is the theme?

—What are the major problems?

—What solutions were given?

—How does it apply to my life today?

Next, do a chapter study. First summarize the chapter and outline it. Start with the first chapter and go through each verse. Compare these verses in several translations to fully understand what the author intended. Next, look at how each chapter relates to the other chapters and to the entire book. Make notes in your personal journal of particular phrases or ideas that you believe God is impressing on you. Set simple goals that you can easily achieve. Start with a simple book like Jonah and progress to the more complex books like Ezekiel and Revelation.

God wants His Word in you, and book studies are an excellent way to accomplish this. You don't have to try to tackle the whole Bible at once; allow the Holy Spirit to lead you in what to study. He knows what you need and what those with whom you come into contact will need.

- Studying the Psalms

The psalms provide a rich Bible study because they are a collection of inspired Hebrew poetry which describe the worship and spiritual experiences of the Jewish people. David is considered to be the author of a majority of the psalms. Many of the psalms show man pouring out his heart in prayer and praise to God for Who He is and for what He has done for man. Generally throughout the psalms, the authors praise and worship God in all circumstances when times are good or bad.

There are several approaches to studying the psalms. One is to start from the beginning and study them as you would any other book. A second approach is to study them according to the six types of psalms:

—Psalms of instruction

—Psalms of praise and adoration

—Psalms of thanksgiving

—Devotional psalms

—Messianic psalms

—Historical psalms

Find the central message or theme of the psalm. Notice the action verbs used. Always look for applications to your own life.

Another approach is to do a word study as you study the psalms (see "Word Studies" on pages 18 and 19).

Notice the words that are frequently used, such as the word *blessed*. Also, notice how often certain verses or words or phrases are repeated over and over for emphasis.

- Studying the Proverbs

The best book on practical wisdom to live by is the book of Proverbs. The purpose of the book stated in the beginning is to impart wisdom. These timeless principles are as important today as they were in the day when they were written. Proverbs says that the beginning of wisdom is the fear of the Lord. (Prov. 9:10.)

There are several approaches to studying Proverbs. Look for the major theme as you would with the psalms study. Then look for repeated phrases or words used for emphasis. Answer the question, "What is the lesson taught and how does it apply to my life?"

Proverbs is filled with practical word studies on topics such as wisdom, self-control, marriage, immorality, strong drink, a good name, youth and discipline, business matters, friendship, and words and the tongue.

- Studying With the Holy Spirit

Another way of studying the Bible is to sit and read it aloud to yourself. Reading aloud will still your mind so that it must listen to what the Scripture is saying. Read a whole book at a time to grasp the flavor of what is being said. Remember that, especially in the New Testament, many of the books are actually letters written to people.

The Bible tells us that the Holy Spirit will teach us things (John 14:26.) For the Holy Spirit to teach you, He needs some material with which to work. This is why Christians need to fill themselves with God's Word. The Holy Spirit will never reveal anything that cannot be confirmed by the Word of God.

Certain prayers that Paul prayed for other Christians in his epistles (Eph. 1:18-20, Eph. 3:14-20, and Col.1:9-11) will allow the Holy Spirit to illuminate God's Word to your heart and mind. Look up these prayers and pray them for yourself, putting your name in the prayer. This allows the Holy Spirit the opportunity to reveal the Word to you.

One important point to remember when studying the Bible is to prepare for revelation. Paul wrote in First Corinthians 3:6 that he planted, and Apollos watered, but God gave the increase. What did Paul plant with? What did Apollos water with? The Word of God. It is our job to plant the Word of God and water with the Word of God, but it is God's job to give the increase. Do your part by reading the Bible, and let God increase your knowledge.

Remember, you cannot give yourself deeper understanding; another man cannot give you deeper understanding; only the Holy Spirit can give you deeper understanding. Don't push for it; just prepare. Read the Word of God, pray the Word of God and wait on the Word of God. It will reveal itself to you.

These methods are simply plans and ideas for reading the Bible. They are to help make your study times easier and more efficient, but they cannot do the reading for you. It is up to you to make a conscious effort to read and study God's Word. You have the key to great victory, joy, love, and eternal life in your hands. Don't neglect this opportunity to know your Father more than ever before. May God bless and quicken you as you study His Word.

[1] James Strong, *The Exhaustive Concordance of the Bible* (Nashville: Abingdon, 1890).

[2] W.E. Vine, *Expository Dictionary of Old and New Testament Words* (Old Tappan: Fleming H. Revell, 1981).

Prayer for Studying the Word

Father, I pray and confess Your promises over my Bible study. I ask that You grant me the diligence and patience to study and show myself approved unto You. As I search the Scriptures daily, I ask that the Holy Spirit help me to discern rightly the word of truth, preparing me to receive all of Your Word. I am aware that all Scripture is Your inspiration, and that it is profitable for doctrine, reproof, correction and instruction and it opens me to good works.

I pray that You order my progress through the Word. Father God, I gladly choose to make Your commandments my standards, and will trust and rely upon the incorruptible seed of Your Word. I am open to Your Word and pray for understanding and knowledge, confessing that Your Word was sent to heal and deliver Your people from any destruction.

Father, I thank You that as I hear Your Word, my faith increases and I experience greater wisdom, becoming a doer of the Word, not a hearer only. As I study Your Word and treasure it in my heart, I have the strength to resist sin and realize that whatever I ask of You, You will do. Thank You, Lord, for the strength and wisdom which come from Your Word!

Part I is taken from *The Word Bible* (Tulsa: Harrison House, 1990), pp. xx-xxiv.

PART II

GETTING INTO THE WORD

SALVATION

Conversion and Soulwinning

I'll guarantee you that if you will make it a practice to win souls for God, the sweet tender compassion of the Lord will boil up out of your spirit like a spray of water—a well of water springing up out of your innermost being.

— Norvel Hayes

Greek and Hebrew Word Studies

OLD TESTAMENT—*YESHUW'AH*

And he said, It is a light thing that thou shouldest be my servant to raise up the tribes of Jacob, and to restore the preserved of Israel: I will also give thee for a light to the Gentiles, that thou mayest be my *salvation (yeshuw'ah)* unto the end of the earth.

Isaiah 49:6

NEW TESTAMENT—*EPISTREPHO*

Let him know, that he which *converteth* (*epistrepho*) the sinner from the error of his way shall save a soul from death, and shall hide a multitude of sins.

James 5:20

You are not supposed to think opposite from the Spirit. When you lose your vision of winning lost souls for God, then you are no longer thinking like the Holy Spirit—you're thinking like yourself.

That which is born of the Spirit is spirit. You are supposed to have the same kind of vision that the Holy Spirit has, the same kind of compassion and faithfulness that the Lord Jesus Christ Himself had, because you have the same Spirit in you that He had in Him.

If the Spirit of God is in your heart, then you will be moved to share Jesus with others. If you have not been doing that, then it's time to begin. You can do it. God's power is available to you to save people or heal them or do anything else that needs to be done for them.

— Norvel Hayes
The Word Bible[1]

Salvation—*Yeshuw'ah*

The Old Testament is a vibrant record of the salvation God demonstrated continually for His people. The saving acts (or deliverances) of God were rehearsed in poems, sung in praises, and danced about in celebrations. They were taught by parents to their eager children every Passover, recounted in prayers, and taught by the elders. They were referred to—and prophesied about—by the prophets, and generally were in the mouths of the Israelites day and night!

There are several Hebrew words for "deliver," "rescue" and "save." The main word in which we are interested now is *yeshuw'ah* (pronounced "yesh-oo′-aw"), #3444 in *Strong's*. It is a feminine passive participle formed from the verb *yasha'* ("yaw-shah′"), #3467 in *Strong's*, meaning to save, rescue, deliver, help, preserve; to bring into a spacious or broad place; to be set free from danger, distress, or tightly confined places.

From *yasha'*, the verb, are derived two important nouns, both pronounced similarly. The masculine noun is the name *Yeshuwa'* ("yay-shoo′-ah"), #3442 in *Strong's*. This was a name of several Israelites in both Testaments. But, most importantly, it is the name by which our Lord was known throughout His lifetime on earth.

Yeshuwa' is transliterated *Iesous* in Greek and from there *Iesus* in Latin, *Jesu* in German, and finally *Jesus* in English. By the time the name *Jesus* arrived in the English language, it had passed through all the above languages, changing each time the Scriptures were translated into a new tongue. But *Yeshuwa'* was His name.

The feminine passive participle *yeshuw'ah* has only a final "h" at the end to distinguish it from the name *Yeshua*. This participle is the main subject of our study. It has been translated "deliverance, victory, rescue, salvation, help, saving health, welfare, liberation." This marvelous participle is found 77 times in the Old Testament. Many times it occurs in beloved and familiar passages.

Its first occurrence was in Genesis 49:18, found among the last words of Jacob: "I have waited for thy *salvation*, O Lord."

Compare Isaiah 25:9: **"And it shall be said in that day, Lo, this is our God; we have waited for him, and he will save us: this is the Lord; we have waited for him, we will be glad and rejoice in his *salvation*."** Notice that the context (vv. 6-8) refers to the coming of Jesus the Savior to judge the world, resurrect the dead, and turn dishonor away from Israel.

How precious is their response to these immeasurable kindnesses: "This is our God!"

The word *yeshuw'ah* refers both to those deliverances which a human hero can achieve for his people, and to those saving deeds which God accomplishes. However, in Scripture there are only a handful of examples wherein *yeshuw'ah* is used to describe a deliverance brought about by a human champion. (The Heavenly Champion, the Savior, is the same One Whose name *is* "Salvation—*Yeshuwa'*, the Lord—able to save us to the uttermost degree.)

While the false gods are derided in Hebrew Scripture as being unable to save, the Lord God of Israel is mighty to save. His praises reflect this very aspect of His power. Deuteronomy 33:29 says, **"Happy art thou, O Israel: who is like unto thee, O people *saved* by the Lord, the shield of thy help, and who is the sword of thy excellency!"**

Several verses state that God is our *salvation*. Psalm 27:1 says: **"The Lord is my light and my *salvation*; whom shall I fear? the Lord is the strength of my life; of whom shall I be afraid?"** Compare the beautiful prayer of David in Psalm 35:3 in which he prays for deliverance from his enemies and beseeches

God, *"...say unto my soul, I am thy salvation."* (See also Job 13:16.)

The Old Testament presents salvation in several levels. There are the saving deeds of the Lord, which is rescue or deliverance from danger. He accomplished this on an individual level, as when He saved David out of the hands of his enemies, and on a national level, as at the Red Sea.

The eventual salvation of Israel is a fundamental promise of both the Old and New Testaments. It will mean their deliverance, finally and forever, from all satanic attempts to annihilate, harass, condemn, belittle, and oppress them. That salvation will eternally be theirs when the Redeemer comes to Zion and turns away ungodliness from Jacob. (Rom. 11:26.)

It is a part of God's plan of redemption which is so vitally connected to His heart that there can be no destruction to His plan for Israel's full salvation without destroying His overall plan for the human race! Jesus was declaring plainly God's integral role for the people of Israel in the plan of salvation when He declared to the Samaritan lady, *"...salvation is of the Jews"* (John 4:22).

Jesus was ordained from the beginning to be Israel's Savior and Redeemer, and there is abundant witness to this unchangeable fact in hundreds of Scripture verses. What makes our theme verse such a key Scripture for understanding God's means of salvation is that it shows the Lord's thoughts on Israel's salvation relative to world salvation.

> **And he said, It is a light thing that thou shouldest be my servant to raise up the tribes of Jacob, and to restore the preserved of Israel: I will also give thee for a light to the Gentiles, that thou mayest be my *salvation* (yeshuw'ah) unto the end of the earth.**

Isaiah 49:6

In this verse the Lord God addresses the Messiah. He informs Him that the honor of being Israel's Savior, awesome though that is, will not in itself be adequate to honor Zion's Redeemer the way God desires to honor Him. So Messiah must also become God's salvation to all nations!

The New Testament maintains this dual purpose for our Savior's sacrificial death in many instances. One example is that Jesus is called both the Savior of Israel and the Savior of the world. It is of further interest that the apostles took God's words in Isaiah 49:6 and pluralized the prophecy to include themselves as messengers who would help further its fulfillment. (Acts 13:47-49.)

Let us briefly look at a few more verses in which *yeshuw'ah* appears.

In Isaiah 12:2,3 we find that the Lord Jehovah **"is become my *salvation* (*yeshuw'ah*)."** This is a clear indication that God would *become* salvation for us and that the Deliverer's name would be *Salvation*. Verse 3 exclaims that the result of God's becoming our salvation is joy as we draw water from salvation's wells. Who can miss the Messianic applications of these verses after comparing John, chapter 4, and John 7:37-39?

Isaiah 51:6,8 shows God's salvation will be an everlasting salvation, one that endures through unending generations.

Isaiah 52:7 indicates the Messiah's message would be salvation. For Him to publish or spread the Good News, His beautiful feet would have to walk from mountain to mountain, from village to town, and into Jerusalem itself.

Verse 10 in the same chapter prophesies that God's salvation is something the entire world will someday see. It is not going to be hidden in some corner; it is going to be a dazzling, splendid display of God's goodness which every nation on earth shall behold.

The Author of that salvation shall all the tribes of the earth seek, and His rest shall be glorious! Thank God forever! His salvation is so much more magnificent than we have ever dreamed.

Ezekiel 37:23 should be mentioned, for in this verse we have an Old Testament reference to being saved from sins. The Old Testament records God's deliverance from all kinds of dangers, something from which we need to be rescued. But this verse shows that the Hebrews also understood how God delivers us from sin.

For further examples of *yeshuw'ah*, see its use in Isaiah 59:17, Psalm 18:50 (translated "deliverance"), Psalm 67:2 ("saving health") and Psalm 149:4.

There are several Old Testament words for "deliver" and others for "redeem," most notably *gaal* ("gaw-al"), #1350 in *Strong's*. The word "redeemer" comes from this primary root and occurs in such verses as Job 19:25 and Isaiah 59:20. But *yeshuw'ah* is the most pertinent Hebrew word for describing God's loving, saving, protecting, rescuing way with His creation, most especially with His children, those whom He redeems or rescues from the hand of the enemy.

The final reference we will quote is Psalm 21:1, describing David's delight in the salvation of God: "The king shall joy in thy strength, O Lord; and in thy *salvation* how greatly shall he rejoice!"

Greek Words for *Convert/Conversion* in the *Authorized Version*

Three Greek words are translated "convert/conversion" in the *Authorized Version*. They are *strepho*, *epistrophe*, and *epistrepho*. In many verses the words *turn*, *turn around*, and *turn back* are used frequently in the *Authorized Version*. Our English word *apostrophe* originates from this series of words.

Strepho—Verb

Matthew 18:3 says, **"Verily I say unto you, Except ye be *converted (strepho)*, and become as little children, ye shall not enter into the kingdom of heaven."**

Strepho ("streff'-o"), #4762 in *Strong's*, appears 18 times in the *Authorized Version*. Only once is it translated "converted." The remaining 17 times the word "turn" is used. Turning around is the basic thought behind *strepho*.

Grammarians define *strepho* as twisting, reversing, turning around, to change course, to change direction, to steer animals, to turn soldiers around, to wheel horses around to alter or transform a person, and to turn a non-believer into a believer.

Hermann Cremer in his *Theological Dictionary* implies that *strepho* is a moral and religious transformation that contrasts what you are changing to with what you have been changed from.[2] In other words, what we were changed from makes the conversion experience more emphatic.

Other grammarians define *strepho* as a turn over, an alteration, adopting a new course of life, and becoming another man.

Strepho says, "God says, 'Repent (change your mind) and be converted (change your direction).'" We cannot save ourselves, but we can cooperate with the Lord. His salvation enables us to change our minds and also helps us to change our direction. We confess our sins and our need for salvation, acknowledging Him as the only One Who can save us. Then His blood cleanses us and His Spirit witnesses to us that we have been accepted by Him, forgiven by Him and regenerated.

Strepho describes the whole process of turning from the downward road to hell to the upward road to heaven. John 1:12 and Romans 1:16 tell us that only the power of God can produce the turnaround.

Epistrepho—Verb

Epistrepho ("ep-ee-stref'-o"), #1994 in *Strong's*, appears 39 times in the *Authorized* and *Revised English Versions*. In James 5:20 we read, **"Let him know, that he which *converteth (epistrepho)* the sinner from the error of his way shall save a soul from death, and shall hide a multitude of sins."**

Epistrepho is more intensive than *strepho*. *Epi* means "towards," as in epicenter, epilogue, or epigram. *Strepho* means "turn." The lexicons define *epistrepho* as turning back, returning, a complete turnaround to correct a situation by returning to your original state, and personally turning from ignorance and error to the true worship of the Living God.

Epistrepho is not a mere external change from one religion to another. In the New Testament it always means the whole-hearted turning of your total personality from pride, rebellion and a lawless lifestyle to right living, with God having full control of your life.

Epistrepho is the best word to describe the dramatic change when we turn from darkness to light, from

Satan to the Savior, from death to life. In Luke 22:32 Jesus told Peter, **"...when thou art *converted (epistrepho)*, strengthen thy brethren."**

It is not enough to turn back to God. We must also turn others. Not only can we share in the work of converting sinners to Jesus Christ, but we can rejoice every time we hear of souls brought into the Kingdom of God. *Epistrepho* is an ongoing work of redemption in the world. As Christians we all are a part of this great plan of saving the lost.

Epistrepho tells us as Jesus told Peter, "After you have been *converted*, you are now ready to strengthen the weak and struggling people in your society by imparting the good news that they too can be *converted*." It is a spiritual version of "sharing the wealth," or passing on to others what the Lord has given to us. This includes forgiveness, peace of mind, joy, hope, strength, faith, and courage. *Epistrepho* says succinctly, **"...freely ye have received, freely give"** (Matt. 10:8).

Epistrophe—Noun

Epistrophe ("ep-is-trof-ay"), #1995 in *Strong's*, appears only once: Acts 15:3. **"...they passed through Phenice and Samaria, declaring the *conversion (epistrophe)* of the Gentiles."** This word describes the moral revolution involved in masses of people becoming Christians from out of the world system.

Epistrephe is defined as a complete turnaround, a counterrevolution, reversing directions, a turn of affairs, turning from the falseness of idolatry and toward the True and Living God, and changing from the worst possible conditions (alienation from God) to the best possible circumstances (the friendship and intimacy of being in God's family).

Epistrephe as used in Acts 15:3 describes how pagan Gentiles were converted in every country visited. They turned from the bondage they were in by their heathen practices to the glorious liberty that goes with the conversion process.

Some grammarians describe *epistrophe* as a returning to a loving and living heavenly Father. It is likened to the prodigal son who left the family nest and steadily regressed until he ended up impoverished, hungry, friendless, and feeding swine. He came to his senses, did a complete about-face *(epistrophe)*, and returned to his father's house. He was welcomed back with a feast and treated like a family member who had come back from the dead. His father was saying: "He which was lost is now found! He which left the family has now returned!" (Luke 15:11-32.)

In the original Garden the family scene between God and man was complete. Then the entrance of sin severed their relationship and produced an alienation. Jesus Christ came to reconcile the shattered family and bring us all together again. *Epistrophe* is the word describing turning from the lordship of Satan to the Lordship of our God.

Colossians 1:13, describing the *epistrophe* process, says, He **"hath delivered us from the power of darkness, and hath translated us into the kingdom of his dear Son."** W. E. Vine when explaining *epistrophe* stated that the word implies "a turning from and a turning to" and that divine grace is the motivating power and human agency is the responding effect.[3]

Not only does *epistrophe* cause the forgiveness of all sins; it also lets God's original purpose in creating us be realized. Conversion to Jesus Christ is a majestic awe-inspiring and profound word that leaves us forever grateful for His compassionate grace and mercy.

Scriptures

Declare His glory among the nations, his wonders among all peoples.

1 Chronicles 16:24 NKJV

Ask of Me, and I will give You the nations for Your inheritance, and the ends of the earth for Your possession.

Psalm 2:8 NKJV

For salvation comes from God. What joys he gives to all his people.

Psalm 3:8 TLB

The fruit of the righteous is a tree of life, and he who is wise wins souls.

Proverbs 11:30 NAS

Come, let's talk this over! says the Lord; no matter how deep the stain of your sins, I can take it out and make you as clean as freshly fallen snow. Even if you are stained as red as crimson, I can make you white as wool!

Isaiah 1:18 TLB

I, the LORD, have called you in righteousness; I will take hold of your hand. I will keep you and will make you to be a covenant for the people and a light for the Gentiles.

Isaiah 42:6 NIV

[25] I, even I, am He who blots out your transgressions for My own sake; and I will not remember your sins.

²⁶ Put Me in remembrance; let us contend together; state your case, that you may be acquitted.

Isaiah 43:25,26 NKJV

⁶ All we like sheep have gone astray; we have turned, every one, to his own way; and the LORD has laid on Him the iniquity of us all.

⁷ He was oppressed and He was afflicted, yet He opened not his mouth; He was led as a lamb to the slaughter, and as a sheep before its shearers is silent, so He opened not his mouth.

⁸ He was taken from prison and from judgment, and who will declare His generation? For He was cut off from the land of the living; for the transgressions of My people He was stricken.

⁹ And they made His grave with the wicked—but with the rich at His death, because He had done no violence, nor was any deceit in His mouth.

¹⁰ Yet it pleases the LORD to bruise Him; He has put Him to grief. When You make His soul an offering for sin, He shall see His seed, He shall prolong His days, and the pleasure of the LORD shall prosper in His hand.

¹¹ He shall see the travail of His soul, and be satisfied. By His knowledge My righteous Servant shall justify many, for He shall bear their iniquities.

¹²Therefore I will divide Him a portion with the great, and He shall divide the spoil with the strong, because He poured out His soul unto death, and He was numbered with the transgressors, and He bore the sin of many, and made intercession for the transgressors.

Isaiah 53:6-12 NKJV

Seek the Lord while you can find him. Call upon him now while he is near.

Isaiah 55:6 TLB

¹ The Spirit of the Sovereign LORD is on me, because the LORD has anointed me to preach good news to the poor. He has sent me to bind up the brokenhearted, to proclaim freedom for the captives and release for the prisoners,
² to proclaim the year of the LORD's favor and the day of vengeance of our God, to comfort all who mourn,
³ and provide for those who grieve in Zion—to bestow on them a crown of beauty instead of ashes, the oil of gladness instead of mourning, and a garment of praise instead of a spirit of despair. They will be called oaks of righteousness, a planting of the LORD for the display of his splendor.

Isaiah 61:1-3 NIV

I will cleanse them from all the guilt of their sin against me, and I will forgive all the guilt of their sin and rebellion against me.

Jeremiah 33:8 RSV

[18] If you refuse to warn the wicked when I want you to tell them, you are under the penalty of death; therefore repent and save your life—they will die in their sins, but I will punish you. I will demand your blood for theirs.

[19] But if you warn them, and they keep on sinning, and refuse to repent, they will die in their sins, but you are blameless—you have done all you could.

[20] And if a good man becomes bad, and you refuse to warn him of the consequences, and the Lord destroys him, his previous good deeds won't help him—he shall die in his sin. But I will hold you responsible for his death, and punish you.

[21] But if you warn him and he repents, he shall live and you have saved your own life too.

Ezekiel 3:18-21 TLB

And she will have a Son, and you shall name him Jesus (meaning 'Savior'), for he will save his people from their sins.

Matthew 1:21 TLB

"Come, follow me," Jesus said, and I will make you fishers of men.

Matthew 4:19 NIV

[25] For whoever desires to save his life will lose it, but whoever loses his life for My sake will find it. [26] For what is a man profited if he gains the whole world, and loses his own soul? Or what will a man give in exchange for his soul? [27] For the Son of Man will come in the glory of His Father with His angels, and then He will reward each according to his works. [28] Assuredly, I say to you, there are some standing here who shall not taste death till they see the Son of Man coming in His kingdom.

Matthew 16:25-28 NKJV

[12] What do you think? If a man owns a hundred sheep, and one of them wanders away, will he not leave the ninety-nine on the hills and go to look for the one that wandered off? [13] And if he finds it, I tell you the truth, he is happier about that one sheep than about the ninety-nine that did not wander off. [14] In the same way your Father in heaven is not willing that any of these little ones should be lost.

Matthew 18:12-14 NIV

[27] But first they took him into the armory and called out the entire contingent.

[28] They stripped him and put a scarlet robe on him,

[29] and made a crown from long thorns and put it on his head, and placed a stick in his right hand as a scepter and knelt before him in mockery. "Hail, King of the Jews," they yelled.

[30] And they spat on him and grabbed the stick and beat him on the head with it.

[31] After the mockery, they took off the robe and put his own garment on him again, and took him out to crucify him.

[32] As they were on the way to the execution grounds they came across a man from Cyrene, in Africa—Simon was his name—and forced him to carry Jesus' cross.

[33] Then they went out to an area known as Golgotha, that is, "Skull Hill,"

[34] where the soldiers gave him drugged wine to drink; but when he had tasted it, he refused.

[35] After the crucifixion, the soldiers threw dice to divide up his clothes among themselves.

[36] Then they sat around and watched him as he hung there.

[37] And they put a sign above his head, "This is Jesus, the King of the Jews."

³⁸ Two robbers were also crucified there that morning, one on either side of him.

³⁹ And the people passing by hurled abuse, shaking their heads at him and saying,

⁴⁰ "So! You can destroy the Temple and build it again in three days, can you? Well, then, come on down from the cross if you are the Son of God!"

⁴¹⁻⁴³ And the chief priests and Jewish leaders also mocked him. "He saved others," they scoffed, "but he can't save himself! So you are the King of Israel, are you? Come down from the cross and we'll believe you! He trusted God—let God show his approval by delivering him! Didn't he say, 'I am God's Son?'"

⁴⁴ And the robbers also threw the same in his teeth.

⁴⁵ That afternoon, the whole earth was covered with darkness for three hours, from noon until three o'clock.

⁴⁶ About three o'clock, Jesus shouted, "Eli, Eli, lama sabachthani?" which means, "My God, my God, why have you forsaken me?"

⁴⁷ Some of the bystanders misunderstood and thought he was calling for Elijah.

⁴⁸ One of them ran and filled a sponge with sour wine and put it on a stick and held it up to him to drink.

⁴⁹ But the rest said, "Leave him alone. Let's see whether Elijah will come and save him."

⁵⁰ Then Jesus shouted out again, dismissed his spirit, and died.

⁵¹ And look! The curtain secluding the Holiest Place in the Temple was split apart from top to bottom; and the earth shook, and rocks broke,

⁵² and tombs opened, and many godly men and women who had died came back to life again.

⁵³ After Jesus' resurrection, they left the cemetery and went into Jerusalem, and appeared to many people there.

⁵⁴ The soldiers at the crucifixion and their sergeant were terribly frightened by the earthquake and all that happened. They exclaimed, "Surely this was God's Son."

Matthew 27:27-54 TLB

¹ Early on Sunday morning, as the new day was dawning, Mary Magdalene and the other Mary went out to the tomb.

² Suddenly there was a great earthquake; for an angel of the Lord came down from heaven and rolled aside the stone and sat on it.

³ His face shone like lightning and his clothing was a brilliant white.

⁴ The guards shook with fear when they saw him, and fell into a dead faint.

⁵ Then the angel spoke to the women. "Don't be frightened!" he said. "I know you are looking for Jesus, who was crucified,

⁶ but he isn't here! For he has come back to life again, just as he said he would. Come in and see where his body was lying....

⁷ And now, go quickly and tell his disciples that he has risen from the dead, and that he is going to Galilee to meet them there. That is my message to them."

⁸ The women ran from the tomb, badly frightened, but also filled with joy, and rushed to find the disciples to give them the angel's message.

⁹ And as they were running, suddenly Jesus was there in front of them! "Good morning!" he said. And they fell to the ground before him, holding his feet and worshiping him.

¹⁰ Then Jesus said to them, "Don't be frightened! Go tell my brothers to leave at once for Galilee, to meet me there."

Matthew 28:1-10 TLB

⁷ He came as a witness to testify concerning that light, so that through him all men might believe.

[8] He himself was not the light; he came only as a witness to the light.

[9] The true light that gives light to every man was coming into the world.

[10] He was in the world, and though the world was made through him, the world did not recognize him.

[11] He came to that which was his own, but his own did not receive him.

[12] Yet to all who received him, to those who believed in his name, he gave the right to become children of God—

[13] children born not of natural descent, nor of human decision or a husband's will, but born of God.

John 1:7-13 NIV

[1,2] After dark one night a Jewish religious leader named Nicodemus, a member of the sect of the Pharisees, came for an interview with Jesus. "Sir," he said, "we all know that God has sent you to teach us. Your miracles are proof enough of this."

[3] Jesus replied, "With all the earnestness I possess I tell you this: Unless you are born again, you can never get into the Kingdom of God."

[4] "Born again!" exclaimed Nicodemus. "What do you mean? How can an old man go back into his mother's womb and be born again?"

[5] Jesus replied, "What I am telling you so earnestly is this: Unless one is born of water and the Spirit, he cannot enter the Kingdom of God.

[6] "Men can only reproduce human life, but the Holy Spirit gives new life from heaven;

[7] so don't be surprised at my statement that you must be born again!"

John 3:1-7 TLB

[21] Just as the Father raises up the dead and gives them life—makes them live on—so the Son also gives life to whomever He wills and is pleased to give it.

[22] Even the Father judges no one; for He has given all judgment—the last judgment and the whole business of judging—entirely into the hands of the Son;

[23] So that all men may give honor (reverence, homage) to the Son, just as they give honor to the Father. [In fact] whoever does not honor the Son, does not honor the Father Who has sent Him.

[24] I assure you, most solemnly I tell you, the person whose ears are open to My words—who listens to My message—and believes and trusts

in and clings to and relies on Him Who sent Me has (possesses now) eternal life. And he does not come into judgment—does not incur sentence of judgment, will not come under condemnation—but he has already passed over out of death into life.

25 Believe Me when I assure you, most solemnly I tell you, The time is coming and is here now when the dead shall hear the voice of the Son of God, and those who hear it shall live.

26 For even as the Father has life in Himself and is self-existent, so He has given to the Son to have life in Himself and be self-existent.

27 And He has given Him authority and granted Him power to execute (exercise, practice) judgment, because He is a Son of man [very man].

28 Do not be surprised and wonder at this; for the time is coming when all those who are in the tombs shall hear His voice,

29 And they shall come out; those who have practiced doing good [will come out] to the resurrection of [new] life; and those who have done evil will be raised for judgment—raised to meet their sentence.

30 I am able to do nothing from Myself—independently, of My own accord—but as I am

taught by God and as I get His orders. [I decide as I am bidden to decide. As the voice comes to Me, so I give a decision.] Even as I hear, I judge and my judgment is right (just, righteous), because I do not seek or consult My own will— I have no desire to do what is pleasing to Myself, My own aim, My own purpose—but only the will and pleasure of the Father Who sent Me.

[31] If I alone testify in My behalf, My testimony is not valid and can not be worth anything.

[32] There is Another Who testifies concerning Me and I know and am certain that His evidence on My behalf is true and valid.

[33] You yourselves have sent an inquiry to John and he has been a witness to the truth.

[34] But I do not receive [a mere] human witness—the evidence which I accept on My behalf is not from man. But I simply mention all these things in order that you may be saved (made and kept safe and sound).

[35] John was the lamp that kept on burning and shining [to show you the way], and you were willing for a while to delight (sun) yourselves in his light.

[36] But I have as My witness something greater (weightier, higher, better) than that of John; for the works that the Father has appointed Me to accomplish and finish, the very same works that I am now doing, are a witness and proof that the Father has sent Me.

[37] And the Father Who sent Me has Himself testified concerning Me. Not one of you has ever given ears to His voice, or seen His form (His face, what He is like).—You have always been deaf to His voice and blind to the vision of Him.

[38] And you have not His word (His thought) living in your hearts, because you do not believe and adhere to, and trust in, and rely on Him Whom He has sent.—That is why you do not keep His message living in you, because you do not believe in the Messenger Whom He has sent.

[39] You search and investigate and pore over the Scriptures diligently, because you suppose and trust that you have eternal life through them. And these [very Scriptures] testify about Me!

[40] And still you are not willing (but refuse) to come to Me, so that you might have life.

41 I receive not glory from men—I crave no human honor, I look for no mortal fame.

42 But I know you and recognize and understand that you have not the love of God in you.

43 I have come in My Father's name and with His power and you do not receive Me—your hearts are not open to Me, you give Me no welcome. But if another comes in his own name and his own power and with no other authority but himself, you will receive him and give him your approval.

44 How is it possible for you to believe—how can you learn to believe—who [are content to seek for and] receive praise and honor and glory from one another, and do not seek the praise and honor and glory which come from Him Who alone is God?

45 Put out of your minds the thought and do not suppose [as some of you are supposing] that I will accuse you to the Father. There is one who accuses you; it is Moses, the very one on whom you have built your hopes—in whom you trust.

46 For if you believed in and relied on Moses, you would believe in and rely on Me, for he wrote about Me [personally].

47 But if you do not believe and trust his writings, how then will you believe and trust

My teachings—how shall you cleave to and rely on My words?

John 5:21-47 AMP

I am the Door. Anyone who enters in through Me will be saved—will live; he will come in and he will go out [freely], and will find pasture.

John 10:9 AMP

²¹ But anyone who asks for mercy from the Lord shall have it and shall be saved.

²² O men of Israel, listen! God publicly endorsed Jesus of Nazareth by doing tremendous miracles through him, as you well know.

²³ But God, following his prearranged plan, let you use the Roman government to nail him to the cross and murder him.

²⁴ Then God released him from the horrors of death and brought him back to life again, for death could not keep this man within its grip.

²⁵ King David quoted Jesus as saying: "I know the Lord is always with me. He is helping me. God's mighty power supports me.

²⁶ "No wonder my heart is filled with joy and my tongue shouts his praises! For I know all will be well with me in death—

²⁷ "You will not leave my soul in hell or let the body of your Holy Son decay.

[28] "You will give me back my life and give me wonderful joy in your presence."

Acts 2:21-28 TLB

[10] Then know this, you and everyone else in Israel: It is by the name of Jesus Christ of Nazareth, whom you crucified but whom God raised from the dead, that this man stands before you completely healed.
[11] He is "the stone you builders rejected, which has become a capstone."
[12] Salvation is found in no one else, for there is no other name under heaven given to men by which we must be saved.

Acts 4:10-12 NIV

[47] For this is as the Lord commanded when he said, "I have made you a light to the Gentiles, to lead them from the farthest corners of the earth to my salvation."
[48] When the Gentiles heard this, they were very glad and rejoiced in Paul's message; and as many as wanted eternal life, believed.

Acts 13:47,48 TLB

[15] That is why I am so eager to preach the gospel also to you who are at Rome.

¹⁶ I am not ashamed of the gospel, because it is the power of God for the salvation of everyone who believes: first for the Jew, then for the Gentile.

Romans 1:15,16 NIV

⁶ When we were utterly helpless with no way of escape, Christ came at just the right time and died for us sinners who had no use for him.

⁷ Even if we were good, we really wouldn't expect anyone to die for us, though, of course, that might be barely possible.

⁸ But God showed his great love for us by sending Christ to die for us while we were still sinners.

⁹ And since by his blood he did all this for us as sinners, how much more will he do for us now that he has declared us not guilty? Now he will save us from all of God's wrath to come.

¹⁰ And since, when we were his enemies, we were brought back to God by the death of his Son, what blessings he must have for us now that we are his friends, and he is living within us!

¹¹ Now we rejoice in our wonderful new relationship with God—all because of what our Lord Jesus Christ has done in dying for our sins—making us friends of God.

¹² When Adam sinned, sin entered the entire human race. His sin spread death throughout

all the world, so everything began to grow old and die, for all sinned.

[13] [We know that it was Adam's sin that caused this] because although, of course, people were sinning from the time of Adam until Moses, God did not in those days judge them guilty of death for breaking his laws—because he had not yet given his laws to them nor told them what he wanted them to do.

[14] So when their bodies died it was not for their own sins since they themselves had never disobeyed God's special law against eating the forbidden fruit, as Adam had. What a contrast between Adam and Christ who was yet to come!

[15] And what a difference between man's sin and God's forgiveness! For this one man, Adam, brought death to many through his sin. But this one man, Jesus Christ, brought forgiveness to many through God's mercy.

[16] Adam's one sin brought the penalty of death to many, while Christ freely takes away many sins and gives glorious life instead.

[17] The sin of this one man, Adam, caused death to be king over all, but all who will take God's gift of forgiveness and acquittal are kings of life because of this one man, Jesus Christ.

¹⁸ Yes, Adam's sin brought punishment to all, but Christ's righteousness makes men right with God, so that they can live.

¹⁹ Adam caused many to be sinners because he disobeyed God, and Christ caused many to be made acceptable to God because he obeyed.

²⁰ The Ten Commandments were given so that all could see the extent of their failure to obey God's laws. But the more we see our sinfulness, the more we see God's abounding grace forgiving us.

²¹ Before, sin ruled over all men and brought them to death, but now God's kindness rules instead, giving us right standing with God and resulting in eternal life through Jesus Christ our Lord.

Romans 5:6-21 TLB

⁸ For salvation that comes from trusting Christ—which is what we preach—is already within easy reach of each of us; in fact, it is as near as our own hearts and mouths.

⁹ For if you tell others with your own mouth that Jesus Christ is your Lord, and believe in your own heart that God has raised him from the dead, you will be saved.

¹⁰ For it is by believing in his heart that a man becomes right with God; and with his mouth he tells others of his faith, confirming his salvation.

[11] For the Scriptures tell us that no one who believes in Christ will ever be disappointed.

[12] Jew and Gentile are the same in this respect: they all have the same Lord who generously gives his riches to all those who ask him for them.

[13] Anyone who calls upon the name of the Lord will be saved.

[14] But how shall they ask him to save them unless they believe in him? And how can they believe in him if they have never heard about him? And how can they hear about him unless someone tells them?

[15] And how will anyone go and tell them unless someone sends him? That is what the Scriptures are talking about when they say, "How beautiful are the feet of those who preach the Gospel of peace with God and bring glad tidings of good things." In other words, how welcome are those who come preaching God's Good News!

Romans 10:8-15 TLB

[12] Giving thanks to the Father who has qualified us to be partakers of the inheritance of the saints in the light.

[13] He has delivered us from the power of darkness and translated us into the kingdom of the Son of His love,

[14] in whom we have redemption through His blood, the forgiveness of sins.

Colossians 1:12-14 NKJV

Prayer for Salvation

Father, in the name of Jesus, we come before You in prayer and in faith, believing. It is written in Your Word that Jesus came to save the lost. You wish all men to be saved and to know Your Divine Truth. Therefore, Father, we bring _____ before You this day.

Satan, we bind you in the name of Jesus and loose you from the activities in _____'s life!

Father, we ask the Lord of the harvest to thrust the perfect laborer into his/her path, a laborer to share Your gospel in a special way so that he/she will listen and understand it. As Your laborer ministers to him/her, we believe that he/she will come to his/her senses, come out of the snare of the devil who has held him/her captive, and make Jesus the Lord of his/her life.

Your Word says that You will deliver those for whom we intercede, who are not innocent, through the cleanness of our hands. We're standing on Your Word, and from this moment on, Father, we shall praise You and thank You for his/her salvation. We have committed this matter into Your hands and with our faith we see _____ saved, filled with Your Spirit, with a full and clear knowledge of Your Word. Amen—so be it!

(Each day after praying this prayer, thank the Lord for this person's salvation. Rejoice and praise God for the victory! Confess the above prayer as done! Thank Him for sending the laborer. Thank Him that Satan is bound. Hallelujah!)

Scripture References

Luke 19:102   Timothy 2:26

Matthew 18:18   Job 22:30

Matthew 9:38

---

[1] pp. 1149, 1150.

[2] Hermann Cremer, *Biblico-Theological Lexicon of New Testament Greek*, 4th English ed. (Edinburgh: T.& T. Clark, 1895), p. 880.

[3] W. E. Vine, *Expository Dictionary of Biblical Words* (Nashville: Thomas Nelson Publishers, 1985), p. 128.

THE AUTHORITY OF THE BELIEVER

Binding/Loosing

The believer who thoroughly understands that the power of God is backing him can exercise his authority and face the enemy fearlessly.

— Kenneth E. Hagin

Greek and Hebrew Word Studies

OLD TESTAMENT—*MASHAL*

Thou madest him to have dominion (*mashal*) over the works of thy hands; thou hast put all things under his feet.

Psalm 8:6

NEW TESTAMENT
BINDING—*DEO*, LOOSING—*LUO*

Verily I say unto you, Whatsoever ye shall *bind* (*deo*) on earth shall be *bound* (*deo*) in

heaven: and whatsoever ye shall *loose (luo)* on earth shall be *loosed (luo)* in heaven.

Matthew 18:18

No earthly commander-in-chief is going to issue military orders or give assignments without giving the authority to carry them out. The fact that he has given those duties and responsibilities to men under him means that the authority to carry them out is inherent in the orders.

If earthly commanders would not expect an order to be carried out without authority, how much more would not our heavenly Commander-in-Chief expect it? Without the authority to carry them out, orders are not worth any more than the paper on which they are written. Without the power of God, the authority of the believer would be useless. Jesus gave the authority. You exercise that authority in obedience. God supplies the power and the ability. (Luke 10:19.)

— Jerry Savelle
The Word Bible[1]

The Believer's Authority

If we wish to truly understand the Scripture teachings about the authority of the believer, we should start with the creation of man. What does Scripture say about the creation of our race? Why did God create us in the first place? What were His expectations of us? What were His original goals for us to achieve? To answer these questions correctly we must take our cue from the manner in which Jesus dealt with certain difficult questions.

Our Lord Jesus directed the attention of Bible readers to God's *original intent* for the world as revealed in the creation record in Genesis. When the sticky issue of divorce was presented to Him, He was not content to let the divorce provision in the Law of Moses be the final word, since it was not the first word. He directed His listeners' hearts to God's motives in making male and female humans in the first place.

Although Moses provided for divorce laws due to the heart-hardening conditions of life in this world, Jesus assures us that **"from the beginning it was not so."** (Matt. 19:3-8.)

Similarly, Jesus answered the question of evil in the world by pointing out that the Devil is **"a murderer from the beginning"** (John 8:44). How long has Satan been killing and hindering God's beautiful design? He has been killing, stealing, and destroying since the beginning of human history. So in reference to the gift of authority which has been bestowed on us, we must start our pursuit of knowledge in the testimony of Scripture concerning the authority of man.

One of the most majestic descriptions of God's purpose in creating humanity is found in Psalm 8:4-7.

What is man, that thou art mindful of him? and the son of man, that thou visitest him?

For thou hast made him a little lower than the angels, and hast crowned him with glory and honour.

Thou madest him to *have dominion* (mashal) over the works of thy hands; thou hast put all things under his feet.

Mashal (pronounced "maw-shal'"), #4910 in *Strong's*, means to rule, to have dominion, to exercise power.

This Scripture teaches that man was made to rule over the works of God's hands, particularly the natural world (animals, fish, and birds are specifically mentioned here). If the whole world were a park, man would be the park superintendent. When man was created, it was not exactly a park but a garden he was to oversee.

"The Lord God took the man, and put him into the garden of Eden to dress it and to keep it" (Gen. 2:15). The word *keep* is the strong word *shamar* (pronounced "shaw-mar'"), #8104 in *Strong's*, which means to guard, protect, watch, keep. Man's two tasks were to tend the Garden and to *guard* it.

In this latter duty—to guard—Adam somehow fell short and was not diligent enough to guard against all intrusion into that very sphere over which he had complete God-given authority: the Garden.

Nonetheless, God's original intention for man's creation (and placement in the Garden as a manager) included several facets which are presented in Scripture. Man was created for God's fellowship, for God's glory and for God's own pleasure. (Rev. 4:11.)

How seldom do we grasp that we have the potential to bring the utmost joy and pleasure to our Creator! We may feel awkward or inadequate and are uncomfortable with the concept that the Infinite has chosen to share His heart's needs with the highly limited little creature He has made. Still, it is inescapably true that God wants something from us which—if we can learn to give Him—will produce enormous happiness for Him.

God also specifically instructed the first human couple to exercise rulership over the earth, as well as **"the fish of the sea...the fowl of the air...and over every creeping thing that creepeth upon the earth"** (Gen. 1:26). Their authority was over vegetable, mineral, animal and all other created things.

Man was to be the most authoritative creature on this globe. Yet we must realize he was not initially given authority over his fellow man, neither his spouse nor any other human made in God's image.

The rulership of husband over wife was a part of the Curse, the sad effects of the rupture in God's perfect order of the original Creation. Domineering of spouse, oppression of children or other human beings, slaveholding, suppression of citizens by king or authoritarian ruler, conquest of one race by another—these occur continually in this world. And, sadly, each is defended by Scripture-quoting people who discover the Word makes matter-of-fact mention of these tendencies in human culture, various societies, and this sin-filled world.

But from the beginning it was not so. A husband was not created to rule over his wife, but to rule together with her. Not until the Fall did the present unnatural imbalance come into being because of sin. (Gen. 3:16.)

Man became confused about his God-given role and authority. And the world today is in much disruption because of that original sin which clouded human ability to properly exercise authority.

Sometimes people tend to fear authority. Thus they put it into the hands of dictators or spiritual or governmental leaders, who are expected to do all the ruling over everyone else. Or they themselves tend to obsessively crave authority and the potential to exercise power over others. Both these fundamental errors concerning authority are sinful, evil, and dangerous.

Some of the symptoms of sin's ill effects include divorce, spousal hatred and abuse, fighting, coercion, domineering of husband over wife (or vice versa), child abuse, and violence of children against parents.

But it is not just family relations which have suffered as a result of the Fall. It is not just human relations which are poisoned by man's shameful mishandling of his authority. And it is not merely race relations which have reflected the ugly character of man's cancerously destructive authoritarian impulses. (Genocide—the wholesale slaughter of one nation by another—slavery or other forms of servitude, oppression, dispossession, clan feuds, malicious oligarchies, and a score of other brutal quests for domination are manifestation of the sinful distortion of man's God-given capacity to rule and lead.)

In addition to all these things, man is confused and deeply disturbed in his relationship to the Lord God, the highest authority of all. People either run and hide from God, imagining He is abusive in His authority, or they try to exalt their will over His, and thus become like the devil in revolting against God's rightful authority. That foolish reaction brings sickness of mind as an inevitable result.

All these problem areas point to the sad fact that man is still messed up when it comes to exercising authority. Many haunting questions remain: How much authority should be used? When? How? Why?

Fortunately, the gospel rectifies every misconception, every frailty and every failure. And it teaches us to exercise great power and godly authority with a meek, humble, trustworthy heart and a right spirit.

Jesus knew when to submit to authority and when to refuse to honor false authority. Compare Matthew 17:24-27 and Luke 2:48-52 with Luke 23:8-10 and John 19:8-11.

Jesus was *very* gentle and meek. Yet He overthrew the moneylenders' tables, which were a provocation and a dishonor to His Father's name. (Matt. 21:12,13.)

He commanded His disciples to submit to the Pharisees' religious pronouncements, but He also publicly humiliated the Pharisees and denounced their hypocrisy. (Matt. 23:1-3,13-33.)

Jesus was called "a servant of rulers" (Isa. 49:7), and He even paid taxes. Yet He drove out thousands of demons with His words, and by His command He stilled the wind and the tempestuous sea. (Matt. 8:16,26,31,32.) He exercised authority over demons and over nature.

Jesus even knocked down 600 soldiers[2] with the powerful declaration, **"I am he"** (John 18:6). He nevertheless went away, led by those same soldiers, and submitted to death. Being a submissive son, He was granted all authority in heaven and in earth. Jesus was perfectly balanced, whole, pure, trustworthy, and true. He is our example in submission and in authority.

There is no authority outside of submission. The two go hand in hand. Adam was steward in the Garden and ruler of the earth, and he was in submission to God. All human woes result from his *mishandling* his authority and stepping out of God's will, thus plunging his descendants into confusion and disorder.

So, before we continue to examine the exciting biblical truths of the vast authority God wishes us to have, let us quickly establish two facts.

First, Jesus was not pleased with the disciples' excitement over having evil spirits subject to them. He told them not to rejoice about that, but instead to rejoice that their names were written in heaven. (Luke 10:17-20.)

Evil spirits are *supposed* to fall before God's anointed people. That is the way God has ordered it, and there really is nothing noteworthy about it.

What is truly amazing though, and what should keep us continually humble, thrilled, and shouting for joy, is that God redeems and repairs fallen human beings and records their names in heaven.

This is a privilege the Lord forever withholds from fallen angels. When God saves a mortal human being, the angels rejoice. (Luke 15:7.) But they also are amazed by it and are filled with curiosity about the whole subject, particularly wondering about God's love and attachment to our race. (1 Peter 1:12.)

If the angels, who see God's face daily, are surprised by our salvation, should we treat it as a usual thing? No. Jesus said we should rejoice over this great privilege more than over our spiritual authority. (And we certainly are not to abuse it on one hand or create chaos on the other as did Adam in *failing* to exercise it.)

But Jesus also expects us to derive pleasure not as much from our authority as from our relationship to God. When Adam forfeited his relationship with God, he lost not only that close fellowship, but most of his authority as well! Authority and fellowship with God, authority and submission—these are parts of a greater whole.

The second fact which must be stated now is that our authority was never intended to be 100 percent unlimited, nor shall it ever be. It will always be anchored in the will (or permission) of God. The New Testament admonishes us not to announce our plans and speak all about the things we are going to do, but rather to say, **"If the Lord wills, we shall live and do such things."** (James 4:15.)

We may request something earnestly, only to hear God state He has a purpose for willing something else. (Both our Lord Jesus and the apostle Paul experienced this dreadful crisis in life.) Then we must say, as did our Lord Jesus, "May Your will—not mine—be done."

God is good *always*. He is kind-hearted and does not willingly grieve the children of men. Yet these accounts are in Scripture for a reason: There are times when neither our rightful authority nor our prayers can change a matter anchored in God's determination and plan for us. We are to have great faith, great authority, and great power in prayer, but we are also to pray according to His will. (1 John 5:14,15.)

In the Old Testament several Hebrew words have to do with ruling, having authority, having dominion, and exercising power.

Mashal is just one of these words, yet we have chosen to examine it because it is the finest example for a study on authority. *Mashal* occurs about 100 times in the Old Testament and is used in a variety of contexts.

In Genesis 1:18 we read that God set the great lights in the heavens to *rule* over the day and night, and to divide light from darkness. In Genesis 3:16 God told Eve her husband would *rule* over her.

In Judges 8:22,23 *mashal* occurs four times:

Then the men of Israel said unto Gideon,
***Rule* thou over us, both thou, and thy son,**

**and thy son's son also: for thou hast deliv-
ered us from the hand of Midian.**

**And Gideon said unto them, I will not *rule*
over you, neither shall my son *rule* over you:
the Lord shall *rule* over you.**

Here Gideon declined to receive the kingship over
God's people even though they were pressing him to
take it. However, Gideon knew that rulership over
God's people is the *Lord's* prerogative.

Esther 9:1 is a thrilling verse, the latter part of
which states: **"...the enemies of the Jews hoped to
have power over them, (though it was turned to the
contrary, that the Jews *had rule* over them that
hated them)."** This is a magnificent verse dealing
with the authority of the believers. By the hand of
God their situation was reversed so that they ruled
over their oppressors.

This verse is one of several biblical indicators that
God wishes us to be delivered from whoever or
whatever threatens to destroy us. We must see the
roles reversed so that our enemies fearfully submit
themselves to the Lord's authority exercised through us.

Quite similar in thought is the divine command to
the Messiah in Psalm 110:2,3. **"The Lord shall send**

the rod of thy strength out of Zion: *rule thou* in the midst of thine enemies. Thy people shall be willing in the day of thy power...." Please read all seven verses of this powerful psalm, a passage much quoted in the New Testament.

Psalm 110 reveals a conquering, authoritative Messiah. He is seated at the right hand of God, ruling over His enemies. He is harnessing the will of God's people and exercising eternal priestly duties. He is slaughtering heathen kings (anti-Christ government) and sending judgments upon the nations which result in uncountable deaths in the day of His wrath. (And both Testaments show there is wrath of the Lamb which shall bring the nations to their knees in unspeakable fear and terror.) Finally He is a Messiah Who rides on into eternity with His head lifted high.

There is nothing mild about Zion's King in the day of His power when He subdues the world and makes it His footstool. If this is not a picture of the authority of the Righteous One, then what is?

All power in heaven and in earth has been given to the Lord Jesus, and He will grant the overcomers to sit with Him in His throne. So we should look admiringly and reverently at what is stated about Christ's eternal authority. We will have a share in it when we have been proven faithful.

Of the many verses in which *mashal* appears, let us look briefly at just a few.

Isaiah 14:1,2 speaks of the time when the House of Jacob is returned to full favor with God. Notice the last part of verse 2: **"...and they shall take them captives, whose captives they were; and they shall rule over their oppressors."** (Compare Proverbs 12:24.) Proverbs 16:32 states, **"...he that *ruleth* his spirit (is better) than he that taketh a city."** Proverbs 29:2 says, **"When the righteous are in authority, the people rejoice: but when the wicked *beareth rule*, the people mourn."** How true this is! When God-fearing people rule, everyone benefits. But whole nations have been reduced to misery, enduring untold sorrows, because their ruler—perhaps a dictator or other self-willed ruler—is wicked.

The final passage in this study of *mashal* is Second Samuel 23:2-4. This is one of the most magnificent utterances in all the Bible, and certainly one which deserves much more attention than it has received.

These words were spoken by David at the end of his long and amazing lifetime of service to God. In this passage, David relates what the Spirit of God has taught him about ruling and exercising authority. This Scripture explains to us what kind of person God considers fit or trustworthy for receiving authority. David writes:

The Spirit of the Lord spake by me, and his word was in my tongue.

The God of Israel said, the rock of Israel spake to me, He that *ruleth (mashal)* over men must be just, ruling in the fear of God.

And he shall be as the light of the morning, when the sun riseth, even a morning without clouds; as the tender grass springing out of the earth by clear shining after rain.

What a revelation! Anyone who wishes to exercise authority must be just, righteous, fair, impartial, and consistent; and he must rule in the fear of God. Other types of rulership seriously miss the mark and go astray.

O God, give us leaders for the Church, for the family and for human government who are fair and righteous, and who do all things out of reverence for You, O Lord, our God. Amen and amen!

Greek Words for *Binding*

Eight words in the Greek New Testament are translated "bind," "binding," or "bound." In the *King*

James Version the main word we want to study in-depth is *deo* (pronounced "deh'-o"), #1210 in *Strong's*. This word is used in binding and loosing as found in Matthew 16:19 and 18:18. The other seven words are colorful and descriptive, even though they are not necessarily dealing with the authority of the believer. We will discuss these seven first, then look at *deo*.

Desmeuo

Desmeuo (pronounced "des-myoo'-o"), #1195 in *Strong's,* appears twice in the New Testament.

In Matthew 23:4 Jesus is faulting the scribes and Pharisees for binding *(desmeuo)* heavy legal burdens on people without themselves helping to carry the load.

In Acts 22:4 Paul is telling how he persecuted Christians prior to his conversion: **"I persecuted this way unto the death, *binding (desmeuo)* and delivering into prisons both men and women."**

Desmeuo in Matthew 23:4 is likened to a beast of burden that is being loaded down with heavy things to carry. The Pharisees caused their followers to be overloaded or overburdened with legalistic rules. Jesus tells them their system is burdensome compared to His gospel.

Desmeuo in Acts 22:4 means to put into chains, fetter, lock up or throw into prison. Paul uses the word to describe how he abused Christians prior to his conversion to Christ.

Desmeuo is not a happy word. It is a sad word describing how a human being created by God to be free ends up being bound spiritually or physically.

Desmeo

Desmeo ("des-mey'-o"), #1196 in *Strong's,* appears only once in the New Testament: in Luke 8:29 concerning the Gadarene demoniac. It states, **"...he was kept bound** *(desmeo)* **with chains and in fetters."**

Desmeo has the same meaning as *desmeuo.* With the passage of time, one replaced the other. This happened in our language as "honour" became *honor* and "colour" became *color.* The definitions given to *desmeo* are the same as *desmeuo.* Of 16 lexicons, 13 state: "same as *desmeuo,* since both words originate from *desmos,* 'a chain.'" *King James* translators simply used "bonds," "bound," or "bondage" for both words, literally and symbolically.

Katadeo

Katadeo ("kat-ad-eh'-o"), #2611 in *Strong's,* appears only once: in Luke 10:34, which describes the Good

Samaritan helping the man who fell among thieves. He **"went to him, and bound *(katadeo)* up his wounds, pouring in oil and wine...."** This is a medical term describing the dressing of wounds.

The definition of *katadeo* is to close up, to bind the lips or edges of a wound, to enclose an object by wrapping a bandage around it, to tie down or to wrap up. Sometimes it describes stopping the flow of blood from an open wound or firmly binding flesh that has been lacerated. It includes starting the curative process and the recovery of an injured person.

The Good Samaritan took a man left for dead and bound *(katadeo)* his wounds. This gives a descriptive picture of our salvation and its recovery process.

Perideo

Perideo ("per-ee-deh'-o"), #4019 in *Strong's*, is used only once. In the last part of John 11:44, it describes the resurrected Lazarus as still having on grave clothes. Then it states, **"....and his face was bound *(perideo)* about with a napkin."**

The word is a compound of *peri* ("around") and *deo* ("to bind").The definition of *perideo* is to enwrap, to tie around, or to wrap an object around something.

In the case of Lazarus it was used of the napkin tied around his face. Jesus not only raised him from the dead, He ordered the removal of all the grave clothes still hanging on him. This included the cloth in which his face and head were wrapped.

This is a good description of our conversion to Jesus Christ. We were dead in trespasses and sins. Not only did He give us eternal life, He replaced our "grave" clothes with robes of righteousness. (Isa. 61:10.)

Proteino

Proteino ("prot-i'-no"), #4385 in *Strong's,* appears once: in Acts 22:25. Paul is about to be scourged by soldiers when he tells the centurion in charge that his Roman citizenship should keep him from this kind of treatment. **"...as they *bound (proteino)* him with thongs, Paul said unto the centurion that stood by, Is it lawful for you to scourge a man that is Roman, and uncondemned?"**

Proteino describes a cruel process of stretching out a person's hands and legs, holding them with leather thongs as a preparation for the painful scourging to be inflicted.

The definition of *proteino* is to stretch full length on a rack, to tie to a beam or pillar ready to be flogged, to put into a tense posture, to tie up a body and expose it to danger, to protend or extend the hands, or to stretch the body forward.

While this preparation for whipping was taking place, Paul asked the question that ultimately caused his release. Cicero, an early Roman writer, stated, "It was a high crime that a Roman citizen be *bound.*"[3] Paul knew this to be a fact. His being set free was a case of saying the right word to the right person at the right time. We have been promised the same ability in Isaiah 50:4.

Sundeo

Sundeo ("soon-deh'-o"), #4887 in *Strong's*, is found only once: Hebrews 13:3. **"Remember them that are in bonds, as *bound with (sundeo)* them...."** The word is a compound: *sun* ("together") and *deo* ("to bind").

Sundeo links us with the martyrs in concentration camps, political prisoners incarcerated in countries where witnessing for Jesus Christ is forbidden, and also Christians worldwide who must meet underground to worship Him.

Sundeo is defined as fellow captives jointly bound with fellow prisoners, to fasten together, to unite in a caring way, to be bound jointly in heart, and remembering those who are in prison as though you were in prison with them.

A song that describes *sundeo* is "Bind us together Lord, bind us together with cords that cannot be broken."[4] With this word we are linked with Christians worldwide. We can rejoice with those that rejoice, and we can weep with those that weep. (Rom. 12:15.)

Sundeo is a network word bringing all Christians together with one common bond: a love for the Lord Jesus Christ!

Hupodeo

Hupodeo ("hoop-od-eh'-o"), #5265 in *Strong's,* is used three times in the New Testament: Mark 6:9, Ephesians 6:15 and Acts 12:8.

Mark 6:9 describes the Twelve going on a mission and being shod *(hupodeo)* with sandals.

Ephesians 6:15 has to do with believers putting on the equipment of a heavily armed infantryman and fighting the good fight of faith, having their feet shod *(hupodeo)* with the preparation (or readiness) of the gospel of peace.

In Acts 12:8 Peter in prison is sleeping the night before his execution. (Would you be sleeping the night before your "hanging"? You could and you would with the Lord's presence to help you!) The angel of the Lord awakens him and commands, "Gird thyself, and *bind (hupodeo)* on thy sandals." When Peter responded, the angel further added, **"Cast thy garment about thee, and follow me."**

In this verse *hupodeo* is defined as putting on shoes; to bind under one's feet; to tie on boots, shoes or sandals; to bind beneath one's feet the necessary wear for moving. It includes all the materials needed for the foot to be prepared for a journey.

Hupodeo is a compounded word: *hupo* ("underneath") and *deo* ("to bind," or literally "to under-bind" referring to the feet).

Hupodeo is used in the middle voice, which means, "Do this for yourself!" The angel could do for Peter things he could not do for himself. He could wake up Peter, break chains off him, keep the guards asleep, and swing open the outer gate automatically *(automatos)*. But he left Peter to do the things he could do for himself: "Wake up! Stand up! Put on your clothes! Put on your shoes! Follow me!"

It is a wonderful teamwork between the Lord and us. He expects us to do the things we can do and to trust Him for the things we cannot do.

Hupodeo—binding on our shoes—is one of these things the Lord expects us to do. Opening the iron gate that stands between us and total freedom is one of those things He delights in doing for us.

Greek Words for *Loosing*

Seven words in the Greek New Testament are translated "loose" or "loosing" in the *King James Version*. The word we want to look at thoroughly, because of its association with binding and loosing in Matthew 16:19 and 18:18, is the word *luo*. We will look first at the other "loosing" word following the chronological numbering of *Strong's Concordance*.

Airo

Airo ("ah'-ee-ro"), #142 in *Strong's*, appears 102 times in the Greek New Testament. In Acts 27:13 a reference is made to the departure of the ship that Paul, the prisoner, is taking to Rome: **"When the south wind blew softly, supposing that they had**

obtained their purpose *loosing (airo)* thence, they sailed close by Crete."

Airo is defined as taking up an anchor to get under way for a trip, sailing away, departing—or as we would say, "anchors aweigh."

Over 75 times in the *Authorized Version, airo* is translated "take," "take up," and "take away." Only once is it translated "loose." (Acts 27:13.) Other newer translations seem to prefer the words "to weigh anchor" over the *King James* "loosing." The thought of removal by lifting up is resident in the word.

There is a parallel between our past lives being held down by the weight of our own sins and salvation loosing the weights holding us down. Setting sail on the old ship of Zion can be compared to *airo*, or getting under way.

Anago

Anago ("an-ag'-o"), #321 in *Strong's*, appears 24 times. Six times it is associated with "bringing." Ten times it refers to sailing. Three times it is translated "loose." (Acts 13:13; 16:11; 27:21.) Acts 16:11 reads, **"Therefore *loosing (anago)* from Troas, we came with a straight course to Samothracia."**

Anago is a compound: *ana* means "up" and *ago* means "to lead." The word is defined as to bring up, to lead up, to lead from a lower place to a higher place. It is a nautical term for putting a ship out to sea. The sea as seen from the shore appears to rise. *Anago* was the word used to describe Paul "loosing" from a port and sailing the sea. Launching out or sailing away gave the illusion of rising to a higher plane, thus the word *anago* ("to lead up") was the best choice to use.

Apoluo

Apoluo ("ap-ol-oo'-o"), #630 in *Strong's*, appears 69 times in the *Authorized Version*. It is a motion word with these factors: dismissing, pardoning, sending away, detaining no longer, setting free, and fully releasing a person. In Luke 13:12 Jesus told the woman bound by infirmity for 18 years, **"Woman, thou art *loosed* (apoluo) from thine infirmity."** She was immediately healed.

Apoluo is a compound word: *apo* means "from" and *luo* means "unbinding or releasing." Dr. Bloomfield's Lexicon (1835 A.D.) stated about *apoluo*: "Disease is considered as a bondage. Healing is a release from the bond."[5] Thayer's Lexicon says *apoluo* means to loose the bonds of a captive and give him the liberty to go.[6] By releasing or setting free a person so he is detained no longer in his bonds, one makes the person free to return home.

How many times have circumstances put a bind on us, leaving us with the feeling of being locked up or tied down? Jesus breaks the chains and releases us to come back to our home base. What a Deliverer we have in our Savior! With Him we can always be home free. *Apoluo* is a liberating word.

Aniemi

Aniemi ("an-ee'-ay-mee"), #447 in *Strong's,* is used four times in the *Authorized Version:* Acts 16:26; 27:40; Ephesians 6:9; Hebrews 13:5. Acts 16:26 says, **"...immediately all the doors were opened, and every one's bands were loosed *(aniemi)*."**

Aniemi is defined as to loosen, to slacken, to unfasten chains, to release, letting go that which has been held fast, and the loosening of bonds.

In Acts 27:40 *aniemi* is used in a nautical sense.

In Ephesians 6:9 it is an admonition for employers to forbear *(aniemi)*, let up or slacken the work load of those in their employ ("masters/servants" is the terminology).

Hebrews 13:5 declares concerning the Lord's care for us, **"...he hath said, I will never *leave (aniemi)* thee,**

nor forsake thee." In this reference He is promising
we will be so bonded and welded in His loving care
that no one person or no one thing will be able to
sever the relationship.

Aniemi is a word describing prison bonds being
unfastened. It also assures us that the melding love of
God fastens us to Him without the fear of removal.

Katargeo

Katargeo ("kat-arg-eh'-o"), #2673 in *Strong's,* is
used 27 times. Over 20 times it is associated with the
idea of abolishing or doing away with. The *Authorized
Version* uses the word *loosed* only once: in Romans 7:2.
Paul is saying of a married woman that the marriage
covenant is binding "till death do them part." He
states, **"...if the husband be dead, she is *loosed (katargeo)* from the law of her husband."**

Katargeo says that in case of bereavement the
marriage covenant is rendered inactive. The wife is no
longer connected in marriage; the husband's death
has voided her status as a wife. This is the only time
the word *loosed* is used by *katargeo.*

The word has great implications in its other usages.
I suggest you look at Hebrews 2:14 and see how *katargeo* is used to render Satan's power null and void,

abolishing death. It is a powerful word. Looking at all the *Authorized Version* usages of *loosed,* we included it even though the great power base of *katargeo* was not fully developed in this study.

Lusis

Lusis ("loo'-sis"), #3080 in *Strong's,* appears only once in the *Authorized Version.* First Corinthians 7:27 asks the question: **"Art thou bound unto a wife? seek not to be *loosed* (lusis)."**

Lusis is defined as a dissolution, a release, a disjunction from any tie, a separation of the conjugal tie, or specifically a divorce.

Lusis is closely related to the main word of this "loose" series: *luo.* Originally *lusis* meant a loosing or delivering from anything that binds us or impedes action. Figuratively, it is defined as freeing one from evil of any kind of constraint or slavery.

Because Paul uses it in a context of the marriage tie, some scholars assume he is anti-matrimony or recommends celibacy. This is not what Paul is saying.

By reading First Corinthians 7:26-40 you will readily see that (1) life was very precarious and uncertain in his day, and (2) the Christians were expecting the return of Jesus Christ at any moment.

Reading the context conveys an overview. Paul is saying: "The time is too short, and things are not stable enough to make any drastic changes with this in mind. Abide in your calling, and keep on doing what you do best." Then he is saying, "If you are married, don't seek to be loosed *(lusis)* from that tie."

Twice—in verses 20 and 24—he urges them to stay with what they have going for them. In this setting *lusis* is the dissolving of a marriage. He urges them to remain in marriage despite the brevity of time and the impending era of coming persecution.

Lusis, or loosing, sets us up for the word used in the spiritual authority of the believer: *luo*. All the preceding words—*airo, anago, aniemi, apoluo, katargeo,* and *lusis*—are only the prelude to the word *luo* used in binding and loosing.

The Main Greek Word for *Loosing* in Binding and Loosing—Luo

...whatsoever thou shalt *loose (luo)* on earth shall be *loosed (lug)* in heaven.

Matthew 16:19, 18:18

Luo ("loo'-o"), #3089 in *Strong's,* appears 43 times in the *Authorized Version.* For 30 of those times *King*

James uses the words *loose, loosing* or *unloose* when used in the rabbinic sense of synagogue structure, morals or community life. It is defined as to abrogate, to annul, to declare lawful, to declare allowable, to admit to privileges, to abolish, to invalidate, or bring to an end what was formerly prohibited.

For the New Testament believer, *luo* means more than ecclesiastical structure and church government. It has to do with life in the Spirit and the freedom that goes with New Testament redemption.

Luo is a rich word that continually points to Jesus Christ's liberating work from man's imprisonment to sin, suffering, Satan and the wretched consequences of living in a flawed, defective, and imperfect world.

Jesus spoke to the woman bound for 18 years with curvature of the spine, and pronounced, **"Woman, thou art loosed (apoluo) from thine infirmity"** (Luke 13:12). This was an illustrated example of what *luo* can mean in our life of faith and prayers for people who use binding and loosing as part of their spiritual weaponry.

Luo can be defined as to dissolve, to break up, to destroy, to melt, to put off, to release, free from bondage, to discharge from prison, to restore a person to health, to liberate, to undo the chains, and to set free. Spiritually, it is making Satan's power null and void.

The Main Greek Word for *Binding* in Binding and Loosing—Deo

> ...whatsoever thou shalt *bind (deo)* on earth shall be *bound (deo)* in heaven....

> **Matthew 16:19, 18:18**

Deo ("deh'-o"), #1210 in *Strong's*, appears 44 times in the New Testament. For 37 times the *Authorized Version* translators used the words *bind* or *bound*.

Deo has two different applications. In the rabbinic setting of the New Testament, it referred to church discipline, morals and government. It is like a group of censors banning a movie or an immoral play. When used in this sense, *deo* is defined as to prohibit, to forbid, to declare unlawful or illicit, to impose a ban, or to expel (as in excommunication).

Deo has a second application which can be used in spiritual warfare, prayer, intercession, and fighting the good fight of faith. Jesus said in Matthew 12:29, **"...how can one enter into a strong man's house, and spoil his goods, except he first *bind (deo)* the strong man? and then he will spoil his house."** In this powerful promise the believer has been given great authority for waging victorious conflict against the powers of darkness.

In this spiritual arena *deo* is defined as to chain down, to hinder, to tie up hand and foot, to keep in bonds, to imprison, to take captive, and to fetter a furious person. In classic Greek it was used for putting a leash on a dog or roping a free-spirited horse.

It is encouraging to know we have the power and authority in Jesus' name to bind *(deo)* all of Satan's strategies and assaults. He goes around as a roaring lion, seeking whom he may devour, but the blood of Jesus negates his power. We are advised in Scripture to give him no place *(topos*—topography), not one inch of ground.

We are also promised that if we resist or vigorously oppose the devil, he will flee *(pheudo*—be the fugitive). Jesus said, "In my name, you will cast out (or expel) demons." (Mark 16:17.)

So binding *(deo)* the strong man can be accomplished by the weapons the Lord has given us. Following are the four main successful weapons:

1. The blood of Jesus. (Rev. 12:11.)

2. The name of Jesus. (Mark 16:17.)

3. The promises of God. (Eph. 6:17.)

4. Militant praises while going forth to battle. (2 Chron. 20:21,22.)

Some Added Comments on Binding and Loosing From Matthew 16:19 and 18:18

The first time the statement is made, Jesus is speaking to Peter. The second time He is speaking to the Twelve, and ultimately to all disciples.

Matthew Henry states: "This is a great honor that Christ, here, puts on the believer. He will not only take notice of their statements but will also confirm them.[7] The power to bind and loose is actually the power to shut and open."[8]

Since Spirit-led believers are attuned to victorious Christian living, we can emphasize the dynamics of binding and loosing for winning the victory in our fight of faith.

Here are some interesting comments from Bible scholars of the past:

A.T. Robertson, a Southern Baptist theologian in 1930 A.D., stated: "The more personal we make these great words, the nearer we come to the mind of Christ. The more ecclesiastical we make them the further we drift from Him."[9]

Bishop Westcott, an Anglican scholar in 1900 A.D., wrote that there was nothing in the context to confine this to the Apostles or any particular group of men and that this commission must be regarded properly as the commission of the whole Christian society and not of the Christian ministry only.[10]

A diseased person is one held in bondage by Satan. Thayer's Greek Lexicon says that *luo* lets a person be freed from the bondage of disease and be restored to health. *Luo* also releases those bound by the chains of sin.[11]

The Lutheran Commentary states, "Your sentence, dictated by the Holy Ghost, will be equivalent to a divine judgment."[12]

Barnes' Notes say that we bind and loose things, not people. It is *whatsoever,* not *whosoever.*"[13]

So the real effectiveness in binding and loosing is not attacking people, but attacking the spirit motivating those people to act in a manner that is contrary to the Word of God. Jesus gave us power and authority over all the power of the Enemy. (Luke 10:19.) No one need be a victim when Jesus told us to be victors.

Examples of Binding and Loosing Being Proclaimed Verbally

Say these words:

In the name of Jesus,
I bind confusion and release peace...
I bind fear and release faith...
I bind sickness and release health...
I bind poverty and release prosperity...
I bind accidents and release safety...
I bind discouragement and release confidence...
I say no to Satan's will to steal, kill and destroy; I say
* yes to God's will to give me life more abundantly...*
All this is in Jesus' mighty name!

Let God arise, let his enemies be scattered....

Psalm 68:1

You have good biblical authority for being aggressive in prayer and using binding and loosing for personal victorious living. Some militant praying saints call it "pressing the battle to the gate" (Isa. 28:6), knowing Jesus promised us the gates of hell would not prevail!

Scriptures

²⁶ Then God said, "Let us make a man—someone like ourselves, to be the master of all life upon the earth and in the skies and in the seas."

[27] So God made man like his Maker. Like God did God make man; man and maid did he make them.
[28] And God blessed them and told them, "Multiply and fill the earth and subdue it; you are masters of the fish and birds and all the animals."

Genesis 1:26-28 TLB

Then the Lord God took the man and put him into the garden of Eden to cultivate it and keep it.

Genesis 2:15 TLB

So Balaam said to Balak, "Behold, I have come now to you! Am I able to speak anything at all? The word that God puts in my mouth, that I shall speak."

Numbers 22:38 NAS

[4] What is man that you are mindful of him, the son of man that you care for him?
[5] You made him a little lower than the heavenly beings and crowned him with glory and honor.
[6] You made him ruler over the works of your hands; you put everything under his feet:
[7] all flocks and herds, and the beasts of the field,
[8] the birds of the air, and the fish of the sea, all that swim the paths of the seas.

Psalm 8:4-8 NIV

The heavens belong to the Lord, but he has given the earth to all mankind.

Psalm 115:16 TLB

Death and life are in the power of the tongue, and they who indulge it shall eat the fruit of it [for death or life].

Proverbs 18:21 AMP

⁷ Keep on asking and it will be given you; keep on seeking and you will find; keep on knocking [reverently] and the door will be opened to you. ⁸ For everyone who keeps on asking receives, and he who keeps on seeking finds, and to him who keeps on knocking it will be opened.

Matthew 7:7,8 AMP

For He was teaching them as one having authority, and not as their scribes.

Matthew 7:29 NAS

⁸ But the centurion answered and said, "Lord, I am not worthy for You to come under my roof, but just say the word, and my servant will be healed. ⁹ "For I, too, am a man under authority, with soldiers under me; and I say to this one, 'Go!' and he goes, and to another, 'Come!' and he comes, and to my slave, 'Do this!' and he does it."

¹⁰ Now when Jesus heard this, He marveled, and said to those who were following, "Truly I say to you, I have not found such great faith with anyone in Israel."

Matthew 8:8-10 NAS

He called his twelve disciples to him and gave them authority to drive out evil spirits and to heal every disease and sickness.

Matthew 10:1 NIV

⁷ And preach as you go, saying, "The kingdom of heaven is at hand,"
⁸ Heal the sick, raise the dead, cleanse lepers, cast out demons. You received without paying; give without pay.

Matthew 10:7,8 RSV

Truly, I tell you, whatever you forbid and declare to be improper and unlawful on earth must be what is already forbidden in heaven, and whatever you permit and declare proper and lawful on earth must be already permitted in heaven.

Matthew 18:18 AMP

¹⁸ He told his disciples, "I have been given all authority in heaven and earth.

¹⁹ Therefore go and make disciples in all the nations, baptizing them into the name of the Father and of the Son and of the Holy Spirit, ²⁰ and then teach these new disciples to obey all the commands I have given you; and be sure of this—that I am with you always, even to the end of the world."

Matthew 28:18-20 TLB

And they were amazed at His teaching; for He was teaching them as one having authority, and not as the scribes.

Mark 1:22 NAS

Calling the Twelve to him, he sent them out two by two and gave them authority over evil spirits.

Mark 6:7 NIV

³⁸ John said to Him, "Teacher, we saw someone casting out demons in Your name, and we tried to hinder him because he was not following us." ³⁹ But Jesus said, "Do not hinder him, for there is no one who shall perform a miracle in My name, and be able soon afterward to speak evil of Me.

⁴⁰ "For he who is not against us is for us."

Mark 9:38-40 NAS

[17] And those who believe shall use my authority to cast out demons, and they shall speak new languages.

[18] They will be able even to handle snakes with safety, and if they drink anything poisonous, it won't hurt them; and they will be able to place their hands on the sick and heal them.

Mark 16:17,18 TLB

And amazement came upon them all, and they began discussing with one another saying, "What is this message? For with authority and power He commands the unclean spirits, and they come out."

Luke 4:36 NAS

Then calling the Twelve together He conferred on them power and authority over all the demons and to cure diseases; and sent them out to proclaim the Kingdom of God and to cure the sick.

Luke 9:1 WEYMOUTH

[1] Now after this the Lord appointed seventy others, and sent them two and two ahead of Him to every city and place where He Himself was going to come.

[2] And He was saying to them, "The harvest is plentiful, but the laborers are few; therefore

beseech the Lord of the harvest to send out laborers into His harvest.

[3] "Go your ways; behold, I send you out as lambs in the midst of wolves.

[4] "Carry no purse, no bag, no shoes; and greet no one on the way.

[5] "And whatever house you enter, first say, 'Peace be to this house.'

[6] "And if a man of peace is there, your peace will rest upon him; but if not, it will return to you.

[7] "And stay in that house, eating and drinking what they give you; for the laborer is worthy of his wages. Do not keep moving from house to house.

[8] "And whatever city you enter, and they receive you, eat what is set before you;

[9] and heal those in it who are sick, and say to them, 'The kingdom of God has come near to you.'"

Luke 10:1-9 NAS

[19] And I have given you authority over all the power of the Enemy, and to walk among serpents and scorpions and to crush them. Nothing shall injure you!

[20] However, the important thing is not that demons obey you, but that your names are registered as citizens of heaven.

Luke 10:19,20 TLB

³¹ Jesus therefore was saying to those Jews who had believed Him, "If you abide in My word, then you are truly disciples of Mine;

³² and you shall know the truth, and the truth shall make you free."

John 8:31,32 NAS

¹² Truly, truly, I say to you, he who believes in Me, the works that I do shall he do also; and greater works than these shall he do; because I go to the Father.

¹³ And whatever you ask in My name, that will I do, that the Father may be glorified in the Son.

¹⁴ If you ask Me anything in My name, I will do it.

John 14:12-14 NAS

But Peter said, "I do not possess silver and gold, but what I do have I give to you: In the name of Jesus Christ the Nazarene—walk!"

Acts 3:6 NAS

And Peter said to him, "Aeneas, Jesus Christ heals you; arise, and make your bed." And immediately he arose.

Acts 9:34 NAS

But Peter sent them all out and knelt down and prayed, and turning to the body, he said,

"Tabitha, arise." And she opened her eyes, and when she saw Peter, she sat up.

Acts 9:40 NAS

³ As Paul gathered an armful of sticks to lay on the fire, a poisonous snake, driven out by the heat, fastened itself onto his hand!
⁴ The people of the island saw it hanging there and said to each other, "A murderer, no doubt! Though he escaped the sea, justice will not permit him to live!"
⁵ But Paul shook off the snake into the fire and was unharmed.

Acts 28:3-5 TLB

I have strength for all things in Christ Who empowers me—I am ready for anything and equal to anything through Him Who infuses inner strength into me, [that is, I am self-sufficient in Christ's sufficiency].

Philippians 4:13 AMP

⁹ For it is in Christ that the fulness of God's nature dwells embodied,
¹⁰ and in Him you are made complete, and He is the Lord of all princes and rulers.

Colossians 2:9,10 Weymouth

These, then, are the things you should teach. Encourage and rebuke with all authority. Do not let anyone despise you.

Titus 2:15 NIV

Prayer:
Commitment To Put on the Armor of God

In the name of Jesus, I put on the whole armor of God, that I may be able to stand against the wiles of the devil, for I wrestle not against flesh and blood, but against principalities, powers, the rulers of the darkness of this world, and against spiritual wickedness in high places.

Therefore, I take unto myself the whole armor of God, that I may be able to withstand in the evil day, and having done all, to stand. I stand, therefore, having my loins girt about with truth. Your Word, Lord, which is truth, contains all the weapons of my warfare which are not carnal, but mighty through God to the pulling down of strongholds.

I have on the breastplate of righteousness, which is faith and love. My feet are shod with the preparation of the gospel of peace. In Christ Jesus I have peace, and pursue peace with all men. I am a minister of reconciliation proclaiming the good news of the gospel.

I take the shield of faith, wherewith I am able to quench all the fiery darts of the wicked, the helmet of salvation (holding the thoughts, feeling, and purpose of God's heart) and the sword of the Spirit, which is the Word of God. In the face of all trials, tests, temptations, and tribulation, I cut to pieces the snare of the enemy by speaking the Word of God. Greater is He that is in me than he that is in the world.

Thank You, Father, for the armor. I will pray at all times—on every occasion, in every season—in the Spirit, with all [manner of] prayer and entreaty. To that end I will keep alert and watch with strong purpose and perseverance, interceding in behalf of all the saints. My power and ability and sufficiency are from God Who has qualified me as a minister and a dispenser of a new covenant [of salvation through Christ]. Amen.

<u>*Scripture References*</u>

Ephesians 6:11-14a	*Ephesians 6:16,17* AMP
John 17:17b	*Ephesians 6:14b,15* AMP
2 Corinthians 10:4	*Ephesians 2:14*
Psalm 34:14	*1 John 4:4b*
2 Corinthians 5:10	*2 Corinthians 3:5,6* AMP

¹ p. 1143.

² Finis Jennings Dake, *Dake's Annotated Reference Bible*, (Lawrenceville, Georgia: Dake Bible Sales, 1963), p. 116-lh.

³ John Parkhurst and Hugh James Rose, *A Greek and English Lexicon to the New Testament* (London: C.J.G. and F. Rovington, 1829), p. 742.

⁴ *Scripture in Song, Songs of Praise*, Vol. 1 (Maryborough: Australian Print Group, 1979), p. 185.

⁵ Samuel Thomas Bloomfield, 6th ed., *The Greek New Testament* (London: Longman, Brown, Green and Longman, 1845).

⁶ Joseph Henry Thayer, *Greek-English Lexicon of the New Testament* (Grand Rapids: Baker Book House, 1980), p. 66.

[7] Matthew Henry, *Commentary on the Whole Bible* (Old Tappan: Fleming H. Revell Co., 1982), p. 261.

[8] Ibid., p. 233.

[9] Archibald Thomas Robertson, *World Pictures in the New Testament* (Nashville: Broadman Press, 1930), p. 135.

[10] B. F. Westcott, *The Gospel According to St. John* (London: John Murray, 1898), p. 295.

[11] Joseph Henry Thayer, *Greek-English Lexicon of the New Testament* (Grand Rapids: Baker Book House, 1980), p. 384.

[12] Charles F. Schaeffer, *Annotations on the Gospel According to St. Matthew* (New York: The Christian Literature Co., 1895), p. 13.

[13] Albert Barnes, *Notes on the New Testament* (Grand Rapids: Baker Book House), p. 171.

PRAYER

Prayer must become as natural as breathing. With such prayer, men defeat spiritual forces arrayed against them that no human means could overcome.

— Gordon Lindsay

Greek and Hebrew Word Studies

OLD TESTAMENT—*PALAL*

Hearken unto the voice of my cry, my King, and my God: for unto thee will I *pray (palal)*.

Psalm 5:2

NEW TESTAMENT—*ENTEUXIS*

For it is sanctified by the word of God and *prayer (enteuxis)*.

1 Timothy 4:5

You cannot pray effectively or intelligently without knowing the will of God. We know the will of God by knowing the Word of God, because God's will is revealed in God's Word.

If you do not know God's will, then you have not been reading the Bible, because that is how He makes His will available to you.

First John 5:14,15 says: "And this is the confidence that we have in him, that, if we ask any thing according to his will, he heareth us: And if we know that he hear us, whatsoever we ask, we know that we have the petitions that we desired of him." If you have confidence that you prayed according to God's will, you should also be confident that He heard you.

— Fred Price
The Word Bible[1]

Prayer—*Palal*

Prayer is one of the most vital subjects in the Scriptures and it receives extensive mention in both Old and New Testaments. Prayer expresses a rightful understanding of the one true God and Who He is, of our special relationship to Him, and of our total dependence upon Him.

Our entire foundation for understanding prayer is established by the Hebrew Scriptures, and the New Testament confirms and builds upon what the Old Testament has established.

There are about twelve Hebrew words translated "prayer," "pray," and "praying," in the *King James Version* of the Old Testament. Several of these words have similar or overlapping definitions. Some are very specific in their designated meanings. Let us take a brief look at each of the Hebrew words for "pray."

The Hebrew word *be'ah* (pronounced "beh-aw'"), #1156 in *Strong's*, means to ask, desire and make petition. The verb *chanan* ("khan-an'"), #2603 in *Strong's*, means to be gracious; to make supplication. A noun form of this word sometimes spelled is the shorter form *chen* (pronounced "khane"), #2580 in *Strong's*, and means grace, favor, and beauty.

There are two forms of this word family used in Zechariah 12:10: **"I will pour upon the...inhabitants if Jerusalem, the spirit of *grace* and of *supplications*: and they shall look upon me whom they have pierced...."** This beloved verse shows the close linguistic tie between *grace* and *supplication*—an appeal for graciousness and favor. (The Hebrew words used in

119

this verse are *chen* and the plural of *tachanuwn* (tak-han-oon'), #8469 in *Strong's,* respectively.)

Another word translated "pray" is *sha'al* ("shaw-al'"), #7592 in *Strong's,* which literally means to ask, to inquire about, to seek to know the condition of someone or something. This verb is used in Psalm 122:6: **"Pray for the peace of Jerusalem: they shall prosper that love thee."** This should be understood to mean, "Ask concerning Jerusalem's welfare; inquire as to how peaceful she is." It is a command to be concerned and involved, and to make the effort to check on Jerusalem's condition.

There are several words which are translated "pray," but are used infrequently in the Old Testament.

Lu' ("loo"), #3863 in *Strong's,* means, "Pray that..." or "Would to God...," and expresses a strong appeal for something.

'Anna' (awn'-naw), #577 in *Strong's,* means, I beseech Thee.

Na' (naw), #4994 in *Strong's,* means now. This emphatic cry is the last syllable of the Hebrew prayer and exclamation found in Psalm 118:25, I beseech thee, O Lord, save now. "Save now" is *hoshiya-nah!* In the New Testament we find the attempt to spell *hoshiya-nah* in the Greek alphabet, which has no means for writing the sound of "sh." Thus we have hosanna.

Other relevant words include *'athar* ("aw-thar'"), #6279 in *Strong's*, which means to burn incense, to entreat or pray; and *lachash* ("lakh'-ash"), #3908 in *Strong's*, which means to chant, whisper, pray.

Another highly interesting word is *siyach* ("see'-akh"), #7878 in *Strong's*, which means to meditate, pray, talk with, muse aloud. *Siyach* is used frequently in the Psalms. For example, Psalm 77:6 states, **"...I *commune* with mine own heart: and my spirit made diligent search."** Another example is Psalm 119:78: **"...will *meditate* in thy precepts."** The word is translated "pray" in Psalm 55:17: **"Evening, and morning, and at noon, will I pray, and cry aloud: and he shall hear my voice."**

Our main word is *palal* ("paw-lal'"), #6419 in *Strong's*, which occurs 84 times as a verb (to pray, to intercede) and more than 75 times in its noun form *tephillah* ("tef-il-law'"), #8605, meaning prayer.

There are quite a number of theories as to why *palal* means "to pray." Scholars are not agreed about its primary linguistic thrust. Some trace it to a verb meaning to fall down, suggesting it refers to falling down before a sovereign and presenting one's petition. Others note the verb often means to present a case in favor of someone; to pray or intercede on behalf of another.

There are other linguistic curiosities about the way in which *palal* functions in Hebrew. But the important thing is that it almost always occurs in the reflexive case, which suggests a strong sense of taking it upon oneself to pray or intercede earnestly and intensely.

In Job 42:10, when Job "prayed for his friends," it was not a casual prayer described. Rather, the verbal stem alone shows Job's great personal involvement in that intercessory prayer for his tormenting, accusatory friends. What a picture of intercession as it ought to be!

Jesus likewise interceded for transgressors, including those who wronged Him personally. (Isa. 53:12.) In His teaching, He commanded that we should likewise pray for those who abuse us. (Matt. 5:44.)

It would seem logical to us that the greatest prayer is the dynamic call from a great servant of God, answered by fire from heaven, the stoppage of rain and its reappearance, the parting of the waters, and the interference with the movements of heavenly bodies. Actually, Scripture shows that some of the men who accomplished such things in prayer were no different from the rest of us. (See James 5:17,18.)

The truth is, the highest mountain ever climbed in prayer is the intercession for and sincere pleading on behalf of one's tormentors. David climbed that mountain. (Ps. 35:12-14.) So did Moses and Stephen. (Ex. 32:11-14,31-34; Acts 7:59,60.) Most triumphantly and majestically, our beloved Messiah climbed that mountain. (Luke 23:33,34,35-43.)

From the verb *palal* comes the noun *tephillah*. The plural of this noun is *tephillim* (prayers). *Tefillim* also refers to the items worn by devout Jewish men when they go to prayer. Jesus Himself wore the prayer garments prescribed by the Law of Moses. The fringes, *tsiytsith* ("tsee-tseeth'"), #6734 in *Strong's*, required in Numbers 15:38 are specifically referred to in the original Greek wording of Matthew 9:20. In that reference, a woman was healed when she touched the fringes or tassels of Jesus' clothing.

Scripture teaches so extensively on the subject of prayer that one could spend a lifetime examining its many revelations. Any study of prayer is apt to be incomplete. The subject is vast. This is one reason we made reference to the large number of words translated "pray" or "prayer" in the Old Testament. These words show the enormous variation in the nature, circumstance, style, position, sound and purpose prayer may take. But remember, prayer is conversing with a

Person. He is the One Who brings the joys of a satisfying prayer life.

A deeper study of prayer from both Old and New Testaments will lead us to see that our Western view of prayer quite often is distant from what the Bible records it to be. Let's take an example.

We teach our little ones, "Fold your hands, close your eyes and get ready to talk to God." This may be well and good, but it is entirely non-scriptural.

First of all, the pressing of the palms of the hands together is completely unknown in Bible history. This form of hand positioning for prayer comes to us entirely from Hinduism, and was not practiced by believers in either Old or New Testament times. It was added to "Christian" tradition centuries after the close of the New Testament writings.

As for closing one's eyes in prayer, it is recorded on numerous times that Jesus lifted up His eyes to heaven in prayer (that is, He prayed looking upward), but it is not stated even once that He closed His eyes in prayer!

These things are mentioned only to cause us to reflect for a moment on the truth that our religious traditions in Christendom contain many elements which may or may not be healthy, but are (in any case) foreign to Scripture! We can never be misled by following God's Word, but we can certainly become confused by traditions of men. Careful observation about the Lord's manner of prayer will teach us a great deal. His *understanding* and His *example* are perfect.

Finally, as a devotional thought, it should be noted that when a person has spent a lifetime talking with the Lord, there is a depth and a power in his or her prayers which reflect a deep knowledge of God, His ways, His will, His nature, and His presence.

How often have we heard an elderly saint begin to lead in prayer with an address as simple as "Dear Lord" or "Lord Jesus" and have the room charged with power and flooded with God's presence before the next word can be breathed! The years of communing with God bring an unmistakable authority, depth, and sweetness to a believer.

It also is true that the prayers of a young child are often pure and sincere, being marvelously free of intellectual, cultural and traditional hindrances! Jesus made pointed reference to the Scripture which declares that God will perfect praise, ordain strength and **"still the enemy and the avenger"** (Ps. 8:2) out of the mouths of babes and nursing children!

It is seriously suggested that when a congregation reaches a critical impasse or some spiritual crisis relating to "the enemy," the young children who are filled with the Holy Spirit should lead in prayer, praise, and subduing "the avenger." In Matthew 21:12-16 Jesus chided the adults who hindered such a response from the youths, and rejoiced and gave thanks that such was the Father's way! (See Matthew 11:25,26; Luke 10:21.)

Let us proceed joyfully and victoriously to new and broader dimensions of prayer, intercession, and coming to know God clearly.

The Greek Words for *Prayer* In the *King James Version*

The subject of prayer covers a wide range of expressions: thanksgiving, praise, intercession, pleas for spiritual help, requests for healing or material blessings, immediate relief from distress, danger or disaster, or seeking guidance.

The Bible encourages both public and private prayers. Public prayers can be structured liturgies or spontaneous extemporaneous utterances. Private prayers can be done kneeling, standing, sitting, or being prostrate.

All nine Greek words in this study use the word *prayer*, as well as other words chosen by the *King James* translators. Since our subject is prayer, we have confined ourselves to these nine words. Other valid prayer words in the *King James*—such as *ask, petition, supplication, seek* and *request*—are not included in this study.

Through the ages scholars have attempted to categorize prayer by a particular Greek word. Since the Reformation, most scholars see various aspects of prayer rather than a chronological order. For example, a sequence is given in First Timothy 2:1: "**...supplications, prayers, intercessions, and giving of thanks, be made for all men.**"

Early church fathers, like Augustine and Origen, tried to build a bridge of increasing intensity or chronological dynamism in the order of the words. Reformation writers, from Calvin on, see the words as looking at the subject of prayer from different perspectives.

The order of these words follows the *Strong's Concordance* numbering, except for *intercession (enteuxis)*. This was a fascinating word, filled with such interesting information and good potential that it is placed last. The first eight words will be basically defined. The last word, *enteuxis*, will be studied in more depth.

Deesis

Deesis ("deh'-ay-sis") is #1162 in *Strong's*. A good example is found in James 5:16: **"...the effectual fervent *prayer (deesis)* of a righteous man availeth much."** This word is used by Paul 13 times, by Luke four times, by James once and by Peter once.

It is not exclusively a religious word like many of the prayer words. Sometimes it is used for asking or making a request of a fellow man. However, all 19 times *deesis* is in the New Testament, it is used as a prayer to the Lord.

Deesis is defined as a petition, a supplication, an asking, an entreating, a beseeching, a wanting, a specific thing requested, and imploring God's aid. *Deesis* stresses (1) our need; (2) our inability or insufficiency to meet that need; and (3) God's willingness to hear, respond and meet the need.

Deesis is not an appeal to God's reluctance, but an appeal to His willingness. Man's extremity becomes God's opportunity to hear and answer prayer.

Deomai

Deomai ("deh'-om-ahee") is #1189 in *Strong's*. A good example is found in Acts 4:31: **"And when they had *prayed (deomai)*, the place was shaken where** they were assembled together; and they were all filled with the Holy Ghost, and they spake the word of God with boldness."

Used 22 times, *deomai* involves humbly and earnestly praying for an urgent need or a specific need. It includes desires and longings as well as needs.

Scholars point out that *deomai* has a warm and winsome attractiveness about it. The individual who prays is deeply aware of his personal needs. *Deomai* is his asking for specific help. The word includes expecting a definite answer for external needs or spiritual blessings.

There is in the word *deomai* a sense of urgency, an earnestness, and soliciting eagerly. You can feel the intensity in the words of First Thessalonians 3:10, where Paul states, **"Night and day *praying (deomai)* exceedingly that we might see your face, and might perfect that which is lacking in your faith."** A definition of *deomai* could easily be emphatic and intensive prayer.

Erotao

Erotao ("er-o-tah'-o") is #2065 in *Strong's*. A good example of *erotao* is found in John 17:20: **"Neither *pray (erotao)* I for these alone, but for them also which shall believe on me through their word."**

Used 58 times in the New Testament, *erotao* is defined as to interrogate or question, to ask a favor, to make a request, to seek information, or to try to get an answer.

Erotao is a relationship word. In Luke 14:32, it is one king making a request of another king. Because of its usage in passages where Jesus is speaking *of* His Father or *to* His Father (John 14:16; 16:26; 17:5,9,21), some scholars see a familiarity or equality in the word that would exclude us. However, in 1 John 5:16 the word *erotao* is used for our praying regarding disciplinary matters.

Erotao could easily be defined as prayer that asks questions, confident that answers will come.

Euche

Euche ("yoo-khay'") is #2171 in *Strong's*. An example of *euche* is found in James 5:15: **"The *prayer (euche)* of faith shall save the sick, and the Lord shall raise him up."** This word is only used three times in the New Testament. Twice it is translated vow (Acts 18:18, 21:23), and once as the "prayer of faith" (James 5:15).

There is a seriousness about the word *euche*. People who make vows are serious about their votive commitment. People who are seriously ill can pray a serious prayer *(euche)* and find healing.

There are not many definitions of *euche* in Greek lexicons. A simple definition could be an all-out prayer that looks seriously at circumstances. According to James 5:15, this is the kind of prayer that causes the Lord to heal and raise up someone from the sick bed.

Euchomai

Euchomai ("yoo'-khom-ahee") is #2172 in *Strong's*. This word is used seven times in the New Testament. Five times it is translated as a wish. A good example is 3 John 2: **"Beloved, I *wish* (euchomai) above all things that thou mayest prosper and be in health, even as thy soul prospereth."**

Phrases like *I wish* (Rom. 9:3) and *I would to God* (Acts 26:29) use *euchomai* as a prayer word associated with strong desires, hopes, aspirations, and longings. In 3 John 2, a strong wish for the Lord to bless them spirit, soul, and body is equivalent to a heartfelt and sincere prayer.

Parakaleo

Parakaleo ("par-ak-al-eh'-o"), #3870 in *Strong's*, has three definitions: (1) to call to one's side for help;

(2) exhorting; and (3) comforting. Of the 106 times it is used in the New Testament, 39 times words like *beseech, entreat, desire* and *pray* are used. The rest of the time it uses *comfort* and *exhort*.

Parakaleo as a prayer word is defined as asking for help, to call for someone to come alongside, to assist, to summon aid, and earnest appealing for added urgent support.

One example of *parakaleo* is found in Matthew 26:53. In the Garden of Gethsemane when Jesus is arrested, He says, **"Thinkest thou that I cannot now *pray (parakaleo)* to my Father, and he shall presently give me more than twelve legions of angels?"** He was saying, "If I but call, thousands of angels will come alongside to help and support me." *Parakaleo* was the choice word to use.

Another good example of *parakaleo* is in Acts 16:9: **"And a vision appeared to Paul in the night; there stood a man of Macedonia, and *prayed (parakaleo)* him, saying, Come over into Macedonia, and help us."** Again, the word *parakaleo* is the appropriate word.

Parakaleo, meaning "to call alongside for assistance," is used many times in the Gospels when people appeal to Jesus for help. Bible translators use the word for implying a greater degree of urging than normal prayer words. A good definition of *parakaleo* could easily be appealing to someone to come alongside and give you the extra support needed for completing your task.

Proseuche

Proseuche ("pros-yoo-khay'"), the noun, is #4335 in *Strong's*. *Proseuche* appears 37 times in the New Testament. Relationship is the undergirding quality of this word. It carries with it a general feeling of devotion to the Lord. It also emphasizes the power of the One to Whom we are praying.

Proseuche is the generic Greek word for prayer. Unrestricted as to its contents, it is the most general term for offering prayers to the Lord in the New Testament. *Pros* is "towards" and *euche* is "prayer." It includes requests for spiritual blessings, prayer poured out in an intercessory way, praise and thanksgiving, presenting needs that only God can supply, and asking for strength which He alone bestows.

In addition, Acts 16:13,16 shows that *proseuche* denotes a place of prayer. Our words *prayer chapel* describe this word. *Proseuche* could easily be defined as the sacred word for drawing near to God with our requests. In our dependent state there are needs always present that God alone can meet.

A good example of *proseuche* is found in Revelation 5:8: **"...four and twenty elders fell down before the Lamb, having every one of them harps, and golden vials full of odours** (incense), **which are the *prayers (proseuche)* of saints."** In heaven our tears are bottled up for eternity (Ps. 56:8) and our prayers are kept as bottles of perfume. (Ps. 141:2; Rev. 5:8.)

Imagine the bliss of eternal life as the Lord lets us inhale as an aromatic fragrance which in our earthly journey was tears of sorrow and prayers of need. All our prayers have been heard, kept, remembered, and bottled with God's stamp of beauty. The bottled prayers of the saints cannot be matched by any rare or exotic perfume on our planet. How beautiful heaven must be, filled with an aroma from our prayer containers! Truly more things are wrought by prayer than this world ever knows.

Proseuchomai

Proseuchomai ("pros-yoo'-khom-ahee"), the verb, is #4336 in *Strong's*. *Proseuchomai* appears 87 times and is always used of prayer to God—petitionary prayer that removes all formality and stiffness. It is a word used to describe prayer not as a structured or legalistic obligation but as a warm and genuine conversation with the Lord.

A good example of *proseuchomai* is found in 1 Timothy 2:8: **"I will therefore that men *pray* (*proseuchomai*) every where, lifting up holy hands, without wrath and doubting."** A strong element of worship is included in this prayer word.

Enteuxis—Prayer as Intercession

Enteuxis ("ent'-yook-sis"), #1783 in *Strong's*, appears twice in the New Testament: First Timothy 2:1 and 4:5.

First Timothy 2:1 says, **"I exhort therefore, that, first of all, supplications, prayers, *intercessions* (*enteuxis*), and giving of thanks, be made for all men."**

First Timothy 4:5 concerns our praying over food before eat: **"For it is sanctified by the word of God and prayer (*enteuxis*)."**

Enteuxis has an interesting history. It first had to do with meeting a person either by prearrangement or by chance. Early grammarians define the word as coming together, joining someone on a journey, falling in with, meeting with, catching up with, interviewing with, visiting with, and approaching someone for the purpose of dialogue. It also includes the idea of catching up with someone for whom you are looking.

In the Old Testament, the word is *paga'* (paw-gah'), #6293 in *Strong's,* (to light upon, to meet together). An example is Isaiah 64:5: **"Thou *meetest (pagah)* him that rejoiceth...."** Literally, "You light upon, meet with, or overtake the rejoicing believer."

Enteuxis progresses to the actual conversation carried on. When speaking to the Lord, *enteuxis* is raised to a level of intimacy, communing with the Lord and entering into familiar speech and heart-warming audience with Him. It is similar to a subject being invited to enter into the audience chamber of a king. The access and the good fortune of coming together with a king carries with it petitions, requests and interceding on behalf of yourself or someone else.

In *enteuxis* the distinctive feature of the word is freedom of access, confidence, and holy intimacy, as we boldly approach the Lord to present our requests, and needs.

Bishop Ellicott in his commentary on First Timothy states: "Prayer in its most individual and urgent form; prayer in which God is, as it were, sought in audience and personally drawn nigh to."[2] We are not making our requests to God from a great distance or across some infinity of space. ("Is there anybody up there?") *Enteuxis* is defined as the privilege of having a personal sacred interview because of His gracious love for us.

Enteuxis also includes approaching God and asking Him for some great thing. An example would be Joshua commanding the sun to stand still. (Josh. 10:12.) *Trench's Synonyms* says, *enteuxis* "refers to free intimate prayer that boldly draws near to God."[3]

Years ago, the word *intercession* started being described as storming heaven, praying till you pray through, tearing down the strongholds of resistance, overcoming all obstacles, and standing in the gap. All these phrases are scriptural and factual realities. They add another dimension to the meaning of *intercession (enteuxis)*.

We are in intimate and loving conversation as we present our petitions, our pleas, our prayers. *Enteuxis* says, "Prayer has tremendous privileges and is answered with tremendous displays of power."

William Barclay stated: *Enteuxis* is prayer that is "nothing less than entering into the presence of the Almighty and receiving all the resources of the Eternal."[4]

When *enteuxis* is used in First Timothy 4:5, Paul is giving a biblical approach to praying over food about to be consumed. He warns that some will command the abstaining of certain foods. Paul tells us everything God created is good and no food need be denied provided it is received with the giving of thanks.

Paul says the food **"is sanctified** (or set apart for consumption) **by the word of God and** *prayer"* *(enteuxis).* The construction in the original language could read, "by praying words of Scripture over the food."

Early-day believers offered up praise verses before eating their meals. This is no doubt how the practice of "saying grace" over food began. This verse encourages our grace to be actual portions of God's Word applicable to the occasion.

The *Goodspeed Translation* renders it, **"Nothing need be refused, provided it is accepted with thanksgiving, for then it is consecrated by prayer and the Scripture used in it."** When praying for our food, we are encouraged to quote Scripture over it.

Since *enteuxis* in First Timothy 4:5 suggests the use of verses of Scripture, it might add a dimension to our approach to the Lord to fill our intercession with Scripture promises. It is possible to change things through intercession made by quoting verses to the Lord!

The bottom line on *enteuxis (prayer)* is relationship.

1. We meet with the Lord. (Practiced continuously, a discipline becomes a habit.)

2. It would be easy to paraphrase Isaiah 40:31 as *They that wait upon the Lord shall exchange their strength, theirs for His.*

3. An unhurried intimacy is developed. We share our gratitude, our appreciation, and our thanks for His merciful longsuffering and gracious benefits He has bestowed upon us.

4. He invites us to present our petition, our plea, our prayer, and our interceding for someone in great need.

The whole concept of intercession *(enteuxis)* is more than rushing into God's presence with a big list of urgent needs. It is an ongoing process of *waiting on* the Lord, *waiting with* the Lord and *waiting for* the Lord.

> Thou art coming to a King,
> Large petitions with thee bring;
> For His grace and power are such
> None can ever ask too much.[5]

Scriptures

[4] Make the Eternal your delight, and he will give you all your heart's desire.

⁵ Leave all to him, rely on him, and he will see to it.

Psalm 37:4,5 Moffatt

¹⁸ If I had cherished iniquity in my heart, the Lord would not have listened.
¹⁹ But truly God has listened; he has given heed to the voice of my prayer.
²⁰ Blessed be God, because he has not rejected my prayer or removed his steadfast love from me! To the choirmaster: with stringed instruments.

Psalm 66:18-20 RSV

¹⁸ If I had cherished sin in my heart, the Lord would not have listened;
¹⁹ but God has surely listened and heard my voice in prayer.
²⁰ Praise be to God, who has not rejected my prayer or withheld his love from me!

Psalm 66:18-20 NIV

¹⁸ The Eternal is near all who call on him, who call on him sincerely;
¹⁹ he satisfies his worshippers, he hears their cry and helps them.

Psalm 145:18,19 Moffatt

[11] "For I know the plans that I have for you," declares the Lord, "plans for welfare and not for calamity to give you a future and a hope.
[12] "Then you will call upon Me and come and pray to Me, and I will listen to you.
[13] "And you will seek Me and find Me, when you search for Me with all your heart."

Jeremiah 29:11-13 NAS

Call to me and I will answer you and tell you great and unsearchable things you do not know.

Jeremiah 33:3 NIV

But I say to you, Love your enemies and pray for those who persecute you.

Matthew 5:44 RSV

[7] Ask and it will be given to you; seek and you will find; knock and the door will be opened to you.
[8] For everyone who asks receives; he who seeks finds; and to him who knocks, the door will be opened.
[9] Which of you, if his son asks for bread, will give him a stone?
[10] Or if he asks for a fish, will give him a snake?
[11] If you, then, though you are evil, know how to give good gifts to your children, how much

more will your Father in heaven give good gifts to those who ask him!

Matthew 7:7-11 NIV

[18] Truly, I say to you, whatever you bind on earth shall be bound in heaven, and whatever you loose on earth shall be loosed in heaven.

[19] Again I say to you, if two of you agree on earth about anything they ask, it will be done for them by my Father in heaven.

[20] For where two or three are gathered in my name, there am I in the midst of them.

Matthew 18:18-20 RSV

[21] Jesus replied, I tell you the truth, if you have faith and do not doubt, not only can you do what was done to the fig tree, but also you can say to this mountain, Go, throw yourself into the sea, and it will be done.

[22] If you believe, you will receive whatever you ask for in prayer.

Matthew 21:21,22 NIV

[1] And it came about that while He was praying in a certain place, after He had finished, one of His disciples said to Him, "Lord, teach us to pray just as John also taught his disciples."

² And He said to them, "When you pray, say: 'Father, hallowed be Thy name. Thy kingdom come.
³ 'Give us each day our daily bread.
⁴ 'And forgive us our sins, for we ourselves also forgive everyone who is indebted to us. And lead us not into temptation.'"

Luke 11:1-4 NAS

Then Jesus told his disciples a parable to show them that they should always pray and not give up.

Luke 18:1 NIV

Be always on the watch, and pray that you may be able to escape all that is about to happen, and that you may be able to stand before the Son of Man.

Luke 21:36 NIV

¹³ And whatever you ask in My name, that will I do, that the Father may be glorified in the Son.
¹⁴ If you ask Me anything in My name, I will do it.
¹⁵ If you love Me, you will keep My commandments.
¹⁶ And I will ask the Father, and He will give you another Helper, that He may be with you forever.

John 14:13-16 NAS

If you remain in me and my words remain in you, ask whatever you wish, and it will be given you.

John 15:7 NIV

²³ In that day you will ask nothing of me. Truly, truly, I say to you, if you ask anything of the Father, he will give it to you in my name. ²⁴ Hitherto you have asked nothing in my name; ask, and you will receive, that your joy may be full.

John 16:23,24 RSV

¹³ For this reason the man who speaks in a tongue should pray that he may interpret what he says. ¹⁴ For if I pray in a tongue, my spirit prays, but my mind is unfruitful. ¹⁵ So what shall I do? I will pray with my spirit, but I will also pray with my mind; I will sing with my spirit, but I will also sing with my mind. ¹⁶ If you are praising God with your spirit, how can one who finds himself among those who do not understand say "Amen" to your thanksgiving, since he does not know what you are saying?

1 Corinthians 14:13-16 NIV

¹⁵ For this reason I too, having heard of the faith in the Lord Jesus which exists among you, and your love for all the saints,

¹⁶ do not cease giving thanks for you, while making mention of you in my prayers;

¹⁷ that the God of our Lord Jesus Christ, the Father of glory, may give to you a spirit of wisdom and of revelation in the knowledge of Him.

¹⁸ I pray that the eyes of your heart may be enlightened, so that you may know what is the hope of His calling, what are the riches of the glory of His inheritance in the saints,

¹⁹ and what is the surpassing greatness of His power toward us who believe. These are in accordance with the working of the strength of His might

²⁰ which He brought about in Christ, when He raised Him from the dead, and seated Him at His right hand in the heavenly places,

²¹ far above all rule and authority and power and dominion, and every name that is named, not only in this age, but also in the one to come.

²² And He put all things in subjection under His feet, and gave Him as head over all things to the church,

[23] which is His body, the fulness of Him who fills all in all.

Ephesians 1:15-23 NAS

[12] For our struggle is not against flesh and blood, but against the rulers, against the powers, against the world forces of this darkness, against the spiritual forces of wickedness in the heavenly places.

[13] Therefore, take up the full armor of God, that you may be able to resist in the evil day, and having done everything, to stand firm.

[14] Stand firm therefore, having girded your loins with truth, and having put on the breastplate of righteousness,

[15] and having shod your feet with the preparation of the gospel of peace;

[16] in addition to all, taking up the shield of faith with which you will be able to extinguish all the flaming missiles of the evil one.

[17] And take the helmet of salvation, and the sword of the Spirit, which is the word of God.

[18] With all prayer and petition pray at all times in the Spirit, and with this in view, be on the alert with all perseverance and petition for all the saints,

[19] and pray on my behalf, that utterance may be given to me in the opening of my mouth, to make known with boldness the mystery of the gospel.

Ephesians 6:12-19 NAS

[3] I thank my God every time I remember you.
[4] In all my prayers for all of you, I always pray with joy
[5] because of your partnership in the gospel from the first day until now,
[6] being confident of this, that he who began a good work in you will carry it on to completion until the day of Christ Jesus.

Philippians 1:3-6 NIV

[1] First of all, then, I urge that entreaties and prayers, petitions and thanksgivings, be made on behalf of all men,
[2] for kings and all who are in authority, in order that we may lead a tranquil and quiet life in all godliness and dignity.
[3] This is good and acceptable in the sight of God our Savior,
[4] who desires all men to be saved and to come to the knowledge of the truth.

1 Timothy 2:1-4 NAS

Let us then with confidence draw near to the throne of grace, that we may receive mercy and find grace to help in time of need.

Hebrews 4:16 RSV

³ You ask and do not receive, because you ask with wrong motives, so that you may spend it on your pleasures.
⁴ You adulteresses, do you not know that friendship with the world is hostility toward God? Therefore whoever wishes to be a friend of the world makes himself an enemy of God.
⁵ Or do you think that the Scripture speaks to no purpose: "He jealously desires the Spirit which He has made to dwell in us"?
⁶ But He gives a greater grace. Therefore it says, "God is opposed to the proud, but gives grace to the humble."
⁷ Submit therefore to God. Resist the devil and he will flee from you.
⁸ Draw near to God and He will draw near to you. Cleanse your hands, you sinners; and purify your hearts, you double-minded.

James 4:3-8 NAS

¹⁴ Is any one of you sick? He should call the elders of the church to pray over him and anoint him with oil in the name of the Lord.

[15] And the prayer offered in faith will make the sick person well; the Lord will raise him up. If he has sinned, he will be forgiven.
[16] Therefore confess your sins to each other and pray for each other so that you may be healed. The prayer of a righteous man is powerful and effective.
[17] Elijah was a man just like us. He prayed earnestly that it would not rain, and it did not rain on the land for three and a half years.
[18] Again he prayed, and the heavens gave rain, and the earth produced its crops.

James 5:14-18 NIV

Likewise you husbands, live considerately with your wives, bestowing honor on the woman as the weaker sex, since you are joint heirs of the grace of life, in order that your prayers may not be hindered.

1 Peter 3:7 RSV

For the eyes of the Lord are on the righteous and his ears are attentive to their prayer, but the face of the Lord is against those who do evil.

1 Peter 3:12 NIV

Cast all your anxiety on him because he cares for you.

1 Peter 5:7 NIV

And we receive from him whatever we ask, because we keep his commandments and do what pleases him.

1 John 3:22 RSV

[14] And this is the confidence which we have before Him, that, if we ask anything according to His will, He hears us.
[15] And if we know that He hears us in whatever we ask, we know that we have the requests which we have asked from Him.
[16] If anyone sees his brother committing a sin not leading to death, he shall ask and God will for him give life to those who commit sin not leading to death. There is a sin leading to death; I do not say that he should make request for this.

1 John 5:14-16 NAS

[20] But you, dear friends, build yourselves up in your most holy faith and pray in the Holy Spirit.
[21] Keep yourselves in God's love as you wait for the mercy of our Lord Jesus Christ to bring you to eternal life.

Jude 20,21 NIV

Sacrifice from evil men is loathsome to the Eternal, but the prayers of upright men are his delight.

Proverbs 15:8 Moffatt

¹⁶ Be always joyful.

¹⁷ Be unceasing in prayer.

¹⁸ In every circumstance of life be thankful; for this is God's will in Christ Jesus respecting you.

1 Thessalonians 5:16-18 Weymouth

Prayer for the
Commitment To Pray

Father, in the name of Jesus, I offer up thanksgiving that You have called me to be a fellow workman—a joint promoter and a laborer together—with and for You. I commit myself to pray and not to turn coward—faint, lose heart, or give up.

Fearlessly and confidently and boldly I draw near to the throne of grace that I may receive mercy and find grace to help in good time for every need—appropriate help and well-timed help, coming just when I (and others) need it. This is the confidence that I have in You, that, if I ask anything according to Your will, You hear me: and if I know that You hear me, whatsoever I ask, I know that I have the petitions that I desired of You.

When I do not know what prayer to offer and how to offer it worthily as I ought, I thank You, Father, that the (Holy) Spirit comes to my aid and bears me up in my weakness (my inability to produce results). He, the Holy Spirit, goes to meet my supplication and pleads in my behalf with unspeakable yearnings and groanings too deep for utterance. And He Who searches the hearts of men knows what is in the mind of the (Holy) Spirit. The Holy Spirit intercedes and pleads in behalf of the saints according to and in harmony with God's will. Therefore, I am assured and know that (God being a partner in my labor) all things work together and are [fitting into a plan] for my good, because I love God and am called according to [His] design and purpose.

I do not fret or have any anxiety about anything, but in every circumstance and in everything by prayer and petition [definite requests] with thanksgiving continue to make my wants (and the wants of others) known to God. Whatever I ask for in prayer, I believe that it is granted to me, and I will receive it.

The earnest (heartfelt, continued) prayer of a righteous man makes tremendous power available—dynamic in its working. Father, I live in You—abide vitally united to You—and Your words remain in me and continue to live in my heart. Therefore I ask whatever I will and it shall be done for me. When I bear (produce) much fruit (through prayer), You, Father, are honored and glorified. Hallelujah!

Scripture References

I Corinthians 3:9 AMP   James 5:16b AMP

Philippians 4:6 AMP   1 John 5:14,15

Luke 18:1 AMP   John 15:7,8 AMP

Mark 11:24 AMP   Romans 8:26-29 AMP

Hebrews 4:16 AMP

[1] p. 1181.

[2] *Ellicot's Commentaries on the Epistles of Saint Paul* (Minneapolis: The James Family Christian Publishers), p. 42.

[3] Richard Chenevix Trench, *Synonyms of the New Testament* (Grand Rapids: Baker Book House), p. 201.

[4] William Barclay, *New Testament Words* (SCM Press, 1964), p. 86.

[5] Arthur Wallis, *In the Day of Thy Power* (Ft. Washington: Christian Literature Crusade), p. 162.

THE HOLY SPIRIT

The experience of the believer filled with the Spirit and seeking the best gifts will be one of untold and unimagined glory—a consciousness that he has become truly united with God in His work, able in some small way to continue the beneficent ministry of his Master which commenced nearly 2,000 years ago.

This great and sacred heritage of the Spirit is before us; let us go up at once and possess it.

— Howard Carter

Greek and Hebrew Word Studies

OLD TESTAMENT—*RUWACH*

Come ye near unto me, hear ye this; I have not spoken in secret from the beginning; from the time that it was, there am I: and now the Lord God, and his *Spirit (rawach)*, hath sent me.

Isaiah 48:16

155

NEW TESTAMENT—*PNEUMA*

It is the *spirit (pneuma)* that quickeneth; the flesh profiteth nothing: the words that I speak unto you, they are *spirit (pneuma)* and they are life.

John 6:63

There are two functions of the Holy Spirit. One is for the indwelling of the believer, and the other is for the outpouring to help others.

The indwelling of the Holy Spirit is for our benefit as individuals. The Holy Spirit dwells in us to do something for us: to make us become what God intended us to be.

Once we are established in the indwelling of the Holy Spirit, the fullness causes an overflow, the outpouring, that reaches out to others. The outpouring of the Holy Spirit is for the benefit of others, to bring them into the fullness of action of the Holy Spirit.

— Buddy and Pat Harrison
The Word Bible[1]

The Holy Spirit—*Ruwach*

When two languages are as dissimilar as Hebrew and Greek, it is unusual for a particular word or concept to mean the same in both tongues. However, there are a few instances in which this is the case.

One example involves the word for "spirit," which is *pneuma* in Greek and *ruwach* in Hebrew. Both words can have the same three definitions: breath, wind and spirit. Because these meanings are present in the original languages, translators often had to make a decision between two or three possible English words best suited to translation in any particular instance.

"Breath of God," "Wind of God" and "Spirit of God" are possible ways to translate *ruwach elohim* in Genesis 1:2. Also, "evil breath," "evil wind" and "evil spirit" have been considered as the best ways to translate phrases occurring in such verses as First Samuel 16:23. (Compare Judges 9:23.)

It would seem that the concepts—*breath, wind, spirit*—are seldom interchangeable. However, by being cognizant of the fact that biblical writers understood these subjects as closely linked, we can read the Scriptures with a more accurate color or flavor, even in our own English translations.

Ruwach (pronounced "roo'-akh"), #7307 in *Strong's*, occurs nearly 400 times in the Old Testament. When it refers to the human spirit, it sometimes means the innermost and eternal part of man's being. (See Ecclesiastes 12:7, Job 32:8.) As in English, the word *spirit* in Scripture quite often refers to one's heart attitude or condition, or the principle which motivates a person or drives one to action.

Such phrases as *wounded spirit* (like bitter, angry, joyful, contrite, hasty, proud, or timid spirit) need no explanation to the average human being. Several verses show that the spirit of man is something God created for His specific use. (See Proverbs 20:27; Isaiah 57:15,16).

It is likely that when God breathed His breath into Adam a spirit was formed inside him. Man is an eternal being, because the *breath* of God cannot cease. When Adam's spirit was produced, his soul (personality, emotions, self-awareness) naturally switched on like a light, and his body automatically came into full function.

Genesis 2:7 may be helpfully illustrated as follows: "The Lord God formed man of the dust of the ground (that is, his *body),* and breathed into his nostrils the breath of life (God breathed *spirit* into him); and man became a living soul *(nephesh)"* (pronounced neh'-fesh), #5315 in *Strong's. Nephesh* means "a life, a living being").

When these three parts of man were formed, the whole person began to function. The man was wholly alive and perfect. His three parts—spirit, soul and body—correspond to the three parts of his Maker in whose reflection he was made: Spirit (God the Spirit), Soul (God the Father) and Body (God the Son Who came in a body of human flesh). Thus man in his three parts was literally made in God's image and after His likeness.

The spirit of man has a most noble function—if the man is redeemed. It is a house for the Holy Spirit to indwell. But the purpose of this study is not to examine what the Bible says about human spirits, evil spirits or angelic spirits (although Psalm 104:4 presents a magnificent study opportunity for those interested in what the Scripture says about angels). We are concerned here with what the Old Testament teaches about the Holy Spirit of God.

Contrary to that which some people have supposed, the Old Testament presents a great deal of knowledge about the Spirit of God. Moses makes only a few references to the Spirit of God. (See, for example, Genesis 41:38 and Exodus 31:1-11.)

The book of Judges gives a clear indication of how much the empowerment from the Holy Spirit was regarded as essential for the equipping of those deliverers God used to bring rescue to Israel from danger, oppression, servitude, and distress. In Judges 11:29 we read that the Spirit of the Lord came upon Jephthah, and he immediately went forward to defeat the children of Ammon.

Later, we see how the Spirit of God came mightily upon Samson and advanced his mighty exploits. (See Judges 13:25; 14:6,19; 15:14. Compare First Samuel 10:9, 11:6; 16:13.)

The prophets similarly had a clear acquaintance with the power of the Holy Spirit. They record that the Spirit of the Lord spoke through them and caused them to prophesy. Read Second Samuel 23:2,3; Ezekiel 37:1-14; and Daniel 4:8,9. In this last reference, a heathen king acknowledges that Daniel has the power to solve mysteries because the Spirit of the Holy God is in him. Compare also Second Peter 1:21: **"For the prophecy came not in old time by the will of man: but holy men of God spake as they were moved by the Holy Ghost."**

An area of particular beauty is the majestic Old Testament teaching that it would be the Holy Spirit Who would empower the Messiah to proclaim the Good News, to be sent with a message, to do mighty works, and to succeed in His task. Read carefully Isaiah 42:1-4 and Isaiah 61:1,2.

Exactly as prophesied, Jesus did no miracles until the Holy Spirit descended upon Him at His baptism in the Jordan River. The text we selected for this study shows that Jehovah and His Spirit sent the Messiah, Whom we sometimes call "the Sent One." This verse is one of only two or three Old Testament verses in which the Father, Son and Holy Spirit are clearly mentioned in the same verse.

We note joyfully that the passage from Isaiah 61:1,2 was read aloud and publicly by our Lord Jesus in His hometown synagogue. (Luke 4:18,19.) After He finished reading these words, He applied them unmistakably to Himself as the Messiah:

> **The Spirit of the Lord God is upon me; because the Lord hath anointed me to preach good tidings unto the meek; he hath sent me to bind up the brokenhearted, to proclaim liberty to the captives, and the opening of the prison to them that are bound; to proclaim the acceptable year of the Lord.**

Isaiah 11:1-3 likewise speaks of Jesse's great descendent, "the Branch," and how "the spirit of the Lord shall *rest* upon him" (that is to say, "shall *remain* on Him"). This prophecy finds total fulfillment in John 1:33, where God instructs John the Baptist thus:

> **...Upon whom thou shalt see the Spirit descending, and *remaining* on him, the same is he which baptizeth with the Holy Ghost.**

Notice John's testimony in verse 34: **"And I saw, and bare record** (witness) **that this is the Son of God."** What a stunning public tribute to God's Messiah: honor from the Father and the Holy Spirit, and from Jesus' own kinsman, John!

This verse declares too that the Anointed One, the One on which the Holy Spirit remains, is also the Son of God. This truth is forcefully stated by Psalm 2 where in the Hebrew wording the Man Who is called Zion's *King* (v. 6) is called God's *Anointed,* or the Messiah (v. 2), and is furthermore called *the Son* of God (vv. 7,12). The Hebrew word translated *Messiah* in English is *mashiyach* ("maw-shee'-akh"), #4899 in *Strong's.*

The Old Testament consistently expresses a strong emphasis upon the Messiah's close relationship to the Holy Spirit Who anoints Him. The New Testament records and develops this truth in such mighty verses as Acts 10:38: **"How God anointed Jesus of Nazareth with the Holy Ghost and with power: who went about doing good and healing all that were** oppressed of the devil, for God was with him." See also John 3:34—a priceless tribute to Jesus.

In the Old Testament, the Holy Spirit may be called *ruach elohim* (Spirit of God), *ruach yahweh* (Spirit of the Lord) or *haruach ha-qodesh* (the Holy Spirit, or more literally "the Spirit of the Holy One"). In addition to being mentioned in connection with Messiah, the Spirit of God is clearly linked, in no uncertain terms, to the salvation process. Carefully examine the following Scripture references: Ezekiel 36:26,27; Isaiah 32:15-18; 59:20,21; 63:11-14; Joel 2:28; and Zechariah 12:10.

Throughout the entire Bible, the Holy Spirit is revealed as being decidedly involved in the inspiration of Scripture. Let us pause a moment and consider the implications of this. The Holy Spirit gave the Scripture in the first place, and He is a life-giving Spirit.

When the New Testament states that the letter kills but the Spirit gives life (2 Cor. 3:6), it does not under any condition mean the Scripture—which the Holy Spirit breathed into existence—is *intended* to kill. It means simply that Scripture often *will* kill—and does kill—unless it is taught and ministered in the same Spirit Who originally inspired it.

The most devilish, heinous, murderous, and evil institutions and religious systems in human history have publicly bolstered themselves with quotations from the Word of God. But they can only mishandle His Word to their own destruction, as they are enemies of God and are operating in complete opposition to the Holy Spirit.

The mind of fallen man is so corrupt it can scarcely receive revelation from God. The mind of man is so corrupt it can scarcely retain and correctly remember and understand the revelation God has given. Hence the cults, false religions and all sorts of denominationalism and unholy factionalism have developed *purportedly* from that Holy Book which the Holy Spirit of our Holy God gave to an unholy world with the intent that the Holy Savior should be honored!

So to rightly divide the Word of Truth, we need the Spirit of Truth, and that is the Holy Spirit Himself.

In conclusion, the Old Testament shows God's Holy Spirit as active in the creation of the world, active in the salvation of His people, active throughout the prophesied life and ministry of the Messiah, active in giving the Scriptures, inspiring the prophets, empowering the heroes of faith, and governing in unsurpassable wisdom. (See Isaiah 40:12-18.)

O Lord God, allow us to give You glory for Your wonderful Holy Spirit!

The Greek Words for Spirit in the *King James Version*

Phantasma

Phantasma ("fan'-tas-mah"), #5326 in *Strong's*, appears only twice in the *Authorized Version*. Both Matthew 14:26 and Mark 6:49 relate the incident of the disciples seeing Jesus walking on the sea. In their fearful reaction they defined what they saw as a *phantasma*, or a spirit.

In this setting *phantasma* is defined as a ghost, a phantom, a spectacle, an unreality, an apparition, or what we would call a spirit, a spook, or a specter.

The disciples had a mistaken impression of Jesus when they saw Him walking on the sea. No one else in the course of human history had ever walked on water. You can imagine how unreal this must have seemed to them. Their response: "It's an unreality—a *phantasma*, a spirit" (as compared to a physical body). Jesus calmed their fears by speaking to them: **"It is I; be not afraid"** (v. 27).

Phantasma is the only other word for "spirit" in the Greek besides the main word, *pneuma*.

Pneuma

Pneuma ("pnyoo'-mah"), #4151 in *Strong's*, appears 383 times in the *Authorized Version*. The word *spirit* (lowercased) for "spirit of man" is used 151; the word *Spirit* (capitalized) for "Spirit of God" is found 137 times. The Old English term *Holy Ghost* appears 89 times. Most Bible translations after 1611 A.D. replaced the name *Holy Ghost* with *Holy Spirit*.

Pneuma is translated by many respiratory words: to draw breath, the nostrils, inhaling, exhaling, the wind, scent, breeze, gale, blast, air, respiration, aroma, panting, and air set in motion.

In the biblical sense *pneuma* is defined as giving life, giving inspiration, giving illumination, imparting power and anointing for service by the in-breathing of the Spirit of God.

In the New Testament *pneuma* refers to the Holy Spirit, the human spirit and evil spirits. One of the grace gifts of the Spirit in First Corinthians 12:8-10 is the discerning of spirits. This grace gift enables a believer to identify the source of any manifestation or phenomena.

Pneuma **as the Human Spirit**

In your private devotions you can use a three-verse bridge from physical life to life in the spirit.

1. Proverbs 20:27—**"The spirit of man is the candle of the Lord, searching all the inward parts of the belly."**

Man is made of material features, such as his body with its functions. He also is made of the immaterial features, such as spirit, soul, conscience, and sensitivity to the spiritual realm. God as Spirit encounters man and interacts with him by the human spirit, as this verse in Proverbs shows.

2. Romans 8:16—**"The Spirit itself beareth witness with our spirit, that we are the children of God."**

This word shows how God's Spirit and man's spirit have two separate identities, yet in the conversion process blend together harmoniously.

3. John 6:63—**"It is the spirit that quickeneth; the flesh profiteth nothing: the words** (*rhema*) **that I speak unto you, they are spirit, and they are life."**

Life in the spirit reaches an ideal level of proficiency by honoring the Holy Spirit. We can invite

Him to envelop our lives with His attributes and qualities. We can be Spirit-filled, Spirit-led and Spirit-empowered for service.

Pneuma as the Holy Spirit

Pneuma hagion is usually translated *the Holy Spirit*. The article *the* is inserted and capital letters are used. In the Gospels Jesus promised to send the Holy Spirit to the waiting believers to empower them for service. (Acts 1:8.) In Luke 24:49 He calls the coming visitation **"power from on high."** This power enables us:

1. To witness to the world. (Acts 1:8.)

2. To pray correctly. (Rom. 8:26.)

3. To understand Scripture. (Ps. 119:18.)

4. To understand His will for our lives. (Eph. 5:17,18.)

5. To make decisions. (John 16:13.)

6. To know how to worship Him in Spirit and in truth. (John 4:24.)

7. To be healed. (Rom. 8:11.)

8. To work miracles. (Gal. 3:5.)

9. To adequately love God. (Rom. 5:5.)

10. To be anointed for fruitful and productive Christian service. (1 John 2:27.)

These are but a few of the ministries of the Holy Spirit. The Holy Spirit is not a mere influence like "the Spirit of '76" or "team spirit" or the national "spirit" of a country. The Holy Spirit is a Person. He has a personality and is one with the Father and the Son in the Trinity.

There are books in print on the "emblems of the Spirit" that are informational and inspirational. Some of these emblems are water, rain, rivers, the dew, the wind, the oil, the dove, the holy anointing oil, the seal, and the fire.

The Flesh and the Spirit

Much of the New Testament contrasts man's carnality and fleshly nature in contradistinction to the man walking in the spirit. Everything associated with the fleshly man makes him a loser. For example:

The flesh profits nothing. (John 6:63.)

No flesh can glory in His presence. (1 Cor. 1:29.)

In my flesh dwells no good thing. (Rom. 7:18.)

They that are in the flesh cannot please God. (Rom. 8:8.)

By contrast notice the victorious quality of life in the Spirit:

As many as are led by the Spirit are the sons of God. (Rom. 8:14.)

Walk in the Spirit, and you will not fulfill the lusts of the flesh. (Gal. 5:16.)

It is the Spirit that quickens. (Rom. 8:11.)

The Spirit helps our infirmities. (Rom. 8:26.)

You will receive power after the Holy Spirit has come on you, and you will be His witnesses. (Acts 1:8.)

Victory over the flesh comes by being filled with the Spirit. Jesus promised the fullness of the Spirit to all who would ask, according to Luke 11:13.

Pneuma in the English Language

In the English language 151 words start with *pneu*, including 101 words which start with *pneum-*, such as pneumatic, pneumonia and pneumatology. All these English words trace back to *pneuma—spirit*. Christianity is not a form, ritual, or ceremony. It is eternal life in-breathed into all its members by the Holy Spirit *(pneuma)*. (John 20:22.)

<u>Scriptures</u>

Now the earth was formless and empty, darkness was over the surface of the deep, and the Spirit of God was hovering over the waters.

Genesis 1:2 NIV

And I have filled him with the Spirit of God, with skill, ability and knowledge in all kinds of crafts.

Exodus 31:3 NIV

The Spirit of the LORD speaks by me, his word is upon my tongue.

2 Samuel 23:2 RSV

You also gave Your good Spirit to instruct them, and did not withhold Your manna from their mouth, and gave them water for their thirst.

Nehemiah 9:20 NKJV

The Spirit of God has made me; the breath of the Almighty gives me life.

Job 33:4 NIV

Where can I go from Your Spirit? Or where can I flee from Your presence?

Psalms 139:7 NKJV

"As for me, this is my covenant with them," says the LORD. "My Spirit, who is on you, and my words that I have put in your mouth will not depart from your mouth, or from the mouths of your children, or from the mouths of their descendants from this time on and forever," says the LORD.

Isaiah 59:21 NIV

I will put My Spirit within you and cause you to walk in My statutes, and you will keep My judgments and do them.

Ezekiel 36:27 NKJV

[28] After I have poured out my rains again, I will pour out my Spirit upon all of you! Your sons and daughters will prophesy; your old men will dream dreams, and your young men see visions. [29] And I will pour out my Spirit even on your slaves, men and women alike.

Joel 2:28,29 TLB

I indeed baptize you with water unto repentance, but He who is coming after me is mightier than I, whose sandals I am not worthy to carry. He will baptize you with the Holy Spirit and fire.

Matthew 3:11 NKJV

For it is not you who are speaking, but the Spirit of your Father speaking through you.

Matthew 10:20 AMP

But when you are arrested and stand trial, don't worry about what to say in your defense. Just say what God tells you to. Then you will not be speaking, but the Holy Spirit will.

Mark 13:11 TLB

If you then, though you are evil, know how to give good gifts to your children, how much more will your Father in heaven give the Holy Spirit to those who ask him!

Luke 11:13 NIV

[17] He is the Holy Spirit, the Spirit who leads into all truth. The world at large cannot receive him, for it isn't looking for him and doesn't recognize him. But you do, for he lives with you now and some day shall be in you.
[18] No, I will not abandon you or leave you as orphans in the storm—I will come to you.

John 14:17,18 TLB

But the Counselor, the Holy Spirit, whom the Father will send in my name, will teach you all things and will remind you of everything I have said to you.

John 14:26 NIV

When the Holy Spirit, who is truth, comes, he shall guide you into all truth, for he will not be presenting his own ideas, but will be passing on to you what he has heard. He will tell you about the future.

John 16:13 TLB

[1,2] Dear friend who loves God: In my first letter I told you about Jesus' life and teachings and how he returned to heaven after giving his chosen apostles further instructions from the Holy Spirit.

[3] During the forty days after his crucifixion he appeared to the apostles from time to time, actually alive, and proved to them in many ways that it was really he himself they were seeing. And on these occasions he talked to them about the Kingdom of God.

[4] In one of these meetings he told them not to leave Jerusalem until the Holy Spirit came upon them in fulfillment of the Father's promise, a matter he had previously discussed with them.

[5] "John baptized you with water," he reminded them, "but you shall be baptized with the Holy Spirit in just a few days."

[6] And another time when he appeared to them, they asked him, "Lord, are you going to free

Israel [from Rome] now and restore us as an independent nation?"

⁷ "The Father sets those dates," he replied, "and they are not for you to know.

⁸ "But when the Holy Spirit has come upon you, you will receive power to testify about me with great effect, to the people in Jerusalem, throughout Judea, in Samaria, and to the ends of the earth, about my death and resurrection."

Acts 1:1-8 TLB

All of them were filled with the Holy Spirit and began to speak in other tongues as the Spirit enabled them.

Acts 2:4 NIV

¹⁷ And it shall come to pass in the last days, says God, that I will pour out of My Spirit on all flesh; your sons and your daughters shall prophesy, your young men shall see visions, your old men shall dream dreams.

¹⁸ And on My menservants and on My maidservants I will pour out My Spirit in those days; and they shall prophesy.

Acts 2:17,18 NKJV

Then, when that happens, we are able to hold our heads high no matter what happens and know that all is well, for we know how dearly God loves us, and we feel this warm love everywhere within us because God has given us the Holy Spirit to fill our hearts with his love.

Romans 5:5 TLB

[26] And in the same way—by our faith—the Holy Spirit helps us with our daily problems and in our praying. For we don't even know what we should pray for, nor how to pray as we should; but the Holy Spirit prays for us with such feeling that it cannot be expressed in words.
[27] And the Father who knows all hearts knows, of course, what the Spirit is saying as he pleads for us in harmony with God's own will.

Romans 8:26,27 TLB

[10] God has revealed to us through the Spirit. For the Spirit searches everything, even the depths of God.
[11] For what person knows a man's thoughts except the spirit of the man which is in him? So also no one comprehends the thoughts of God except the Spirit of God.
[12] Now we have received not the spirit of the world, but the Spirit which is from God, that we might understand the gifts bestowed on us by God.

¹³ And we impart this in words not taught by human wisdom but taught by the Spirit, interpreting spiritual truths to those who possess the Spirit.
¹⁴ The unspiritual man does not receive the gifts of the Spirit of God, for they are folly to him, and he is not able to understand them because they are spiritually discerned.

1 Corinthians 2:10-14 RSV

Do you not know that you are God's Sanctuary, and that the Spirit of God has His home within you?

1 Corinthians 3:16 Weymouth

Haven't you yet learned that your body is the home of the Holy Spirit God gave you, and that he lives within you? Your own body does not belong to you.

1 Corinthians 6:19 TLB

⁷ But the manifestation of the Spirit is given to each one for the profit of all:
⁸ for to one is given the word of wisdom through the Spirit, to another the word of knowledge through the same Spirit,
⁹ to another faith by the same Spirit, to another gifts of healings by the same Spirit,

[10] to another the working of miracles, to another prophecy, to another discerning of spirits, to another different kinds of tongues, to another the interpretation of tongues.

[11] But one and the same Spirit works all these things, distributing to each one individually as He wills.

[12] For as the body is one and has many members, but all the members of that one body, being many, are one body, so also is Christ.

[13] For by one Spirit we were all baptized into one body—whether Jews or Greeks, whether slaves or free—and have all been made to drink into one Spirit.

1 Corinthians 12:7-13 NKJV

[17] Now the Lord is the Spirit, and where the Spirit of the Lord is, there is freedom.

[18] And we, who with unveiled faces all reflect the Lord's glory, are being transformed into his likeness with ever-increasing glory, which comes from the Lord, who is the Spirit.

2 Corinthians 3:17,18 NIV

[22] But when the Holy Spirit controls our lives he will produce this kind of fruit in us: love, joy, peace, patience, kindness, goodness, faithfulness,

[23] gentleness and self-control; and here there is no conflict with Jewish laws.

Galatians 5:22,23 TLB

Do not get drunk on wine, which leads to debauchery. Instead, be filled with the Spirit.

Ephesians 5:18 NIV

[17] And take the helmet of salvation, and the sword of the Spirit, which is the word of God. [18] With all prayer and petition pray at all times in the Spirit, and with this in view, be on the alert with all perseverance and petition for all the saints.

Ephesians 6:17,18 NAS

This is how you can recognize the Spirit of God: Every spirit that acknowledges that Jesus Christ has come in the flesh is from God....

1 John 4:2 NIV

By this we know that we abide in him and he in us, because he has given us of his own Spirit.

1 John 4:13 RSV

Prayer for the Spirit-Controlled Life

The law of the Spirit of life in Christ Jesus has made _____ free from the law of sin and death. His/her life is governed not by the standards and according to the dictates of the flesh but controlled by the Holy Spirit. _____ is not living the life of the flesh. _____ is living the life of the Spirit. The Holy Spirit of God dwells within, and directs and controls him/her.

_____ is a conqueror and gains a surpassing victory through Jesus Who loved him/her. _____ does not let himself/herself be overcome by evil, but overcomes and masters evil with good. _____ has on the full armor of light. _____ clothes himself/herself with the Lord Jesus Christ, the Messiah, and makes no provision for indulging the flesh.

_____ is a doer of God's Word. He/she has God's wisdom. He/she is peace-loving, courteous, considerate, gentle, willing to yield to reason, full of compassion and good fruits. _____ is free from doubts, wavering, and insincerity. He/she is subject to God.

_____ stands firm against the devil. _____ resists the devil and he flees from him/her. _____ comes close to God and God comes close to him/her.

_____ does not fear, for God never leaves him.

In Christ, _____ is filled with the Godhead: Father, Son, and Holy Spirit. Jesus is his/her Lord!

Scripture References

Romans 8:2,4,9,14,31,37	*James 3:17*
Romans 12:21	*Hebrews 13:5*
Romans 13:12,14	*James 4:7,8*
James 1:22	*Colossians 2:10*

[1] p. 1162.

FAITH

Only believe! God will not fail you, Beloved. It is impossible for God to fail. Believe Him. Rest in Him, for God's rest is an undisturbed place where heaven bends to meet you. God will fulfill the promises made to you in His Word—believe it!

— Smith Wigglesworth

Greek and Hebrew Word Studies

OLD TESTAMENT—*CHASAH/BATACH*

How excellent is thy loving kindness, O God! therefore the children of men put their *trust (chasah)* under the shadow of thy wings.

Psalm 36:7

Trust (batach) in the Lord with all thine heart; and lean not unto thine own understanding.

Proverbs 3:5

NEW TESTAMENT—*PISTIS*

So then *faith (pistis)* cometh by hearing, and hearing by the word *(rhema)* of God.

Romans 10:17

I see so many Christians who are struggling to believe and struggling to have faith. Their focus is all wrong. They're focusing on their ability or inability to believe God, or "trying" to have faith. They should simply start acting like God's Word is true. It will make all the difference in their lives!

It is when we know God's Word is true and act like it's true that it becomes a reality to us. Faith is not something we have so much as it is something we do.

— Kenneth E. Hagin
The Word Bible[1]

Trust/Believe/Faith—*Chasah/Batach*

There are four different words used to describe the Old Testament concept of faith. An Old Testament believer's faith included trust, believing, hope, and a steadfastness that produces faithfulness.

The *King James* translation uses the word *faith* only twice in the Old Testament. In Deuteronomy 32:20, **"...children in whom is no faith"** could also be translated, "children in whom is no faithfulness." A paraphrase of two translations could read, **"they had no loyalty to the Lord and proved unfaithful."**[2]

The second Old Testament use of faith by *King James* is in Habakkuk 2:4: **"...but the just shall live by his faith."** It could easily be translated, "The just shall live by being faithful to Me."

Some people stumble over the fact that the English word *faith* occurs infrequently in the Old Testament. They have concluded that faith was unimportant (or unknown) to Old Testament believers. What could be further from the truth?

Abraham's faith set things in motion that have forever changed the course of human history. Israel could never have survived what she did in Old Testament times without unyielding faith in her God.

All the "heroes of faith" in Hebrews 11, to whom New Testament believers look for inspiration, were Old Testament persons! Tremendous faith was demonstrated in their deeds, but what about their words?

Did they have words for *faith* with which to talk about their strong belief in the Lord? Yes, certainly!

The two words we are examining (generally taken to mean "have confidence in, trust, make refuge") are foremost examples of Old Testament faith. We may think *trust* is a passive or milder form of *faith,* but not so. By simply reading the verses in which *chasah* and *batach* occur, one can be schooled in faith.

Some believers try to demonstrate their "great" faith, and may sincerely think they are full of faith— but they actually don't *trust* the Lord at all. In no biblical sense is it possible to have faith in a God you do not trust. There are elements of faith that go beyond trust, but trust is still at the core. Why else would the Word contain so many references to child-like trust in one's response to God? See especially *batach* in Psalm 22:9, and compare Mark 10:14,15.

The word *emunah* (pronounced "em-oo-naw'"), #530 in *Strong's Exhaustive Concordance*, means faith, belief, firmness, steadfastness, endurance and is used in Habakkuk 2:4, **"...the just shall live by his faith,"** and in a few other references. It refers more to faith-filled actions and steadfastness than to belief or faith as we think of it. This is why we have emphasized these two Hebrew words rather than others which may be translated "faith" in the *King James Version*.

Lexical Analysis of *Chacah* and *Batach*

Chacah

Chacah (pronounced "khaw-saw'"), #2620 in *Strong's* appears 37 times; 26 of these appear in David's writings, and three are in the book of Isaiah.

Chacah is defined by Old Testament grammarians as flee for protection, confide in, trust in someone (especially the Lord), find shelter, turn aside from the presence of danger, find a place of shelter from a rainstorm and remain there for protection, find a shadow or covert from blistering heat, find a shield to protect from missiles being thrown at a person, put confident trust in God. He, above all, is the sole refuge for His people.

Other words used to further our comprehension of *chacah* are our Rock, our Strength, our Fortress, our Hiding Place and our Stronghold.

One grammarian listed four things associated with the progress of *chacah* in our lives:

1. He gives us a word of promise or a word of command.

2. Our attitude changes to one of compliance to His Word as a guideline.

3. The attitude change produces action, and we in obedience act upon the promise or command.

4. The action demonstrates our trust/belief/faith. It starts with an assuring word from the Lord and terminates with a confiding or abiding faith in God and His promises.

Psalm 36:7 is one of the most precious verses in the Old Testament. It explains the basis for our love of the Lord, our faith in the Lord, and our trust in the Lord. **"How excellent is thy lovingkindness, O God! therefore the children of men put their** *trust (chacah)* **under the shadow of thy wings."**

God's tender kindness is so wonderful that the children of men quite naturally run to the shadow of His wings, trustingly putting their hope, confidence, and faith in Him. Why do they do this? Because He is so eminently trustworthy. It is only reasonable to run into the shadow of His wings, near His heart, and make Him the object of our faith and trust.

The English hymn by Wesley offers these stirring words: "Jesus, lover of my soul, let me to Thy bosom fly."[3]

We love Him because He first loved us. We trust Him because of His unsurpassable kindness. We have faith in Him because we know Him.

Compare Psalm 34:22: **"The Lord redeemeth the soul of his servants: and none of them that *trust (chacah)* in him shall be desolate."** This verse accurately portrays the faith-filled relationship of the Old Testament believers to their God. (Also in Psalm 11:2.) Notice the resolute and final quality of the Psalmist's declaration here. (See Psalm 37:40; 91:4.)

Batach

Batach (pronounced "baw-takh'"), #982 in *Strong's*, appears 120 times in the Old Testament. While *chasah* is more precipitous (run, flee, hide, step aside, pursue, search, look) than *batach*, *batach* has a lot going for it.

Batach can be traced back to an Arabic word: to throw a person face down on the ground. Then it included lying extended on the ground. From there, it progressed to lying down on the ground in a posture of rest or repose.

Batach in non-biblical Hebrew is the word for melons that lie upon the ground and grow totally undisturbed. They appear to be resting on the ground.

Batach progressed to mean living securely, calmly, in tranquility, and to lie down in the sense of relying or trusting. It even included a confident trust that would seem as though the trusting person is either unconcerned or incautious. Psalm 22:9 is an example: **"But thou art he that took me out of the womb: thou didst make me *hope (batach)* when I was upon my mother's breasts."** One translation reads, **"You inspired me with *trust* at my mother's breast."**[4]

Trust and safety are closely linked in Hebrew. A child nestled beneath his parent's arm is trusting because he is secure. There is no reason that child cannot trust. Compare Proverbs 3:5: ***"Trust* in the Lord with all thine heart."**

The words *batach* (meaning trust) and *betach* (#983 in *Strong's,* meaning safety) also give rise to the word *bittachown* ("bit-taw-khone'"), #986 in *Strong's,* which means confidence, security, trust. This word occurs infrequently in Scripture. In modern Hebrew it is in the phrase for air travel, "happy landing," which literally means landing in safety and security.

Synopsis

R.B. Girdlestone in his book, *Synonyms of the Old Testament,* has an interesting comment about the faith found in Old Testament believers. He writes:

Faith signifies believing the truth of the Word of God. It relates to some word spoken or some promise made by the Lord. It expresses the belief which a person who hears it has of its being true. He assents (or confesses) to it. He relies upon it. And he acts accordingly. This is faith.

Its fruit will vary according to the nature of the promise received and according to the circumstances of the receiver. It led Noah to build an ark, Abraham to offer up his son, Moses to refuse to be called the son of Pharaoh's daughter, and the Israelites to march around the walls of Jericho. "I believe God that it shall be even as it has been told me." This is a picture of the process which the Bible calls faith.[5]

Faith—*Pistis*

Faith is the New Testament word for the Old Testament word *trust*. *Faith* appears only twice in the Old Testament—Deuteronomy 32:20 and Habakkuk 2:4—while *trust* appears over 105 times. As used in the Old Testament, a better translation of faith would be faithfulness or steadfastness.

Five Greek words are translated "faith" in the New Testament: *elpis, pistos, apistos, oligopistos* and, the main faith word, *pistis.*

The Five Greek Words for *Faith*
Elpis—Hope/Faith

Elpis ("el-peace'"), #1680 in *Strong's*, appears 54 times in the New Testament. Fifty-three times the *Authorized Version* translates it "hope."[6] In Hebrews 10:23 it is translated "faith." "Let us hold fast the profession of our *faith (elpis)."*

Why the 47 authorized translations used *faith* instead of the more common usage of *hope* is fairly easy to understand. At the time of the *King James* translation *hope* was defined as including an expectation of future happenings.

One grammarian consulted stated, "*Elpis* was the dearly cherished and the well-grounded expecting of some desired good."[7] With this in mind, you can readily see that *elpis,* or hope, also embodies a faith element. Faith, as does hope, looks to the future for a favorable outcome.

Pistos—The Faithful

Pistos ("pis-toss'"), #4103 in *Strong's*, is a verbal adjective used 66 times and can be defined objectively as trustworthy, or subjectively as trusting. It can also be defined as active or passive depending upon the meaning of the words.

Passively, *pistos* is defined as and worthy of confidence faithful trusting. When used of persons, it means one on whom we can rely. Jesus Christ, as our Savior from sins and bestower of eternal life, is a good example. When used of things, it means trustworthy, firm, sure, and certain.

Most of the grammarians consulted stated that the Word of God, the sayings of Jesus and the biblical promises given to us are a prime example of *pistos* being defined as reliable and worthy of our trust. We can put our total trust in the sure Word of God.

Actively, *pistos* is defined as trusting and believing. A good example of this is Acts 16:1. Referring to Timothy's mother, it literally reads, "She was a *believing (pistos) Jewess*."

When the word is used of Christians, it is always in sharp contrast with doubters, skeptics and unbelievers. J.H. Thayer states: "In the New Testament *(pistos)* is used of one who trusts in God's promises and is convinced Jesus has been raised from the dead. It is that person who is convinced Jesus is the Messiah and the Author of (our) salvation!"[8]

Pistos could be one who not only believes in the Lord Jesus Christ for eternal salvation, but lives a life of consistent trust and faithful obedience to the Lord on a daily basis. What is why Christians are frequently referred to as "the faithful." It is a complimentary word, though the media sometimes use it in a derogatory way.

Apistos—The Unfaithful

Apistos ("app'-is-toss"), #571 in *Strong's*, is used only 23 times in the *King James Version*.

Words in our English language that start with an "a" coming from a Greek origin usually negate the rest of the word. *Theist* is a person with a god. Put an "a" in front of *theist*, and you have *atheist*—one who has no god. The same can be done with *gnostic*, or a knowing one. *Agnostic* is one who does not know or is not sure. Other "a" words include *amillenial*, *amoral* and, our present study word, *apistos*—one without faith.

Apistos can be defined as disbelieving, distrustful, faithless, lacking in trust, refusing to believe, an unbeliever, and a non-Christian.

In classical or non-biblical Greek, *apistos* is associated with being illiterate. First John 5:10,11 refers to those who believe the record God gave of His Son. It is possible for people to be faithless *(apistos)* because they do not know the Scripture.

New Testament usage infers that the person termed faithless *(apistos)* is one who hears but refuses to believe. New Testament writers call faithless the one who does not believe the Good News about Jesus Christ. It is one who says no to Christ's invitation to come to Him for rest. Second Corinthians 4:4 reads literally, "The god of this world has blinded their *unbelieving (apistos)* minds."

One reason Christians are anxious to convert young people is because of the hardening process of unbelief. The Greek grammarians consulted for this study point out how *apistos* leads from general distrust and unbelief to disobedience. This, in turn, makes a person skeptical, suspicious, and disloyal. The end result is a treacherous lifestyle of rebellion against God.

This must be one of the reasons Ecclesiastes 12:1 says, **"Remember now thy Creator in the days of thy youth...."** This implies it is better to start serving the Lord while young before the heart becomes hardened by the cement of faithlessness *(apistos)*.

Oligopistos—Little Faith

Oligopistos ("oll-igg-opp'-is-toss"), #3640 in *Strong's*, is used only five times in the New Testament. Each time it has been translated, "O you of little faith...." Once it was spoken by Jesus to Peter only. The other four times He was speaking to all twelve disciples.

This word appears only in the synoptic Gospels. It seems to have been coined by Jesus as Greek grammarians cannot locate the word in secular literature. *Patristic* authors in three centuries following New Testament times used the word, but only in the sense Jesus used when He introduced the word for *little faith*.

Oligopistos is a compounded word: *oligos* meaning little, small, brief, or puny and *pistos* meaning "believing faith." *Oligopistos* is defined as little faith, trusting too little, insufficient faith, or lacking confidence in Christ.

The Lord authored this word and used it as a tender rebuke covering four different mind sets of the disciples:

1. Anxiety about needs being met.
   (Luke 12:28; Matt. 6:30.)

2. Fear of accident or harm.
   (Matt. 8:26.)

3. Doubting or fear of failure.
   (Matt. 14:31.)

4. Forgetfulness of previous blessings.
   (Matt. 16:8.)

It is interesting to notice Jesus' stern qualities when speaking of the lack of faith by those who rejected Him (*apistos*—"faithless"). In contrast, the lack of faith by His chosen followers only elicits a mild reproof and a tender rebuke (*oligopistos*—"little faith").

The Lord shows a reaction to hostile unbelief and at the same time a tender compassionate side to struggling believers. Little faith does have the chance of growing into large faith. Unbelief totally shuts the door on a faithful God working for the person.

Pistis—Faith

Pistis ("pis'-tis"), #4102 in *Strong's,* is used 244 times. It is translated "faith" 239 times. The other times "belief," "fidelity," and "assurance" are the *King James* translators' choices. "Faith" is a fascinating word because it covers a broad spectrum of meanings.

"The Faith" is the generic term for Christianity. "Keep the faith" is a more recent phrase coming from a group that seems avant-garde. We will define faith (*pistis*) using the insight of some Greek grammarians who have spent their lifetimes getting to the meaning of the word and clarifying it for all students of the Word.

Smith Wigglesworth, pioneer Pentecostal evangelist with a strong emphasis on divine healing, often preached that faith is an act.

In his recently published book *Christian Words*, Nigel Turner states the same thing when referring to the New Testament use of the word: "The Old Testament word for faith is *passive* (faithfulness) while the New Testament word for faith has an *active* sense."[9]

Christian Faith

Bloomfield wrote his lexicon in 1835 A.D. It is now out of print, but his remarks about faith *(pistis)* are worth repeating:

Faith is not only firmly persuaded that Christ is Who He said He is, but it also includes the idea of hope and expectation. It is called the "Good Faith." Faith is the essential trait of Christian life and character. It is a firm conviction and confiding belief that Jesus as God/man is one with the Father and worthy of our total trust.[10]

Faith never rests in a doctrine but always in the person, Jesus, and the trustworthiness of the person, Jesus Christ.

Action Faith

Romans 10:17 tells us that *"faith (pistis)* **cometh by hearing, and hearing by the word** (rhema) **of God."** Galatians 5:6 states faith *works* by agape love. The two words *coming* and *working* show us a very active side of faith. It has motion to it.

Faith is not a trophy to put on display as an exhibit. It is not an arm band to be worn for impressing people. It is not a commodity to be carried around in a jewel box, then to be brought out and shown to an admiring audience.

Faith *comes,* faith *works,* faith *abides,* faith *continues.* It is God's gift to us to make it through this life, so we can arrive safely and soundly in the other world. **"...this is the victory that overcometh the world, even our** *faith (pistis)"* (1 John 5:4).

Saving Faith

Hebrews 11:6 and Ephesians 2:8,9 tell that God graces us with the ability to come to Him for forgiveness, the cleansing of our past sins, and admission into His family. The faith vitally necessary for our conversion to Jesus Christ is a gifting and a gracing. Some scholars call this *saving faith*.

Keeping Faith

Upon conversion, the new Christian soon finds himself on an upward path requiring a disciplined life and humble trust in God's promises. Romans 12:3 says God has dealt to every man *the measure of faith*. The Greek word for "measure" is *metron*. We get our English word *metric* (or *meter*) from *metron*.

At conversion, a portion of faith is metered out to us. By walking with the Lord, obeying His will, and living in His Word, our particular measure of faith has a growth potential. Some are *weak in faith*. (Rom. 14:1.) Some have *growing faith*. (2 Cor. 10:15.) Some have *steadfast faith*. (1 Cor. 15:58.) Some have *strong faith*. (Rom. 4:20.)

We know faith has a developing quality about it. Romans 1:17 tells us we go *from faith to faith*. That means we are gaining ground, and our measure of faith can increase and grow.

The Gift of Faith

First Corinthians 12:8-10 is a list of nine giftings of the Holy Spirit. In verse nine we read, **"To another faith by the same Spirit."** Richard Weymouth translates this, **"by means of the same Spirit, special** faith." Conybeare calls it, **"wonder-working faith."**[11] H. A. W. Meyer says, **"a heroism of faith."**[12] Bible scholars remind us that this faith is more than the faith accompanying Christian living.

There are special giftings for special occasions, such as working of miracles, raising the dead, stopping floods, miraculous healings, acts of judgment (Ananias and Sapphira, for example), and everything the Bible calls "signs and wonders."

This gift of faith has never been removed from the Church and is still available today for all Christian activity. The promise is it will remain in the Church body of believers until the Second Coming of Christ, according to First Corinthians 1:7.

The Fruit of Faith

In Galatians 5:22 faith is listed as one of the nine fruit of the Spirit. The more modern translations use the word *faithfulness*. It is a better description of a consistent life of trust and abiding confidence in the Lord and in His promises.

Faith for the Rest of our Journey

Unbelief is going to be every Christian's opponent from now till the coming of the Lord. The love of many will wax cold as iniquity abounds. But we are also promised that where sin abounds, grace does *much more abound* (Rom. 5:20).

The Lord asked in the parable of the unjust judge, **"When the Son of man comes will He find (persistence in) the faith on the earth?"** (Luke 18:8 AMP.) He answers His own question with a declaration of faith found in Daniel 11:32 AMP: **"...the people who know their God shall prove themselves strong and shall stand firm, and do exploits [for God]."**

Your personal faith is a dynamic force that demands constant adjustment and self-adjustment. Jesus prayed for Peter that his faith would not fail him. (Luke 22:32.) As our Intercessor, He is saying to us: "Live in My Word and let My promises live in you. None of these will ever fail you!"

Your faith in God and His promises is your support system from now until the Second Coming of Jesus Christ. Trust Him!

Scriptures

Abram believed the LORD, and he credited it to him righteousness.

Genesis 15:6 NIV

³ You will keep him in perfect peace, whose mind is stayed on You, because he trusts in You. ⁴ Trust in the LORD forever, for in YAHWEH, the LORD, is everlasting strength.

Isaiah 26:3,4 NKJV

Behold, as for the proud one, His soul is not right within him; but the righteous will live by his faith.

Habakkuk 2:4 NAS

⁵,⁶ When Jesus arrived in Capernaum, a Roman army captain came and pled with him to come to his home and heal his servant boy who was in bed paralyzed and racked with pain.
⁷ "Yes," Jesus said, "I will come and heal him."
⁸,⁹ Then the officer said, "Sir, I am not worthy to have you in my home; [and it isn't necessary for you to come]. If you will only stand here and say, 'Be healed,' my servant will get well! I know, because I am under the authority of my superior officers and I have authority over my soldiers, and I say to one, 'Go,' and he goes, and to another, 'Come,' and he comes, and to my slave boy, 'Do this or that,' and he does it. And I know you have authority to tell his sickness to go—and it will go!"

[10] Jesus stood there amazed! Turning to the crowd he said, "I haven't seen faith like this in all the land of Israel!"

[13] Then Jesus said to the Roman officer, "Go on home. What you have believed has happened!" And the boy was healed that same hour!

Matthew 8:5-10,13 TLB

[23] And when He got into the boat, His disciples followed Him.

[24] And behold, there arose a great storm in the sea, so that the boat was covered with the waves; but He Himself was asleep.

[25] And they came to Him, and awoke Him, saying, "Save us, Lord; we are perishing!"

[26] And He said to them, "Why are you timid, you men of little faith?" Then He arose, and rebuked the winds and the sea; and it became perfectly calm.

[27] And the men marveled, saying, "What kind of a man is this, that even the winds and the sea obey Him?"

Matthew 8:23-27 NAS

[22] A Canaanite woman from that vicinity came to him, crying out, "Lord, Son of David, have mercy on me! My daughter is suffering terribly from demon-possession."

²³ Jesus did not answer a word. So his disciples came to him and urged him, "Send her away, for she keeps crying out after us."

²⁴ He answered, "I was sent only to the lost sheep of Israel."

²⁵ The woman came and knelt before him. "Lord, help me!" she said.

²⁶ He replied, "It is not right to take the children's bread and toss it to their dogs."

²⁷ "Yes, Lord," she said, "but even the dogs eat the crumbs that fall from their masters' table."

²⁸ Then Jesus answered, "Woman, you have great faith! Your request is granted." And her daughter was healed from that very hour.

Matthew 15:22-28 NIV

¹⁸ Now in the morning, as He returned to the city, He was hungry.

¹⁹ And seeing a fig tree by the road, He came to it and found nothing on it but leaves, and said to it, "Let no fruit grow on you ever again." And immediately the fig tree withered away.

²⁰ Now when the disciples saw it, they marveled, saying, "How did the fig tree wither away so soon?"

²¹ So Jesus answered and said to them, "Assuredly, I say to you, if you have faith and do not doubt, you will not only do what was done to the fig

tree, but also if you say to this mountain, 'Be removed and be cast into the sea,' it will be done."

Matthew 21:18-21 NKJV

²² One of the synagogue rulers, named Jairus, came there. Seeing Jesus, he fell at his feet
²³ and pleaded earnestly with him, "My little daughter is dying. Please come and put your hands on her so that she will be healed and live."
²⁴ So Jesus went with him. A large crowd followed and pressed around him.
²⁵ And a woman was there who had been subject to bleeding for twelve years.
²⁶ She had suffered a great deal under the care of many doctors and had spent all she had, yet instead of getting better she grew worse.
²⁷ When she heard about Jesus, she came up behind him in the crowd and touched his cloak,
²⁸ because she thought, "If I just touch his clothes, I will be healed."
²⁹ Immediately her bleeding stopped and she felt in her body that she was freed from her suffering.
³⁰ At once Jesus realized that power had gone out from him. He turned around in the crowd and asked, "Who touched my clothes?"

³¹ "You see the people crowding against you," his disciples answered, "and yet you can ask, 'Who touched me?'"

³² But Jesus kept looking around to see who had done it.

³³ Then the woman, knowing what had happened to her, came and fell at his feet and, trembling with fear, told him the whole truth.

³⁴ He said to her, "Daughter, your faith has healed you. Go in peace and be freed from your suffering."

³⁵ While Jesus was still speaking, some men came from the house of Jairus, the synagogue ruler. "Your daughter is dead," they said. "Why bother the teacher any more?"

³⁶ Ignoring what they said, Jesus told the synagogue ruler, "Don't be afraid; just believe."

³⁷ He did not let anyone follow him except Peter, James and John the brother of James.

³⁸ When they came to the home of the synagogue ruler, Jesus saw a commotion, with people crying and wailing loudly.

³⁹ He went in and said to them, "Why all this commotion and wailing? The child is not dead but asleep."

⁴⁰ But they laughed at him. After he put them all out, he took the child's father and mother and

the disciples who were with him, and went in where the child was.

⁴¹ He took her by the hand and said to her, "Talitha koum!" (which means, "Little girl, I say to you, get up!").

⁴² Immediately the girl stood up and walked around (she was twelve years old). At this they were completely astonished.

⁴³ He gave strict orders not to let anyone know about this, and told them to give her something to eat.

Mark 5:22-43 NIV

⁴⁶ And they came to Jericho. And as He was going out from Jericho with His disciples and a great multitude, a blind beggar named Bartimaeus, the son of Timaeus, was sitting by the road.

⁴⁷ And when he heard that it was Jesus the Nazarene, he began to cry out and say, "Jesus, Son of David, have mercy on me!"

⁴⁸ And many were sternly telling him to be quiet, but he kept crying out all the more, "Son of David, have mercy on me!"

⁴⁹ And Jesus stopped and said, "Call him here." And they called the blind man, saying to him, "Take courage, arise! He is calling for you."

⁵⁰ And casting aside his cloak, he jumped up, and came to Jesus.

⁵¹ And answering him, Jesus said, "What do you want Me to do for you?" And the blind man said to Him, "Rabboni, I want to regain my sight!"

⁵² And Jesus said to him, "Go your way; your faith has made you well." And immediately he regained his sight and began following Him on the road.

Mark 10:46-52 NAS

²²,²³ In reply Jesus said to the disciples, "If you only have faith in God—this is the absolute truth—you can say to this Mount of Olives, 'Rise up and fall into the Mediterranean,' and your command will be obeyed. All that's required is that you really believe and have no doubt!

²⁴ "Listen to me! You can pray for anything, and if you believe, you have it; it's yours!

²⁵ "But when you are praying, first forgive anyone you are holding a grudge against, so that your Father in heaven will forgive you your sins too."

Mark 11:22-25 TLB

¹ After he had ended all his sayings in the hearing of the people he entered Capernaum.

² Now a centurion had a slave who was dear to him, who was sick and at the point of death.

³ When he heard of Jesus, he sent to him elders of the Jews, asking him to come and heal his slave.

⁴ And when they came to Jesus, they besought him earnestly, saying, "He is worthy to have you do this for him,

⁵ for he loves our nation, and he built us our synagogue."

⁶ And Jesus went with them. When he was not far from the house, the centurion sent friends to him, saying to him, "Lord, do not trouble yourself, for I am not worthy to have you come under my roof;

⁷ therefore I did not presume to come to you. But say the word, and let my servant be healed.

⁸ For I am a man set under authority, with soldiers under me: and I say to one, 'Go,' and he goes; and to another, 'Come,' and he comes; and to my slave, 'Do this,' and he does it."

⁹ When Jesus heard this he marveled at him, and turned and said to the multitude that followed him, "I tell you, not even in Israel have I found such faith."

¹⁰ And when those who had been sent returned to the house, they found the slave well.

Luke 7:1-10 RSV

⁵ The apostles said to the Lord, "Increase our faith!"
⁶ He replied, "If you have faith as small as a mustard seed, you can say to this mulberry tree, 'Be uprooted and planted in the sea,' and it will obey you.

Luke 17:5,6 NIV

³¹ Simon, Simon, Satan has asked to have you, to sift you like wheat,
³² but I have pleaded in prayer for you that your faith should not completely fail. So when you have repented and turned to me again, strengthen and build up the faith of your brothers.

Luke 22:31,32 TLB

²⁷ Then what becomes of our boasting? It is ruled out absolutely. On what principle? On the principle of doing deeds? No, on the principle of faith.
²⁸ We hold that a man is justified by faith, apart from deeds of the Law altogether.

Romans 3:27,28 Moffatt

³⁰ God treats us all the same; all, whether Jews or Gentiles, are acquitted if they have faith.
³¹ Well then, if we are saved by faith, does this mean that we no longer need obey God's laws?

Just the opposite! In fact, only when we trust Jesus can we truly obey him.

Romans 3:30,31 TLB

³ What does the Scripture say? "Abraham believed God, and it was credited to him as righteousness."
⁴ Now when a man works, his wages are not credited to him as a gift, but as an obligation.
⁵ However, to the man who does not work but trusts God who justifies the wicked, his faith is credited as righteousness.

Romans 4:3-5 NIV

¹¹ And he [Abraham] received the sign of circumcision, a seal of the righteousness of the faith which he had while uncircumcised, that he might be the father of all who believe without being circumcised, that righteousness might be reckoned to them,
¹² and the father of circumcision to those who not only are of the circumcision, but who also follow in the steps of the faith of our father Abraham which he had while uncircumcised.
¹³ For the promise to Abraham or to his descendants that he would be heir of the world was not through the Law, but through the righteousness of faith.

¹⁴ For if those who are of the Law are heirs, faith is made void and the promise is nullified;

¹⁵ for the Law brings about wrath, but where there is no law, neither is there violation.

¹⁶ For this reason it is by faith, that it might be in accordance with grace, in order that the promise may be certain to all the descendants, not only to those who are of the Law, but also to those who are of the faith of Abraham, who is the father of us all,

¹⁷ (as it is written, "A father of many nations have I made you") in the sight of Him whom he believed, even God, who gives life to the dead and calls into being that which does not exist.

¹⁸ In hope against hope he believed, in order that he might become a father of many nations, according to that which had been spoken, "So shall your descendants be."

¹⁹ And without becoming weak in faith he contemplated his own body, now as good as dead since he was about a hundred years old, and the deadness of Sarah's womb;

²⁰ yet, with respect to the promise of God, he did not waver in unbelief, but grew strong in faith, giving glory to God,

21 and being fully assured that what He had promised, He was able also to perform.
22 Therefore also it was reckoned to him as righteousness.
23 Now not for his sake only was it written, that it was reckoned to him,
24 but for our sake also, to whom it will be reckoned, as those who believe in Him who raised Jesus our Lord from the dead,
25 He who was delivered up because of our transgressions, and was raised because of our justification.

Romans 4:11-25 NAS

For through the authority graciously given to me I warn every individual among you not to value himself unduly, but to cultivate sobriety of judgement in accordance with the amount of faith which God has allotted to each one.

Romans 12:3 Weymouth

22 Do you have faith? Have it to yourself before God. Happy is he who does not condemn himself in what he approves.
23 But he who doubts is condemned if he eats, because he does not eat from faith; for whatever is not from faith is sin.

Romans 14:22,23 NKJV

...for we are living a life of faith, and not one of sight.

2 Corinthians 5:7 Weymouth

16 Yet we know that a man is justified or reckoned righteous and in right standing with God, not by works of law but [only] through faith and [absolute] reliance on and adherence to and trust in Jesus Christ, the Messiah, the Anointed One. [Therefore] even we [ourselves] have believed on Christ Jesus, in order to be justified by faith in Christ and not by works of the Law—for we cannot be justified by any observance of [the ritual of] the Law [given by Moses]; because by keeping legal rituals and by works no human being can ever be justified—declared righteous and put in right standing with God.

Galatians 2:16 AMP

5 Does He then, who provides you with the Spirit and works miracles among you, do it by the works of the Law, or by hearing with faith? 6 Even so Abraham believed God, and it was reckoned to him as righteousness. 7 Therefore, be sure that it is those who are of faith who are sons of Abraham.

⁸ And the Scripture, foreseeing that God would justify the Gentiles by faith, preached the gospel beforehand to Abraham, saying, "All the nations shall be blessed in you."
⁹ So then those who are of faith are blessed with Abraham, the believer.

Galatians 3:5-9 NAS

²² But the Scripture declares that the whole world is a prisoner of sin, so that what was promised, being given through faith in Jesus Christ, might be given to those who believe.
²³ Before this faith came, we were held prisoners by the law, locked up until faith should be revealed.
²⁴ So the law was put in charge to lead us to Christ that we might be justified by faith.
²⁵ Now that faith has come, we are no longer under the supervision of the law.
²⁶ You are all sons of God through faith in Christ Jesus.

Galatians 3:22-26 NIV

Because of his kindness, you have been saved through trusting Christ. And even trusting is not of yourselves; it too is a gift from God.

Ephesians 2:8 TLB

Lift up over all the (covering) shield of saving faith, upon which you can quench all the flaming missiles of the wicked [one].

Ephesians 6:16 AMP

But since we belong to the day, let us be self-controlled, putting on faith and love as a breast-plate, and the hope of salvation as a helmet.

1 Thessalonians 5:8 NIV

Cling tightly to your faith in Christ and always keep your conscience clear, doing what you know is right. For some people have disobeyed their consciences and have deliberately done what they knew was wrong. It isn't surprising that soon they lost their faith in Christ after defying God like that.

1 Timothy 1:19 TLB

[1] What is faith? It is the confident assurance that something we want is going to happen. It is the certainty that what we hope for is waiting for us, even though we cannot see it up ahead.
[2] Men of God in days of old were famous for their faith
[3] By faith—by believing God—we know that the world and the stars—in fact, all things—were

made at God's command; and that they were all made from things that can't be seen.

⁴ It was by faith that Abel obeyed God and brought an offering that pleased God more than Cain's offering did. God accepted Abel and proved it by accepting his gift; and though Abel is long dead, we can still learn lessons from him about trusting God.

⁵ Enoch trusted God too, and that is why God took him away to heaven without dying; suddenly he was gone because God took him. Before this happened God had said how pleased he was with Enoch.

⁶ You can never please God without faith, without depending on him. Anyone who wants to come to God must believe that there is a God and that he rewards those who sincerely look for him.

⁷ Noah was another who trusted God. When he heard God's warning about the future, Noah believed him even though there was then no sign of a flood, and wasting no time, he built the ark and saved his family. Noah's belief in God was in direct contrast to the sin and disbelief of the rest of the world—which refused to

obey—and because of his faith he became one of those whom God has accepted.

⁸ Abraham trusted God, and when God told him to leave home and go far away to another land that he promised to give him, Abraham obeyed. Away he went, not even knowing where he was going.

⁹ And even when he reached God's promised land, he lived in tents like a mere visitor as did Isaac and Jacob, to whom God gave the same promise.

¹⁰ Abraham did this because he was confidently waiting for God to bring him to that strong heavenly city whose designer and builder is God.

¹¹ Sarah, too, had faith, and because of this she was able to become a mother in spite of her old age, for she realized that God, who gave her his promise, would certainly do what he said.

¹² And so a whole nation came from Abraham, who was too old to have even one child—a nation with so many millions of people that, like the stars of the sky and the sand on the ocean shores, there is no way to count them.

¹³ These men of faith I have mentioned died without ever receiving all that God had promised them; but they saw it all awaiting them on ahead and were glad, for they agreed

that this earth was not their real home but that they were just strangers visiting down here.

[14] And quite obviously when they talked like that, they were looking forward to their real home in heaven.

[15] If they had wanted to, they could have gone back to the good things of this world.

[16] But they didn't want to. They were living for heaven. And now God is not ashamed to be called their God, for he has made a heavenly city for them.

[17] While God was testing him, Abraham still trusted in God and his promises, and so he offered up his son Isaac and was ready to slay him on the altar of sacrifice;

[18] yes, to slay even Isaac, through whom God had promised to give Abraham a whole nation of descendants!

[19] He believed that if Isaac died God would bring him back to life again; and that is just about what happened for as far as Abraham was concerned, Isaac was doomed to death, but he came back again alive!

[20] It was by faith that Isaac knew God would give future blessings to his two sons, Jacob and Esau.

²¹ By faith Jacob, when he was old and dying, blessed each of Joseph's two sons as he stood and prayed, leaning on the top of his cane.

²² And it was by faith that Joseph, as he neared the end of his life, confidently spoke of God bringing the people of Israel out of Egypt; and he was so sure of it that he made them promise to carry his bones with them when they left!

²³ Moses' parents had faith too. When they saw that God had given them an unusual child, they trusted that God would save him from the death the king commanded, and they hid him for three months and were not afraid.

²⁴,²⁵ It was by faith that Moses, when he grew up, refused to be treated as the grandson of the king, but chose to share ill-treatment with God's people instead of enjoying the fleeting pleasures of sin.

²⁶ He thought that it was better to suffer for the promised Christ than to own all the treasures of Egypt, for he was looking forward to the great reward that God would give him.

²⁷ And it was because he trusted God that he left the land of Egypt and wasn't afraid of the king's anger. Moses kept right on going; it seemed as though he could see God right there with him.

[28] And it was because he believed God would save his people that he commanded them to kill a lamb as God had told them to and sprinkle the blood on the doorposts of their homes so that God's terrible Angel of Death could not touch the oldest child in those homes as he did among the Egyptians.

[29] The people of Israel trusted God and went right through the Red Sea as though they were on dry ground. But when the Egyptians chasing them tried it, they all were drowned.

[30] It was faith that brought the walls of Jericho tumbling down after the people of Israel had walked around them seven days as God had commanded them.

[31] By faith—because she believed in God and his power—Rahab the harlot did not die with all the others in her city when they refused to obey God, for she gave a friendly welcome to the spies.

[32] Well, how much more do I need to say? It would take too long to recount the stories of the faith of Gideon and Barak and Samson and Jephthah and David and Samuel and all the other prophets.

[33] These people all trusted God and as a result won battles, overthrew kingdoms, ruled their people well, and received what God had promised them; they were kept from harm in a den of lions

[34] and in a fiery furnace. Some, through their faith, escaped death by the sword. Some were made strong again after they had been weak or sick. Others were given great power in battle; they made whole armies turn and run away.

[35] And some women, through faith, received their loved ones back again from death. But others trusted God and were beaten to death, preferring to die rather than turn from God and be free—trusting that they would rise to a better life afterwards.

[36] Some were laughed at and their backs cut open with whips, and others were chained in dungeons.

[37,38] Some died by stoning and some by being sawed in two; others were promised freedom if they would renounce their faith, then were killed with the sword. Some went about in skins of sheep and goats, wandering over deserts and mountains, hiding in dens and caves. They were hungry and sick and ill-treated—too good for this world.

[39] And these men of faith, though they trusted God and won his approval, none of them received all that God had promised them;

[40] for God wanted them to wait and share the even better rewards that were prepared for us.

Hebrews 11:1-40 TLB

Only it must be in faith that he asks, with no wavering—no hesitating, no doubting. For the one who wavers (hesitates, doubts) is like the billowing surge out at sea, that is blown hither and thither and tossed by the wind.

James 1:6 AMP

[17] In the same way, faith by itself, if it is not accompanied by action, is dead.

[18] But someone will say, "You have faith; I have deeds." Show me your faith without deeds, and I will show you my faith by what I do.

[19] You believe that there is one God. Good! Even the demons believe that—and shudder.

[20] You foolish man, do you want evidence that faith without deeds is useless?

[21] Was not our ancestor Abraham considered righteous for what he did when he offered his son Isaac on the altar?

²² You see that his faith and his actions were working together, and his faith was made complete by what he did.
²³ And the scripture was fulfilled that says, "Abraham believed God, and it was credited to him as righteousness," and he was called God's friend.
²⁴ You see that a person is justified by what he does and not by faith alone.
²⁵ In the same way, was not even Rahab the prostitute considered righteous for what she did when she gave lodging to the spies and sent them off in a different direction?
²⁶ As the body without the spirit is dead, so faith without deeds is dead.

James 2:17-26 NIV

¹⁴ Is anyone among you sick? Let him call for the elders of the church, and let them pray over him, anointing him with oil in the name of the Lord;
¹⁵ and the prayer offered in faith will restore the one who is sick, and the Lord will raise him up, and if he has committed sins, they will be forgiven him.

James 5:14,15 NAS

For every child of God can obey him, defeating sin
and evil pleasure by trusting Christ to help him.

1 John 5:4 TLB

Prayer of Faith

Lord, I want to thank You that Jesus is the Author
and Finisher of my faith. You which have begun a
good work in me will be faithful to perform or
complete it. Because I am Your workmanship and
handicraft, I know You are teaching me how to
strengthen and develop my faith so I can grow up to
the full stature of Jesus and my faith can be complete
and mature, lacking nothing in Jesus.

Because faith is the victory that overcomes the
world, and You have given me the measure of faith, I
determine in my heart to be a doer of the Word and
not just a hearer, deceiving myself.

Father, because faith comes by hearing and
hearing by the Word of God, I determine to stay in
Your Word and study to show myself approved, a
workman that need not be ashamed.

Thank You, Lord, for giving me the Holy Spirit to
lead, guide, and teach me how to grow and develop
my faith for every area of my life, because the just
shall live by faith.

Your Word says that faith works by love, so I determine to grow in love and mercy so that my faith will develop totally.

Father, You have made it clear that faith is released through my mouth when I speak Your Word. Words can be faith-filled, doubt-filled, or empty and idle. I now consecrate my mouth to speak only words filled with faith, hope, love, power, and joy. No words of doubt, unbelief, death, or hate will cross my lips. I'll speak Your Word and plant it like a grain of mustard seed that will grow and develop so that no mountain can stand before me and nothing will be impossible to me.

Faith calls those things that be not as though they are, so by faith I thank You that my faith is being developed and matured to the place where You desire it to be.

My glad confession is that these things are mine. I have them now in Jesus' Name. Amen.

Scripture References

Philemon 6	*Ephesians 5:17*
John 10:27	*Colossians 4:12*
John 10:5	*Acts 22:14*

[1] p. 1128.

[2] Gerrit Verkuyl, *The Modern Language Bible* (Grand Rapids: Zondervan Bible Publishers). *Holy Bible: International Children's Bible, New Century Version* (Ft. Worth: Sweet Publishing), Deut. 32:20.

[3] *Hymns for the Family of God* (Nashville: Paragon Associates), p. 222.

[4] F. Delitzsch (Grand Rapids: Wm. B. Eerdman's Publishing Co., 1982), p. 301.

[5] R. B. Girdlestone, *Synonyms of the Old Testament*, 3rd ed. (Grand Rapids: Baker Book House, 1983).

[6] In 1611 A.D. the *King James Version* was published involving approximately 47 translations. It is also known as the *Authorized Version*.

[7] E. W. Bullinger, *A Critical Lexicon and Concordance to the English and Greek New Testament* (Grand Rapids: Zondervan Publishing House, 1975), p. 272.

[8] Carl Ludwig and Wilibald Grimm, *Greek-English Lexicon of the New Testament* (New York: American Book Co., 1889).

[9] Nigel Turner, *Christian Words* (Edinburgh: T & T Clark, 1980).

[10] Samuel Thomas Bloomfield, *The Greek New Testament*, 6th ed. (London: Longman, Brown, Green and Longman, 1845).

[11] W. J. Conybeare and J. S. Howson, *The Life and Epistles of St. Paul* (Grand Rapids: Wm. B. Eerdman's Publishing Co., 1987), p. 405.

[12] H. A. W. Meyer, *A Critical Lexegetical Handbook to the Epistle to the Corinthians* (Winona Lake: Alpha Publications), p. 282.

PRAISE AND WORSHIP

Regardless of the limitations and hinderances the enemy, Satan, puts in our path—no matter what means he uses to try to lock us away—we can overcome them all through praise. Prison doors cannot stand as we enter into God's gates with sacrifices of praise and into His courts singing praises.

— David Ingles

Greek and Hebrew Word Studies

OLD TESTAMENT—*TEHILLAH*

I will bless the Lord at all times: his *praise (tehillah)* shall continually be in my mouth.

Psalm 34:1

NEW TESTAMENT—*PROSKUNEO*

...for the Father seeketh such to *worship (proskuneo)* him.

John 4:23

The word *worship* comes from an old Anglo-Saxon word *weorthscipe*, which eventually became *worthship*. English lords in those days were called "Your Worthship" in recognition of their position of authority and their extensive lands and holdings, or worth. As time went by, *worthship* was further shortened to worship.

Thus, to worship means "to ascribe worth or value, or to count worthy." When we worship God, we acknowledge that He is worthy. We acknowledge Who He is and what He is.

— David Ingles
The Word Bible[1]

Praise—*Tehillah*
I will bless the Lord at all times: his *praise* (tehillah) shall continually be in my mouth.

Psalm 34:1

The subject of praise and worship is a major theme, occupying a large place throughout the Bible. Scriptures seem to pulsate with the heartbeat of praise, thanksgiving and worship.

One book of the Bible—the book of Psalms—radiates God's praise above all other portions of Scripture. The Hebrew Bible appropriately titled it "The Book of *Tehillim*" ("praises"). While there are several words translated "praise" or "worship" in the Old Testament, *tehillah* is the word that shall be emphasized in this study.

Tehillah (pronounced "teh-hil-law"), #8416 in *Strong's,* may take either the feminine plural *(tehillot)* or masculine plural *(tehillim)* form when referring to "praises."

The root verb, from which *tehillah* is derived, enables us to better understand the idea of praise. This verb *halal* (pronounced "haw-lal'"), #1984 in *Strong's,* has a range of meaning. It includes celebrating, causing to shine, making splendorous, praising, revelling, spinning wildly, and making someone or something bright, famous, or renowned.

The *King James* translates this verb with a variety of English words, which include "commend," "glory," "praise," "celebrate," "boast," and "shine." The most universally recognized example of the verb *halal* is in the command "Hallelujah," which is an imperative—that is, an order—and means, "All of you must praise

Yah!" *Halal* occurs more than 70 times in the book of Psalms alone.

Psalm 148 contains a list of created things which shall praise God: His people, the sun, the moon and stars, the angels, the heavens, animals of all kinds, mountains, and trees. Just to read or sing this psalm is enough to incite oneself to burst forth in a fountain of praise, making God, in our estimation, more filled with brightness, splendor and glory than He was previously.

Notice that the created universe, and especially the natural world (when not hampered by sinful man), automatically praises the Creator. Scripture declares, **"The dead praise not the Lord, neither any that go down into silence"** (Ps. 115:17). (Compare Isaiah 38:18.) These verses show that praising the Creator is a duty and a privilege of the living, not the dead. But they also may explain how living people in dead traditions tend not to praise God any more than literal corpses do.

Before passing on to other Hebrew words for "praise," let us note that Psalms 22 and 69 have to do with the suffering of Jesus the Messiah, especially those sufferings related to the Crucifixion. In fact, passages from both these psalms are quoted and applied to the Lord Jesus in the Gospels, most extensively so in the accounts of His death.

Let us see then from these two psalms how the Messiah understood the glorious nature of praising God. He even held on to a determined anticipation of leading the multitudes in praise of God, while He was enduring sorrows Himself.

In Psalm 22:3 the suffering Redeemer acknowledges God's holiness, and He properly dwells (literally, "is seated") on the praises of Israel. In verses 22 and 25 He pledges to lead out in praise in the midst of God's vast congregation. In verse 27 He believes the results of His suffering will include the turning of all the world to Jehovah. As a result **"...all the kindreds of the nations shall worship before thee."** Additionally, in verse 26, He is envisioning praise and happiness among God's people.

The Man of Sorrows, the One acquainted with grief, had the glorifying and praising of our praiseworthy God so close to His heart. Certainly we who have so marvelously benefited from His great redemption should never (for any reason) refrain from giving Him praise all our lives. Everyone living and breathing is to praise our glorious God!

Similarly, in Psalm 69 the One on Whom the reproaches fell, the One to Whom they gave gall and vinegar in response to His thirst, still declares, **"I will praise the name of God with a song, and will magnify him with thanksgiving"** (v. 30).

And what was His final concern in this psalm of anguish? His goal was that heaven and earth, and even every creature in the sea, would come to praise God, and that His own people would be redeemed and inherit God's blessings in their land. (vv. 34-36.) What a Savior!

In addition to *tehillah,* there are Hebrew words— like *towdah* and *yadah* (#8426 and #3034 respectively in *Strong's*)—for such concepts as "thank," "thanks," and "thanksgiving." The *King James* translators chose "praise" for these words, which normally have to do with lifting one's hands in thankfulness. One such case is Psalm 50:23, where *towdah* is translated "praise." This family of words is used as extensively as the *hallal/tehillah/tehillim* group.

There are numerous references in Scripture to "magnifying" God. To magnify Him is to make Him larger, grander and more magnificent than He was before in our understanding, our speech, and our lives. The Hebrew word here is *gadal* ("gaw-dal'"),

#1431 in *Strong's*, meaning to be large, great, increased, magnified. It is the exact opposite of the word *despise*, which means to make small, insignificant or little.

This, we read in the New Testament, is how the Savior chose to regard His own humiliations; He "despised" the shame. We can "magnify" our embarrassments and "despise" the Lord Who judges fairly and maintains our cause—or we can "belittle" our own humiliations and make God's honor and concerns and His majestic reputation "magnified" even more.

Finally there are the Hebrew words for worship: *shachah* ("shaw-khaw'"), #7812 in *Strong's*, which means to bow down reverently before God as a means of worship; and *cegid* (pronounced "seg-eed'"), #5457 in *Strong's*, meaning to fall down and worship. The latter form of the verb is from the Aramaic language, and is used in the book of Daniel. The former verb is found throughout the Old Testament with the exception of the book of Daniel.

Two well-known examples of *shachah* are Psalm 29:2, "...worship the Lord in the beauty of holiness," and Psalm 95:6, "**O come, let us worship and bow down: let us kneel before the Lord our maker.**"

The subject of praise and worship is so beautiful and so extensive in Scripture one could easily devote a lifetime to studying it and never learn all there is to know. But in the ages to come we will be even more knowledgeable and skillful in that delightful thing we were created to do: worship and praise Him. (See Psalm 102:18; compare Ephesians 1:4-6.)

May God be praised, thanked, magnified, and worshipped eternally. Amen!

The Greek Words for *Worship* in the *King James Version*

Doxa ("dox'-ah"), #1391 in *Strong's*—to glory, to esteem, to honor, to praise.

> ...then shalt thou have *worship (doxa)* in the presence of them that sit at meat with thee.

> Luke 14:10

Note: Since worship is given to God alone and not to man, later and newer translations insert the words *honor* or *respect* for the word *worship* in the *King James Version.*

Eusebeo ("yoo-seb-eh'-o"), #2151 in *Strong's*—reverence, relating to holy and hallowed things.

...Whom therefore ye ignorantly *worship* (*eusebeo*), him declare I unto you.

Acts 17:23

Therapeuo ("ther-ap-yoo'-o"), #2323 in *Strong's*—to serve, to wait on, to attend, to do service to deity.

Neither is *worshipped* (*therapeuo*) with men's hands, as though he needed anything.

Acts 17:25

Note: Later and newer translations insert the words *supply, minister,* or *served* for the *King James* word *worship.*

Latreuo ("lat-ryoo'-o"), #3000 in *Strong's*—to serve, to be bound to, to minister to the Lord, to render spiritual homage.

For we are the circumcision, which *worship* (*latreuo*) God in the spirit....

Philippians 3:3

Threskeia ("thrace-ki'-ah"), #2356 in *Strong's*—ceremonial observance.

Let no man beguile you of your reward in a voluntary humility and *worshipping* (*threskeia*) of angels.

Colossians 2:18

Neokoros ("neh-o-kor'-os"), #3511 in *Strong's*—one who has charge of a temple, a temple servant.

> ...how that the city of the Ephesians is a **worshipper** *(neokoros)* of the great goddess Diana....
>
> **Acts 19:35**

Note: Later and newer translations insert the words *temple-keeper* or *guardian* for the *King James* word *worshipper*.

Proskuneo ("pros-koo-neh'-o"), #4352 in *Strong's*—to adore, to do reverence, to pay homage to.

> ...for the Father *seeketh* *(proskuneo)* such to worship him.
>
> **John 4:23**

Proskunetes ("pros-koo-nay-tace"), #4353 in *Strong's*—worshipper.

> ...the true **worshippers** *(proskunetes)* shall worship the Father in spirit and in truth.
>
> **John 4:23**

Sebazomai ("seb-ad'-zom-ahee"), #4573 in *Strong's*—to be in awe of or to venerate.

> ...and **worshipped** *(sebazomai)* and served the creature more than the Creator.
>
> **Romans 1:25**

Sebomai ("seb'-om-ahee"), #4576 in *Strong's*—venerate, to pay high regard to.

And a certain woman named Lydia...which worshipped (sebomai) God, heard us: whose heart the Lord opened....

Acts 16:14

Sebasma ("seb'-as-mah"), #4574 in *Strong's*—an object of veneration.

Who opposeth and exalteth himself above all that is called God, or that is worshipped (sebasma)....

2 Thessalonians 2:4

Theosebes ("theh-oss-ebb-ace'"), #2318 in *Strong's*—one who venerates God.

...if any man be a worshipper (theosebes) of God, and doeth his will, him he heareth.

John 9:31

Ethelothreskeia ("eth-el-oth-race-ki'-ah"), #1479 *Strong's*—superstitious observance or will-worship.

Which things have indeed a shew of wisdom in will worship (ethelothreskeia), and humility, and neglecting of the body.

Colossians 2:23

Worship—*Proskuneo*

Of the thirteen Greek words translated "worship" in the *King James*, *proskuneo* ("pros-koo-neh'-oh") is the most expressive and colorful word in the group.

Etymology is used to describe a particular word's origin, history, development, and current idiomatic usage. In English *worship*, as David Ingles points out in *The Word Bible*, was an old Anglo-Saxon word *weorthscipe* which eventually became *worthship*. *Worth* has to do with value; *-ship* is a suffix denoting a state or condition. (Compare other words such as courtship, friendship, township, scholarship and fellowship.)

The word *proskuneo* has an interesting background. *Pros* means in the direction of or towards, and *kuneo* is a word for kiss. At one time it was a word of warm affection describing a puppy kissing the hand or crouching down at the feet of his master.

Proskuneo has an Eastern usage describing kissing the ground in the presence of a potentate or bowing in obedience before a ruler. The word was used to describe the reverence, respect, homage, and adoration given by an individual to a person of high rank.

Proskuneo easily became the New Testament word for offering worship to the Divine Being. *Proskuneo* is the adoration in word, gesture, prayer, confession, songs of praise and thanksgiving, that extols God the Father and Jesus the Son. Strictly speaking, worship is the occupation of the soul with God Himself.

The dominant note in the New Testament worship is that of joy and thanksgiving for God's gracious redemption of mankind in Jesus Christ. In worship the past, present, and future are combined. He Who was, Who is, and Who is to come is present with His people in worship.

We don't start to worship and then conclude it the way we start and conclude a church service. We join worship. It is universal—going on all over the world—and it is going on in heaven too. When we begin to sing praise, give thanks, or extol the beauties of our Savior, we are joining an activity already in progress.

In John 4:20-24 Jesus is clarifying worship to the Samaritan woman at Jacob's well. She mentions a place to worship in contrast to the Jews' worshipping place, Jerusalem. Jesus' tender response is that locality has nothing to do with religious worship.

An ever-present universal God receives universal worship. It is not the place of worship which counts the most, but the object of worship and the spirit of worship.

Proskuneo tells us the spirit of man is the part of his nature that is invisible and immortal. True worship is when man through his spirit attains to friendship and intimacy with God, Who is invisible and immortal.

Colin Brown, in the *Dictionary of New Testament Theology*, writes about *proskuneo* in the book of Revelation:

> The word appears 59 times in the New Testament, and 24 of these are in the Book of Revelation.... In Revelation the *proskuneo* hymns make use of ever-varied language and ideas. They constantly find new titles of dignity with which to praise God. They ascribe to Him the most exalted merits and attributes such as eternity, honor, omnipotence, wisdom, holiness, power, etc., in an attempt to confess His name. Through all these hymns there runs a gloriously universal strain. Frequently this takes the form of royal acclamation, "Thou art worthy."[2]

In the out-of-print *People's Commentary* written by Edwin W. Rice (1891 A.D.), he defines *proskuneo* from John 4:23-25 with these words:

> The time has come when formal outward worship can no longer be accepted as true

worship. These ceremonies, offerings, pilgrimages to some particular sacred place, are not the highest form of worship. They are not the worship God seeks. He wants the homage of the heart, not the natural heart of the flesh, but the heart renewed by the Spirit.

Forms, posture, sacrifices, sacraments, liturgies, holy places, holy days, may be a means to worship...but as forms and expression they are not worship. They may hinder worship such as God seeks.[3]

It is only as the spirit of man communes with God that true worship *(proskuneo)* takes place.

Scriptures

But as for me, I will come into your Temple protected by your mercy and your love; I will worship you with deepest awe.

Psalm 5:7 TLB

[22] I will declare Your name to my brethren; in the midst of the congregation I will praise You. [23] You who fear the LORD, praise Him! All you descendants of Jacob, glorify Him, and fear Him, all you offspring of Israel!

²⁴ For He has not despised nor abhorred the affliction of the afflicted; nor has He hidden His face from Him; but when He cried to Him, He heard.

²⁵ My praise shall be of You in the great congregation; I will pay my vows before those who fear Him.

²⁶ The poor shall eat and be satisfied; those who seek Him will praise the LORD. Let your heart live forever!

²⁷ All the ends of the world shall remember and turn to the LORD, and all the families of the nations shall worship before You.

²⁸ For the kingdom is the LORD's, and He rules over the nations.

²⁹ All the prosperous of the earth shall eat and worship; all those who go down to the dust shall bow before Him, even he who cannot keep himself alive.

Psalm 22:22-29 NKJV

Be glad in the Lord, and rejoice, you [uncompromisingly] righteous—you who are upright and in rightstanding with Him; shout for joy, all you upright in heart!

Psalm 32:11 AMP

¹ I will bless the LORD at all times; his praise shall continually be in my mouth.

² My soul makes its boast in the LORD; let the afflicted hear and be glad.

³ O magnify the LORD with me, and let us exalt his name together!

Psalm 34:1-3 RSV

⁴ There I will go to the altar of God my exceeding joy, and praise him with my harp. O God— my God!

⁵ O my soul, why be so gloomy and discouraged? Trust in God! I shall again praise him for his wondrous help; he will make me smile again, for he is my God!

Psalm 43:4,5 TLB

Great is the LORD, and most worthy of praise, in the city of our God, his holy mountain.

Psalm 48:1 NIV

He who brings an offering of praise and thanksgiving honors and glorifies Me; and he who orders his way aright—who prepares the way that I may show him—to him I will demonstrate the salvation of God.

Psalm 50:23 AMP

[1] Oh come, let us sing to the LORD! Let us shout joyfully to the Rock of our salvation.

[2] Let us come before His presence with thanksgiving; let us shout joyfully to Him with psalms.

[3] For the LORD is the great God, and the great King above all gods.

[4] In His hand are the deep places of the earth; the heights of the hills are His also.

[5] The sea is His, for He made it; and His hands formed the dry land.

[6] Oh come, let us worship and bow down; let us kneel before the LORD our Maker.

[7] For He is our God, and we are the people of His pasture, and the sheep of His hand....

Psalm 95:1-7 NKJV

[1] Sing a new song to the Lord telling about his mighty deeds! For he has won a mighty victory by his power and holiness.

[2,3] He has announced this victory and revealed it to every nation by fulfilling his promise to be kind to Israel. The whole earth has seen God's salvation of his people.

[4] That is why the earth breaks out in praise to God and sings for utter joy!

[5] Sing your praise accompanied by music from the harp.

⁶ Let the cornets and trumpets shout! Make a joyful symphony before the Lord, the King!
⁷ Let the sea in all its vastness roar with praise! Let the earth and all those living on it shout, "Glory to the Lord."

Psalm 98:1-6 TLB

¹ Shout with joy before the Lord, O earth!
² Obey him gladly; come before him, singing with joy.
³ Try to realize what this means—the Lord is God! He made us—we are his people, the sheep of his pasture.
⁴ Go through his open gates with great thanksgiving; enter his courts with praise. Give thanks to him and bless his name.
⁵ For the Lord is always good. He is always loving and kind, and his faithfulness goes on and on to each succeeding generation.

Psalm 100:1-5 TLB

¹ Praise the LORD, O my soul; all my inmost being, praise his holy name.
² Praise the LORD, O my soul, and forget not all his benefits.

Psalm 103:1,2 NIV

[34] I will sing to the LORD as long as I live; I will sing praise to my God while I have my being.
[34] May my meditation be sweet to Him; I will be glad in the LORD.

Psalm 104:33,34 NKJV

[1] O give thanks to the LORD, for he is good; for his steadfast love endures for ever!
[2] Let the redeemed of the LORD say so, whom he has redeemed from trouble.

Psalm 107:1,2 RSV

[1] My heart is steadfast, O God; I will sing and make music with all my soul.
[2] Awake, harp and lyre! I will awaken the dawn.
[3] I will praise you, O LORD, among the nations; I will sing of you among the peoples.
[4] For great is your love, higher than the heavens; your faithfulness reaches to the skies.
[5] Be exalted, O God, above the heavens, and let your glory be over all the earth.

Psalm 108:1-5 NIV

Praise the LORD. I will give thanks to the LORD with my whole heart, in the company of the upright, in the congregation.

Psalm 111:1 RSV

[1] Praise the LORD. Praise the LORD, O my soul.

² I will praise the LORD all my life; I will sing praise to my God as long as I live.

Psalm 146:1,2 NIV

Praise the LORD! For it is good to sing praises to our God; for it is pleasant, and praise is beautiful.

Psalm 147:1 NKJV

¹ Praise the Lord, O heavens! Praise him from the skies!

² Praise him, all his angels, all the armies of heaven.

³ Praise him, sun and moon and all you twinkling stars.

⁴ Praise him, skies above. Praise him, vapors high above the clouds.

⁵ Let everything he has made give praise to him. For he issued his command, and they came into being;

⁶ he established them forever and forever. His orders will never be revoked.

⁷ And praise him down here on earth, you creatures of the ocean depths.

Psalm 148:1-7 TLB

¹ Praise the LORD. Sing to the LORD a new song, his praise in the assembly of the saints.

² Let Israel rejoice in their Maker; let the people of Zion be glad in their King.

³ Let them praise his name with dancing and make music to him with tambourine and harp.

⁴ For the LORD takes delight in his people; he crowns the humble with salvation.

⁵ Let the saints rejoice in this honor and sing for joy on their beds.

⁶ May the praise of God be in their mouths and a double edged sword in their hands,

⁷ to inflict vengeance on the nations and punishment on the peoples,

⁸ to bind their kings with fetters, their nobles with shackles of iron,

⁹ to carry out the sentence written against them. This is the glory of all his saints. Praise the LORD.

Psalm 149:1-9 NIV

¹ Hallelujah! Yes, praise the Lord! Praise him in his Temple, and in the heavens he made with mighty power.

² Praise him for his mighty works. Praise his unequaled greatness.

³ Praise him with the trumpet and with lute and harp.

⁴ Praise him with the tambourines and processional. Praise him with stringed instruments and horns.

⁵ Praise him with the cymbals, yes, loud clanging cymbals.

⁶ Let everything alive give praises to the Lord! You praise him! Hallelujah!

Psalm 150:1-6 TLB

This people I have formed for Myself; they shall declare My praise.

Isaiah 43:21 NKJV

The ransomed of the LORD will return. They will enter Zion with singing; everlasting joy will crown their heads. Gladness and joy will overtake them, and sorrow and sighing will flee away.

Isaiah 51:11 NIV

Heal me, O Lord, and I shall be healed; save me, and I shall be saved; for You are my praise.

Jeremiah 17:14 AMP

Therefore, I will sing out in thanks to the Lord! Praise him! For he has delivered me, poor and needy, from my oppressors.

Jeremiah 20:13 TLB

[12] The next day the great crowd that had come for the Feast heard that Jesus was on his way to Jerusalem.

[13] They took palm branches and went out to meet him, shouting, "Hosanna!" "Blessed is he who comes in the name of the Lord!" "Blessed is the King of Israel!"

John 12:12,13 NIV

That with one accord you may with one voice glorify the God and Father of our Lord Jesus Christ.

Romans 15:6 NAS

Always give thanks for everything to our God and Father in the name of our Lord Jesus Christ.

Ephesians 5:20 TLB

Saying, "I will proclaim thy name to my brethren, in the midst of the congregation I will praise thee."

Hebrews 2:12 RSV

Through Jesus, therefore, let us continually offer to God a sacrifice of praise—the fruit of lips that confess his name.

Hebrews 13:15 NIV

But you are a chosen race, a royal priesthood, a dedicated nation, [God's] own purchased, special people, that you may set forth the wonderful deeds and display the virtues and perfections of Him Who called you out of darkness and into His marvelous light.

1 Peter 2:9 AMP

A Prayer of Praise

O magnify the Lord with me, and let us exalt His name together.

As for God, His way is perfect! The Word of the Lord is tested and tried; He is a shield to all those who take refuge and put their trust in Him.

Let the words of my mouth and the meditation of my heart be acceptable in Your sight, O Lord, my firm, impenetrable rock and my redeemer.

Your Word has revived me and given me life.

Forever, O Lord, Your Word is settled in heaven.

Your Word is a lamp to my feet and a light to my path.

The sum of Your Word is truth and every one of Your righteous decrees endures forever.

I will worship toward Your Holy Temple, and praise Your name for Your loving-kindness and for Your truth and faithfulness; for You have exalted above all else Your name and Your Word, and You have magnified Your Word above all Your name!

Let my prayer be set forth as incense before You, the lifting up of my hands as the evening sacrifice. Set a guard, O Lord, before my mouth; keep watch at the door of my lips.

He who brings an offering of praise and thanks-giving honors and glorifies Me; and he who orders his way aright—who prepares the way that I may show him—to him I will demonstrate the salvation of God.

My mouth shall be filled with Your praise and with Your honor all the day.

Because Your loving-kindness is better than life, my lips shall praise You. So will I bless You while I live; I will lift up my hands in Your name.

Your testimonies also are my delight and my counselors.

Scripture References (AMP)

Psalm 34:3   Psalm 138:2

Psalm 18:30   *Psalm 142:2,3*

Psalm 19:14   *Psalm 50:23*

Psalm 119:50   *Psalm 71:8*

Psalm 119:89   *Psalm 63:3,4*

Psalm 119:105   *Psalm 119:24*

Psalm 119:160

---

[1] p. 1156.

[2] Colin Brown, *Dictionary of New Testament Theology* (Grand Rapids: Zondervan Publishing House, 1975-1978).

[3] Edwin W. Rice, *People's Commentary on the Gospel According to John* (Philadelphia: The American Sunday-School Union, 1891), p. 80,81.

THE DEVIL AND DEMONIC POWERS

I do not spend much time in talking about the devil. The Lord took care of him. Jesus has the keys of hell and death, and He has mastered that individual and that condition once and for all. If you and I had as much faith to believe it as we have to believe the Lord Jesus is our Saviour we would have mighty little trouble with the devil or his power while we walk through this world.

—John G. Lake

Greek and Hebrew Word Studies

OLD TESTAMENT—*HA-SATAN*

And the Lord said unto *Satan (ha-satan)*, The Lord rebuke thee, O Satan; even the Lord that hath chosen Jerusalem rebuke thee...

Zechariah 3:2

NEW TESTAMENT—*DIABLOS*

Then was Jesus led up of the Spirit into the wilderness to be tempted of the *devil (diabolos)*.

Matthew 4:1

Any believer—any born-again person, anyone who knows the Lord Jesus Christ personally—can cast out devils. The instant someone comes into the Kingdom of God, he has Kingdom power and authority—if he knows it and believes it. This ability does not depend upon our own power, strength, faith or name. Jesus said we would cast out devils in His name. (Mark 16:17.)

Let's stand firm in our Christian security and use the power at our disposal to tear down the strongholds of Satan and to "set at liberty them that are bruised" (Luke 4:18).

— Lester Sumrall
The Word Bible[1]

Ha-Satan

The truth that both evil and good exist in this world is something no observant person can deny.

There is a struggle ignited by the friction of these two opposites, which are in continual collision. This struggle is present in every human being in the world.

Scriptures clearly portray the God of Creation as the One Who made everything good and perfect. In Genesis, chapter 1, God paused six times to thoroughly examine His work, and each time He saw that it was good. Then the seventh time, after He had created man, He looked over the whole Creation, including man, and saw that "it was very good" (Gen. 1:31). In Hebrew this is *tov me'od*—"greatly good," "very, very good" or "a hundred times good."

There was nothing wrong with the universe as God created it. However, Genesis 3 shows something *did* go dreadfully wrong. As a result, all tribes, peoples, and individuals for the past few thousand years have been left with a nagging inner emptiness and a desire to return to that Edenic garden of perfection our first parents enjoyed for such a brief moment! Evil came into the world and hastily ruined the perfect order God had made.

The background of evil's inception is not mentioned in Genesis, nor is it clearly explained anywhere in Scripture. There are some hints about the origin of Satan, most notably the denunciation in

Ezekiel 28. Though this is addressed to a human ruler, it contains things which cannot normally pertain to any human being. Consequently, the great majority of believers have understood this chapter to speak of Satan's origin, pride, fall, and destruction.

Although this is a good application of Ezekiel's prophecy, we still must admit that God has not yet given us a detailed account of how, when, and why evil originated. We must face the fact that God has chosen not to give us a full explanation. There are three very good reasons for Him to limit our knowledge at the present time.

First, Scripture was given to glorify our Holy God, to make His name great, and to testify of Jesus the Messiah (Jesus Himself stated this fact in John 5:39). Since the purpose of Scripture is to reveal God and glorify Him alone, it must likewise be true that the purpose of Scripture is not at all to reveal Satan's biography, nor to give him credit or honorable mention. The references to Satan thus must be limited to what is necessary, so that we can be aware and behave wisely.

The second reason God must limit our present understanding of Satan's origins is that much of it would be both hard to grasp and very upsetting. It would provoke many more questions and involve our precious time, which must be spent in the pursuit of holiness. When we reign with Christ, we will be given the full truth (and only then will we be able to fully comprehend). We will be granted the privilege of seeing back into the shrouded past, and we will praise God more and more for His marvelous wisdom, patience, love, and triumphs.

The third reason for our limited knowledge is that this subject is very painful to our God. The grief and distress in God's heart at seeing His beautiful masterpiece—creation generally, and man specifically—horribly disfigured by a hateful and destructive servant-gone-bad, is impossible for Him to portray to us in any language which humans speak or understand.

God's thoughts and ways are as high above ours as the heavens are high above the earth. (Isa. 55:9.) Similarly, His emotions, feelings, griefs, joys, and all such things important to His own heart and soul are infinitely deeper than our own emotions and feelings.

Genesis 6:5,6 records that when God saw the great wickedness expressed through the continually evil thoughts and deeds of fallen man (who was originally His trophy creation), He was deeply grieved in His heart. We may read this quickly and think we relate to it, but we can never see it or feel it as strongly as the Lord does, for it was His personal glory that was marred, and His handiwork dishonored.

There are, unfortunately, countless human beings who have never been (and are not now) grieved over the violence, murder, sorrows, and death which spoil God's creation daily. Should God communicate the private anguish of His heart to dry-eyed human beings who may only casually share His sense of grief? Should a bereaved adult expect a small child to understand the mourning period and allow that child to be burdened with the complexities of adult responses to tragedy? I think not!

This mystery of God's grief over the Fall is one He does not often communicate, though there are certainly indications of it beyond Genesis, chapters 3 and 6. However, God focuses our attention scripturally in another direction. He gives us little information about Satan's origin, but a good deal of information about his ultimate destruction and his final state!

We are therefore wise to involve ourselves not in a study of the enemy's beginnings, but rather in the Lord's plans for us to assist in bringing him to an end. (See Ps. 149:5-9; Zech. 13:2; Matt. 13:39-43; Luke 10:19; Rom. 16:20; 1 Cor. 6:2,3; Rev. 12:7-11.)

The honor of *binding* with chains the king of darkness and *executing* upon him the judgment written is an honor which all His saints shall have. We thus conclude that the casting of the devil into the lake of fire (Rev. 20:10) is an honor the Lord's people must share! May God be praised!

Satan is not mentioned by name in the Old Testament until the book of Job, where he appears eight times in the first two chapters. God speaks of Job, without fail, as one who pleases Him, honors Him, and is perfect and upright. Notice how Satan, without fail, cynically and cruelly judges Job's motives for serving God and accuses him relentlessly, suspiciously, and groundlessly.

It would be wonderful if Christians could *agree* with God about Job's blamelessness rather than support the devil's position by accusing Job, trying to search for his faults, and justify his catastrophe, which God declared to be "without cause" (Job 2:3).

Satan is also mentioned in Psalm 109:6, First Chronicles 21:1 and Zechariah 3:1,2. His appearance and function in each reference is one of a tempter, accuser, hinderer, slanderer, and opponent.

An explanation of the Hebrew meaning of the name *Satan* will be helpful, as it will point out the causes of his ugly behavior. There is a Hebrew root verb *satan* (pronounced "saw-tan'"), #7853 in *Strong's*, meaning to be an opponent or an adversary. This verb occurs six times. Psalm 38:20 is a good example.

From the verb comes the noun *satan* ("saw-tawn"), #7854 in *Strong's*, which means an opponent, enemy, adversary, hater, slanderer. This noun occurs 21 times, and is sometimes translated "an adversary," as in First Kings 11:14. Many times though, it appears with the definite article *the*, which would be *ha-satan*—"the opponent," that is, "the adversary" or "the satan." In these cases it is translated as *Satan*, who is not just "an" enemy—he is "the" enemy.

The linguistic roots of *satan* are informative. Not only does it represent accusation and opposition, but it even contains elements of a word meaning "to hate." Satan is by nature—and by name—cruel, merciless, hateful, jealous, strife-producing, cynical, accusatory, selfish, slanderous, murderous, hindering and, above all, exceedingly malicious to God and to the entire human race.

Satan's most vicious fury has been directed at the Jewish people over the ages and at Bible-believing Christians. Destroying Israel has been Satan's greatest obsession for the past 4,000 years. His reasons are primarily the following:

First, he hates Israel because the Bible, especially the Law of Moses and the prophets, was given by God to them specifically. Thus, what Paul calls their chief advantage (Rom. 3:1,2) is Satan's chief irritation. He wants no people to hear directly from God as did Israel, and he wants to kill and silence the descendants of those who heard God speak at Sinai.

Secondly, he is furious that Israel gave birth to the Messiah, that male Child Who shall rule all nations with a rod of iron (destroying Satan's kingdom, don't you see!) and Who has been caught up to God's throne. Unable to destroy Messiah, Satan turns his wrath on the people who produced him. Read carefully Revelation 12:1-6,13-17.

Thirdly, he reasons that by exterminating all Jews he can sabotage God's promises to Israel (specifically the return of their Savior). If he can prevent the return of Christ, then he can hold on to the world indefinitely. While we know from the mouth of the Lord Jesus that such a thing shall never be, it appears Satan thinks he has a chance of accomplishing it. This is the spiritual force behind anti-Semitism, and it is a most *satanic* phenomenon.

Considering that no people have been more slandered, hated, and accused than have the Jewish people over the centuries, and that Satan's name is slanderer, hater, and accuser, it is not difficult to discern Satan's foul breath in the slander heaped upon God's chosen people.

Fourthly, Satan hates whatever God loves. God loves Israel, so Satan hates Israel. It is just as simple as that.

Satan's reasons for hating—and fearing—Spirit-filled believers is actually quite similar to his reasons for being furious with Israel. Like Israel, we have the written Word of God. We honor the Messiah they produced. We are actively involved in hastening the return of the Lord Jesus Christ. And we are objects of God's infinite, everlasting love. Additionally we will rule with Christ, further demolishing Satan's realm of influence, even to the point of obliterating the memory of his "importance."

No wonder he is so afraid of us! God has *chosen* to give us authority, and this is deeply unsettling to the devil. Furthermore, we have the indwelling Holy Spirit of God, Whose power is shown in supernatural gifts, miracles, knowledge, and so forth. Satan has no way to control Holy Spirit-directed Christians, so he wants to mess us up badly *before* we get to a place of exercising spiritual power.

There are only a few direct references to Satan in the Old Testament, although he does leave some clear tracks in such deeds as are recorded in Second Chronicles 22:10. The same evil spirit who provoked this slaughter of children in an attempt to prevent the birth of the Messiah was still at work in New Testament times. Again, he provoked the slaughter of innocent children in an attempt to kill the Messiah as soon as He was born. (See Matt. 2:3-16; Rev. 12:4.)

In addition to providing indications of satanic activity such as this, the Old Testament also mentions devils, idols, and gods. We know these to be evil spirits, which are much more observable in New Testament references. We are able to see their action and patterns more clearly there, largely because they opposed the Lord Jesus continually—and He opposed them successfully! They were surely at work in earlier times, but the Hebrew text gives them only brief mention.

The Hebrew word *shed*, #7700 in *Strong's*, means "devils" and occurs twice: Deuteronomy 32:17 and Psalm 106:37. The word *sa'ir* ("saw-eer"), #8163 in *Strong's*, is usually translated "goat"; sometimes it is "satyr" or "hairy." In more than one reference though, it is translated "devil," as in Leviticus 17:7. This presumably refers to a satyr—a goat-like devil—venerated by many ancient cultures, including that of the Greeks.

There are a great number of Hebrew words which refer to "idols." In an extensive study of either idolatry or demonology, these words should be quite informative. Sometimes both the idol and the spirit behind the idol are discernable. For now, this study is concerned more with active evil spirits than with the icons behind which they hide and lurk.

Before the conclusion of this part of the study, we will include the following information from the rabbinic writing. It is stated that the light which existed before the world was hidden by God beneath His throne. When Satan questioned God about His light, God answered, "This light is kept for him who shall bring thee to shame." Satan requested to see the Messiah. When he saw Him, he trembled, fell upon his face, and cried, "Verily this is the Messiah who shall hurl me and all the princes of the angels of the peoples down even unto hell" (Pesik. R. iii. 6)[2]

Several things are greatly exciting about this information. It shows that ancient rabbis understood Messiah existed before the creation of the world, that

God intended to use Messiah to destroy Satan's kingdom, and that Satan *clearly grasped* this fact from the moment God first presented it to him! This in itself would explain Satan's *relentless* onslaught against those families who were ancestors of the Messiah, Who is the King of Zion and "Great David's greater Son."

In conclusion, we may be able to hate Satan intensely for all the death, torture, sorrow, and anguish he has caused the human race. We can, should, and must hate him. However, we are unable to hate the devil with the type of destructive anger God holds for this spoiler of His perfect creation. God alone can respond with the perfect vengeance of eternal judgment.

Jesus spoke of that fire He prepared specifically for "the devil and his angels" (Matt. 25:41). It is God Who will rectify the satanic damages inflicted upon the human race and upon all creation. (See Rom. 8:16-23.)

Nevertheless, God allows us to play a special part in bruising Satan, and in bringing that "deceiver of the nations" to the Judgment and into everlasting fire. Let us bruise Satan to the fullest degree possible. Hallelujah! Hallelujah! May God be praised!

Greek Words Translated
Devil or Devils

Five Greek words were translated "devil" or "devils." Four of them have to do with evil spirits or demons. Only one word *diabolos* is translated "devil," being the singular word for Satan. We will list first the four Greek words for "evil spirits" that the *Authorized Version* mistranslated as "devil" or "devils."

Daimon

He (Jesus) had commanded the unclean spirit to come out of the man...and he (the man...was driven of the *devil (daimon)* into the wilderness.

Luke 8:29

Daimon (pronounced "dah'-ee-mown"), #1142 in *Strong's,* appears five times in the New Testament. In non-Christian usage *daimon* refers to an inferior deity or being that is either good or bad. This is how Greek mythology handles the word. But the New Testament always shows *daimon* as an evil spirit with a malignant, hostile, or evil nature.

Daimon is the force behind sorcery and witchcraft. Pagan sacrifices are offerings to demons. (1 Cor. 10:20,21.) Demons are subordinate to Satan and act as his agents. They are active in cultic teaching and inflict harm on people, causing sickness and all misery. Scriptures point to a surge of demonic activity as we approach the end of the age. (1 Tim. 4:1.)

Jesus broke the power of demons through His name and by His word of command. (Mark 16:17, Matt. 8:16.) He also promised all believers that we can nullify the power of demons by declaring the wonder-working power of His shed blood. (Rev. 12:11.)

No Christian should be afraid of demons. The truth is that demons are afraid of Christians!

Daimonion

> **He called his twelve disciples together, and gave them power and authority over all *devils* (*daimonion*), and to cure diseases.**
>
> **Luke 9:1**

Daimonion (pronounced "dahee-mon'-ee-on"), #1140 in *Strong's,* appears 60 times in the Greek New Testament. Definitions of *daimonion* are an evil spirit, a shade, a demonic being, a messenger and minister of the devil, the gods of the Gentiles, the authors of idolatry, those who disseminate cultic error, those who try to seduce Christians from the truth, and the powers of the Evil One who are morally destructive.

Demons tremble before God. They recognize Jesus as Lord and as their future Judge. Christ cast them out by His Word, and His disciples did so in His name. All believers have the same authority. Scripture says we will be present at a gathering of beings in which all the fallen creatures of hell will bow their knee and verbally confess, JESUS IS LORD. (Phil 2:10,11.)

That is why we can cast out evil spirits by the Word, by His name, and by the blood of Jesus. He defeated them all by His death, burial, and triumphant resurrection. The believer should never be intimidated by the presence of evil spirits. Jesus gave all believers authority over them and their malignant works.

Daimonizomai

And at even, when the sun did set, they brought unto him all that were diseased, and them that were possessed *with devils (daimonizomai).*

Mark 1:32

The Greek word *daimonizomai* ("dahee-mon-id'-zom-ahee"), #1139 in *Strong's,* appears 13 times in the New Testament, all in the four Gospels. Eleven times it is translated "possessed with a devil." In

Matthew 15:22, it is rendered "vexed with a devil." In John 10:21 it is rendered "hath a devil."

Lexicons define *daimonizomai* as to be demonized, cruelly tormented by a demon, under the power of an evil spirit, to act under the control of an evil spirit and to be possessed by a demon.

Thayer's Lexicon was written in 1886 A.D. and has been a standard Greek lexicon for over 100 years. His words about *daimonizomai* are forceful:

> In the New Testament *daimonizomai* are persons afflicted with especially severe diseases, either bodily or mental—such as paralysis, blindness, deafness, loss of speech, epilepsy, melancholy (moods), insanity—whose bodies demons had entered. They held possession of them, not only afflicting them with ailments, but also to dethrone the reasoning mind and take its place themselves. The expulsion of the demon was the only cure.

Daimoniodes

This wisdom descendeth not from above, but is earthly, sensual, *devilish* (*daimoniodes*).

James 3:15

Daimoniodes ("dahee-mon-ee-o'-dace"), #1141 in *Strong's,* appears only once in the New Testament: James 3:15. It describes a wisdom that is diabolical, demonic, devil-inspired and aggressively ambitious to work against God's people and thwart God's purposes. It thrives in a climate of strife, envy, turmoil, greed, lust, anger, and deception.

One grammarian stated the word is descriptive of a wisdom that derives its origin from demons. Another says it is demon-like wisdom proceeding from an evil spirit. Much of the occultic practices and teachings originate from *daimoniodes.*

Jesus' wisdom is so pure, peaceful, beneficial, and elevating. What a contrast Jesus and His wisdom are compared to the depravity, degeneracy, and perversion much of modern media, apparently inspired by evil spirits, are spewing out on the world.

Diabolos

Then was Jesus led up of the Spirit into the wilderness to be tempted of the *devil (diabolos).*

Matthew 4:1

Diabolos ("dee-ab'-ol-os"), #1228 in *Strong's,* appears 38 times in the New Testament. The word is a compound *dia* ("through") and *ballo* ("to throw").

It describes our adversary as throwing fiery missiles at us trying to ignite lust, anger, jealousy, wrath, or violence. But we can put up the shield of faith and suppress or suffocate the fiery darts of the devil. (Eph. 6:16.)

There is only one devil but many demons. Revelation 12:9 links the word *devil* with *Satan*. *Diabolos* is defined by malignant words, such as accuser, hater, enemy, adversary, persecutor, murderer, slanderer, degrader, critic, liar, and the Father of Lies. In John 10:10 Jesus lists Satan's activities as stealing, killing, and destroying.

The power-promises giving all believers victory over the devil are found all through the Bible. Especially potent are Luke 10:19; Hebrews 2:14,15; 1 John 3:8; Romans 16:20; Revelation 12:10,11; and James 4:7. Add these promises to your spiritual arsenal. They will help you to pull down the strongholds of the devil. (2 Cor. 10:4.)

One grammarian stated about *diabolos:* "Satan is the malignant enemy of God and man. He accuses man to God (Job 1:6-11), and then he accuses God to man" (Gen. 3).

Besides working physical ailments in people, he also oppresses, depresses, and works to disturb man's peace with God. Since he is unclean, he puts unclean thoughts in men's minds. Since pride was his downfall, he puts proud thoughts in people's minds.

The United Bible Societies have given a wide range of words for Bible translators to use when putting the Bible into new languages where no Scriptures previously existed. Some of their suggested definitions for *diabolos* are "the no-good one," "the barking one," "the truly bad one," "the left-handed one," and "the chief ruler of the evil spirits."[4]

One Greek scholar consulted stated: "Jesus has defeated and disarmed the devil, and can thus rob him of his plunder."[5] Jesus not only heals the sick but is also able to deliver those who are possessed.

The ultimate reason for Satan's total defeat is the blood of Jesus. That is the victory Jesus gave us all through His death on the cross. The empty tomb tells us the god of this world has been dethroned. The battle is the Lord's, but the victory He shares with us!

Scriptures

Then Satan brought disaster upon Israel, for he made David decide to take a census.

1 Chronicles 21:1 TLB

You believe that there is one God. Good! Even the demons believe that—and shudder.

James 2:19 NIV

Little children, you are of God you belong to Him—and have [already] defeated and overcome them [the agents of antichrist], because He Who lives in you is greater (mightier) than he who is in the world.

1 John 4:4 AMP

[12] How you have fallen from heaven, O star of the morning, son of the dawn! You have been cut down to the earth, You who have weakened the nations!

[13] But you said in your heart, "I will ascend to heaven; I will raise my throne above the stars of God, And I will sit on the mount of assembly in the recesses of the north.

[14] "I will ascend above the heights of the clouds; I will make myself like the Most High."

[15] Nevertheless you will be thrust down to Sheol, to the recesses of the pit.

[16] Those who see you will gaze at you, they will ponder over you, saying, "Is this the man who made the earth tremble, who shook kingdoms,

[17] who made the world like a wilderness and overthrew its cities, who did not allow his prisoners to go home?"

Isaiah 14:12-17 NAS

[1] Then he showed me Joshua the high priest standing before the angel of the LORD, and Satan standing at his right side to accuse him.
[2] The LORD said to Satan, "The LORD rebuke you, Satan! The LORD, who has chosen Jerusalem, rebuke you! Is not this man a burning stick snatched from the fire?"

Zechariah 3:1,2 NIV

[1] Then Jesus was led up by the Spirit into the wilderness to be tempted by the devil.
[2] And when He had fasted forty days and forty nights, afterward He was hungry.
[3] Now when the tempter came to Him, he said, "If You are the Son of God, command that these stones become bread."
[4] But He answered and said, "It is written, 'Man shall not live by bread alone, but by every word that proceeds from the mouth of God.'"
[5] Then the devil took Him up into the holy city, set Him on the pinnacle of the temple,
[6] and said to Him, "If You are the Son of God, throw Yourself down. For it is written: 'He shall

give His angels charge over you,' and, 'In their hands they shall bear you up, lest you dash your foot against a stone.'"

7 Jesus said to him, "It is written again, 'You shall not tempt the Lord your God.'"

8 Again, the devil took Him up on an exceedingly high mountain, and showed Him all the kingdoms of the world and their glory.

9 And he said to Him, "All these things I will give You if You will fall down and worship me."

10 Then Jesus said to him, "Away with you, Satan! For it is written, 'You shall worship the Lord your God, and Him only you shall serve.'"

11 Then the devil left Him, and behold, angels came and ministered to Him.

Matthew 4:1-11 NKJV

And when evening had come, they brought to Him many who were demon-possessed; and He cast out the spirits with a word, and healed all who were ill.

Matthew 8:16 NAS

28 When he arrived at the other side in the region of the Gadarenes, two demon-possessed men coming from the tombs met him. They were so violent that no one could pass that way.

²⁹ "What do you want with us, Son of God?" they shouted. "Have you come here to torture us before the appointed time?"

³⁰ Some distance from them a large herd of pigs was feeding.

³¹ The demons begged Jesus, "If you drive us out, send us into the herd of pigs."

³² He said to them, "Go!" So they came out and went into the pigs, and the whole herd rushed down the steep bank into the lake and died in the water.

³³ Those tending the pigs ran off, went into the town and reported all this, including what had happened to the demon-possessed men.

Matthew 8:28-33 NIV

And Jesus summoned to Him His Twelve disciples and gave them power and authority over unclean spirits, to drive them out, and to cure all kinds of disease and all kinds of weakness and infirmity.

Matthew 10:1 AMP

²² Then a demon-possessed man—he was both blind and unable to talk—was brought to Jesus, and Jesus healed him so that he could both speak and see.

[23] The crowd was amazed. "Maybe Jesus is the Messiah!" they exclaimed.

[24] But when the Pharisees heard about the miracle they said, "He can cast out demons because he is Satan, king of devils."

[25] Jesus knew their thoughts and replied, "A divided kingdom ends in ruin. A city or home divided against itself cannot stand.

[26] "And if Satan is casting out Satan, he is fighting himself and destroying his own kingdom.

[27] "And if, as you claim, I am casting out demons by invoking the powers of Satan, then what power do your own people use when they cast them out? Let them answer your accusation!

[28] "But if I am casting out demons by the Spirit of God, then the Kingdom of God has arrived among you.

[29] "One cannot rob Satan's kingdom without first binding Satan. Only then can his demons be cast out!

[30] "Anyone who isn't helping me is harming me."

Matthew 12:22-30 TLB

[43] Now when the unclean spirit goes out of a man, it passes through waterless places, seeking rest, and does not find it.

⁴⁴ Then it says, "I will return to my house from which I came"; and when it comes, it finds it unoccupied, swept, and put in order.
⁴⁵ Then it goes, and takes along with it seven other spirits more wicked than itself, and they go in and live there; and the last state of that man becomes worse than the first. That is the way it will also be with this evil generation.

Matthew 12:43-45 NAS

The enemy who sowed them is the devil, the harvest is the end of the age, and the reapers are the angels.

Matthew 13:39 NKJV

Then he will say to those on his left, "Depart from me, you who are cursed, into the eternal fire prepared for the devil and his angels."

Matthew 25:41 NIV

And these are the ones by the wayside where the word is sown. When they hear, Satan comes immediately and takes away the word that was sown in their hearts.

Mark 4:15 NKJV

⁸ For He had been saying to him, "Come out of the man, you unclean spirit!"

⁹ And He was asking him, "What is your name?" And he said to Him, "My name is Legion; for we are many."

¹⁰ And he began to entreat Him earnestly not to send them out of the country.

¹¹ Now there was a big herd of swine feeding there on the mountain.

¹² And the demons entreated Him, saying, "Send us into the swine so that we may enter them."

¹³ And He gave them permission. And coming out, the unclean spirits entered the swine; and the herd rushed down the steep bank into the sea, about two thousand of them; and they were drowned in the sea.

¹⁴ And their herdsman ran away and reported it in the city and out in the country. And the people came to see what it was that had happened.

¹⁵ And they came to Jesus and observed the man who had been demon-possessed sitting down, clothed and in his right mind, the very man who had had the "legion"; and they became frightened.

¹⁶ And those who had seen it described to them how it had happened to the demon-possessed man, and all about the swine.

¹⁷ And they began to entreat Him to depart from their region.

[18] And as He was getting into the boat, the man who had been demon-possessed was entreating Him that he might accompany Him.

Mark 5:8-18 NAS

And he called his twelve disciples together and sent them out two by two, with power to cast out demons.

Mark 6:7 TLB

The hard path where some seed fell represents the hard hearts of those who hear the words of God, but then the devil comes and steals the words away and prevents people from believing and being saved.

Luke 8:12 TLB

But Peter said, "Ananias, why has Satan filled your heart to lie to the Holy Spirit and keep back part of the price of the land for yourself?"

Acts 5:3 NKJV

And, before long, God the giver of peace will crush Satan under your feet. The grace of our Lord Jesus Christ be with you!

Romans 16:20 Weymouth

To keep Satan from gaining the advantage over us; for we are not ignorant of his designs.

2 Corinthians 2:11 RSV

The god of this age has blinded the minds of unbelievers, so that they cannot see the light of the gospel of the glory of Christ, who is the image of God.

2 Corinthians 4:4 NIV

[13] For such men are false apostles, deceitful workmen, disguising themselves as apostles of Christ. [14] And no wonder, for even Satan disguises himself as an angel of light.
[15] So it is not strange if his servants also disguise themselves as servants of righteousness. Their end will correspond to their deeds.

2 Corinthians 11:13-15 RSV

[11] Put on all of God's armor so that you will be able to stand safe against all strategies and tricks of Satan.
[12] For we are not fighting against people made of flesh and blood, but against persons without bodies—the evil rulers of the unseen world, those mighty satanic beings and great evil princes of darkness who rule this world; and against huge numbers of wicked spirits in the spirit world.

¹³ So use every piece of God's armor to resist the enemy whenever he attacks, and when it is all over, you will still be standing up.

¹⁴ But to do this, you will need the strong belt of truth and the breastplate of God's approval.

¹⁵ Wear shoes that are able to speed you on as you preach the Good News of peace with God.

¹⁶ In every battle you will need faith as your shield to stop the fiery arrows aimed at you by Satan.

¹⁷ And you will need the helmet of salvation and the sword of the Spirit—which is the Word of God.

¹⁸ Pray all the time. Ask God for anything in line with the Holy Spirit's wishes. Plead with him, reminding him of your needs, and keep praying earnestly for all Christians everywhere.

Ephesians 6:11-16 TLB

¹³ For he has rescued us out of the darkness and gloom of Satan's kingdom and brought us into the Kingdom of his dear Son,

¹⁴ who bought our freedom with his blood and forgave us all our sins.

¹⁵ Christ is the exact likeness of the unseen God. He existed before God made anything at all, and, in fact,

[16] Christ himself is the Creator who made everything in heaven and earth, the things we can see and the things we can't; the spirit world with its kings and kingdoms, its rulers and authorities; all were made by Christ for his own use and glory.
[17] He was before all else began and it is his power that holds everything together.

Colossians 1:13-17 TLB

[8] Then this wicked one will appear, whom the Lord Jesus will burn up with the breath of his mouth and destroy by his presence when he returns.
[9] This man of sin will come as Satan's tool, full of satanic power, and will trick everyone with strange demonstrations, and will do great miracles.
[10] He will completely fool those who are on their way to hell because they have said "no" to the Truth; they have refused to believe it and love it, and let it save them,
[11] so God will allow them to believe lies with all their hearts,
[12] and all of them will be justly judged for believing falsehood, refusing the Truth, and enjoying their sins.

2 Thessalonians 2:8-12 TLB

²⁴ And the Lord's servant must not quarrel; instead, he must be kind to everyone, able to teach, not resentful.

²⁵ Those who oppose him he must gently instruct, in the hope that God will grant them repentance leading them to a knowledge of the truth, ²⁶ and that they will come to their senses and escape from the trap of the devil, who has taken them captive to do his will.

2 Timothy 2:24-26 NIV

¹⁴ Since, therefore, [these His] children share in flesh and blood—that is, in the physical nature of human beings—He [Himself] in a similar manner partook of the same [nature], that by [going through] death He might bring to nought and make of no effect him who had the power of death, that is, the devil.

¹⁵ And also that He might deliver and completely set free all those who through the (haunting) fear of death were held in bondage throughout the whole course of their lives.

Hebrews 2:14,15 AMP

Therefore submit to God. Resist the devil and he will flee from you.

James 4:7 NKJV

[8] Be self-controlled and alert. Your enemy the devil prowls around like a roaring lion looking for someone to devour.

[9] Resist him, standing firm in the faith, because you know that your brothers throughout the world are undergoing the same kind of sufferings.

1 Peter 5:8,9 NIV

[8] He who does what is sinful is of the devil, because the devil has been sinning from the beginning. The reason the Son of God appeared was to destroy the devil's work.

[9] No one who is born of God will continue to sin, because God's seed remains in him; he cannot go on sinning, because he has been born of God.

[10] This is how we know who the children of God are and who the children of the devil are: Anyone who does not do what is right is not a child of God; neither is anyone who does not love his brother.

1 John 3:8-10 NIV

[6] And the angels who did not keep their positions of authority but abandoned their own home—these he has kept in darkness, bound with everlasting chains for judgment on the great Day.

[7] In a similar way, Sodom and Gomorrah and the surrounding towns gave themselves up to sexual immorality and perversion. They serve as an example of those who suffer the punishment of eternal fire.

[8] In the very same way, these dreamers pollute their own bodies, reject authority and slander celestial beings.

[9] But even the archangel Michael, when he was disputing with the devil about the body of Moses, did not dare to bring a slanderous accusation against him, but said, "The Lord rebuke you!"

[10] Yet these men speak abusively against whatever they do not understand; and what things they do understand by instinct, like unreasoning animals—these are the very things that destroy them.

[11] Woe to them! They have taken the way of Cain; they have rushed for profit into Balaam's error; they have been destroyed in Korah's rebellion.

Jude 6-11 NIV

[9] And the great dragon was thrown down, the serpent of old who is called the devil and Satan, who deceives the whole world; he was thrown down to the earth, and his angels were thrown down with him.

[10] And I heard a loud voice in heaven, saying, "Now the salvation, and the power, and the kingdom of our God and the authority of His Christ have come, for the accuser of our brethren has been thrown down, who accuses them before our God day and night."

Revelation 12:9,10 NAS

[2] He laid hold of the dragon, that serpent of old, who is the devil and Satan, and bound him for a thousand years;

[3] and he cast him into the bottomless pit, and shut him up, and set a seal on him, so that he should deceive the nations no more till the thousand years were finished. But after these things he must be released for a little while.

Revelation 20:2,3 NKJV

[7] Now when the thousand years have expired, Satan will be released from his prison

[8] and will go out to deceive the nations which are in the four corners of the earth, Gog and Magog, to gather them together to battle, whose number is as the sand of the sea.

[9] They went up on the breadth of the earth and surrounded the camp of the saints and the beloved city. And fire came down from God out of heaven and devoured them.

[10] The devil, who deceived them, was cast into the lake of fire and brimstone where the beast and the false prophet are. And they will be tormented day and night forever and ever.

Revelation 20:7-10 NKJV

Prayer for Defeating the Devil and Demonic Forces

Father, thank You that greater are You Who are in me, than he that is in the world. You are so much, much more powerful than Satan or any demon in hell. Just as light dominates any bit of darkness, so the light of Your Word totally conquers the devil and any bondage of darkness he tries to put on people. For this purpose was the Son of God manifest—that He would destroy all the works of the devil and loose the captives from all Satan's works.

Father, I know how You anointed Jesus with the Holy Ghost and with power and how He went about doing good and healing all that were oppressed of the devil. Satan and all darkness are forced to flee in the presence of Your great light, so I determine to let Your light shine brightly in me, Lord, for all the world to see.

I thank You that You have not given me a spirit of fear but of love and of power and of sound mind, and that perfect love casts out all fear. I determine that I will not be intimidated or bullied by Satan or any demon of hell. In Jesus, I am not afraid of man nor beast and I am surely not afraid of any defeated (spiritually dead) demon. Father, I determine not to fight the devil with my own strength or power, but to enforce his defeat with the Word of God and the weapons and armor that You have given me—the sword of the Spirit, the helmet of salvation, the breastplate of righteousness, the belt of truth and my feet shod with the preparation of the gospel of Jesus.

The weapons of my warfare are not carnal, but mighty through God to the pulling down of all the devil's strongholds.

I thank You, Lord, that I do not need to go looking or searching for demons behind every door, but when the devil manifests himself in or through any person, I know I have authority over every evil spirit in Jesus' name.

As Jesus used the Word to fight Satan (Matt. 4:1-6) so will I use the Word to exercise my authority over him. In Jesus' name I pray, amen.

Scripture References

Hebrews 4:16 2

Ezekiel 22:30

Romans 8:26

Isaiah 58:6

Ephesians 6:16

Matthew 18:18

Mark 16:17

Ephesians 6:12

Colossians 2:15

Matthew 12:29

Hebrews 1:14

Romans 4:17

2 Corinthians 4:18

Corinthians 2:11

James 4:7

Ephesians 4:27

Revelation 12:11

Luke 10:19

Galatians 1:4

Colossians 1:13

Matthew 12:43-45

1 Corinthians 6:12

2 Timothy 2:26

1 John 3:8

Romans 14:17

1 p. 1176.

2 Isidore Singer, *The Jewish Encyclopedia* (New York: Funk and Wagnalls, 1901), p. 70.

3 *Redemption Hymnal With Tunes* (London: Elim Publishing House, 1970), p. 754.

4 Johannes P. Louw and Eugene A. Nida, *Greek-English Lexicon of the New Testament,* Vol. 2 (United Bible Societies), p. 145.

5 Colin Brown, *New Testament Theology* (Grand Rapids: Zondervan Publishing House, 1971), p. 470.

HEALING

W e see, from almost every conceivable angle throughout the Scriptures, that there is no doctrine more clearly taught than that it is God's will to heal all who have need of healing, and that they may fulfill the number of their days, according to His promise.

—F. F. Bosworth

Greek and Hebrew Word Studies

OLD TESTAMENT—*RAPHA*

Heal *(rapha)* me, O Lord, and I shall be *healed (rapha)*; save me, and I shall be saved....

Jeremiah 17:14

NEW TESTAMENT—*THERAPEUO*

There came also a multitude out of the cities round about unto Jerusalem, bringing sick folks, and them which were vexed with unclean spirits: and they were *healed (therapeuo)* every one.

Acts 5:16

The right to pray and receive the answer is given to every believer. (John 14:13,14.)

The ministry of healing was given to "the seventy," who represent the future workers of the Church. (Luke 10:1,9,19.) It was given to all "them that believe" the gospel, them that act on the gospel, and the doers of the Word.

It is committed to "the elders" of the Church. (James 5:14.) It is bestowed upon the whole Church as one of its ministries and gifts until Jesus comes. (1 Cor. 12:9,10.)

Jesus never commissioned anyone to preach the Gospel without including healing for the sick. He said, "Whatever city you enter, heal the sick that are there" (Luke 10:8,9). That command still applies to Gospel ministry today.

—T.L. Osborn
The Word Bible[1]

Healing—*Rapha*

Heal (rapha) me, O Lord, and I shall be *healed (rapha);* save me, and I shall be saved.

Jeremiah 17:14

The nature of God is such that His heart intensely yearns to heal and repair His creation. Mankind has become so terribly marred by sin, sorrow, evil, and the countless disorders which plague the physical, emotional, mental, behavioral, and spiritual components of man's being.

All creation in general—the human race in particular—is groaning and travailing under the complex burdens which result from sin and the Fall. Those burdens include sickness, birth defects, emotional illness, compelling behavioral dysfunctions, death, a host of inexpressible heartaches known to man, alienation, loneliness, famine, bereavement, loss, futility and everything else which is contrary to God's design and desire for creation.

It is for God's own sake that He steadfastly desires to repair these blotches on His beautiful handiwork. Since these griefs abound worldwide, healing, repair, and restoration can never be far from God's thoughts. Restoring creation to its proper function and beauty, and repairing man—the crowning glory of His works— is a desire which originates solely in God's heart.

Thus, He has pledged repeatedly, in both Testaments, that He will completely repair the earth and all creation. He will heal the world's uncountable sorrows and restore the human race to a position of nobility. He will banish sickness and destroy finally and forever His great enemy, Death. God is One Who repairs what He has made, not One Who is inclined to abandon the work of His own hands.

From this broad overview of the Lord's announced plan to remedy the ills of creation, we shall now focus upon His specific healing of human ills as seen in the biblical record.

The Hebrew word for "heal" is the verb *rapha* (pronounced "raw-faw'"), #7495 in *Strong's*, which means to repair, restore health, heal, mend, fix, cure.

Rapha occurs more than 60 times in the Old Testament. Its first occurrence is in Genesis 20:17. Abraham prayed to God on behalf of Abimelech, and God healed him and his household.

Rapha occurs in many famous verses, such as Psalm 103:3, referring to the Lord **"who forgiveth all thine iniquities; who *healeth (rapha)* all thy diseases."** And Psalm 107:20: **"He sent His word, and *healed (rapha)* them."** Its most majestic occurrence is in Isaiah 53:5, which tells us we are healed by the stripes of God's sacrificed Lamb, Jesus the Messiah.

In the book of Leviticus *rapha* is used to describe healing from a sickness or plague, such as leprosy. (Lev. 13:18,37; 14:3,48.)

Some unscholarly disputers of the validity of divine healing have gone out on a limb to maintain that "healing" does not refer to physical healing in the Bible. Aside from the basic nonsense of such a stance, we note that leprosy is a *physical* condition whose cure can only be *physically* verifiable.

Additionally, the participle form of *rapha* is *rophe* ("ro'-fay") which means doctor, physician. Jeremiah 8:22 and Second Chronicles 16:12 clearly portray the work of physicians or doctors as healers, or at least as specialists who are supposed to be able to bring healing. The Lord applies this word to Himself in Exodus 15:26 when He says, **"...I am the Lord that healeth thee."** In other words, "I am Jehovah, your *rophe*,"—that is, your Doctor, your Physician, and your Healer.

The majority of occurrences of the *rapha* word group in Scripture refers to physical healing. However, some of the other references where *rapha* is found will shed greater understanding on this powerful word.

For instance, in one well-known promise—Second Chronicles 7:14—God declares that the repentance and prayer of His people will result in their land being healed! Relatively few saints seem to have a clear grasp of how intensely God yearns to heal the earth. But it is His splendid jewel which reflects His glory. Isaiah 6:3 says, **"...the whole earth is full of his glory."** Thus, whenever the earth is scarred, destroyed, or blighted, it is an assault on His handiwork.

In Second Kings 2:22 Elisha "healed" the undrinkable, poisoned water in the spring at Jericho, and these waters remained permanently healed. Compare the healing of the waters in the Dead Sea. (Ezek. 47:9.)

Psalm 147:3 portrays another use of the word *rapha* by declaring that God heals the "broken in heart." Here is a real condition, one of the most serious a person can face. Yet it cannot be seen with the eye or measured on any medical instrument. It urgently requires healing, and only the Lord can satisfactorily heal this condition called "broken-heartedness."

A similar concept is found in Jeremiah 30:17 where the Lord promises healing for Israel's wounds. The most difficult wounds to heal are the kind no one can see.

A related concept is found in Jeremiah 3:22, where God pledges to "heal" His people of their backslidings.

Here we see an excellent example of a behavioral disorder which God sees as being in need of healing, cure, repair, and restored health. Three Scripture verses— Lamentations 2:13, Jeremiah 6:14 and 8:11—refer to the "hurt" in God's people that has not been healed.

Rapha is considered to be the opposite of "tearing" (Hos. 6:1), "wounding" (Deut. 32:39), and "smiting" (Isa. 19:22). There is a noun formed from *rapha* which is *marpe'* ("marpay'"), #4832 in *Strong's*, translated healing. Its most famous occurrence concerns the rising **"Sun of righteousness...with healing in his wings"** (Mal. 4:2). It also occurs in such verses as Proverbs 4:22, 12:18 and Jeremiah 33:6.

One of the most beautiful uses of *rapha* is in Psalm 41:4. David says, **"Lord, be merciful unto me: heal (rapha) my soul; for I have sinned against thee."** Let us note a few things which can be learned from this verse.

The human soul sometimes needs to be healed. Brokenness, disease or injury of the soul can be caused by sin, and an act of God's mercy brings healing to the soul.

An army of mental health personnel is overburdened as it tries to treat multitudes of mentally injured persons. Sometimes these professionals, who are dedicated to helping the emotionally ill and traumatized, have successful results. And sometimes they cannot bring healing, as if the wounds are so great their repair is beyond the reach of human hands.

The Great Physician is equally comfortable healing both emotional and physical disorders. An old hymn states, "There is a balm in Gilead, to make the wounded whole...to heal the sin-sick soul."

The final example of *rapha* cited in this vein is in First Kings 18:30. Elijah "repaired" the altar of the Lord, which was broken down. English translators might use the words *fix, repair, restore, mend.* Yet the Hebrew word is *heal.* Elijah found God's altar in a state of disrepair and brokenness, and his heart yearned to restore it to its original wholeness and magnificence.

Similarly, the "healing" which God desires to bestow is for man's whole being. It involves repair of the physical body, soul, behavior, life, and even extends outward to nature itself.

As our vision for healing expands from healing of the sick to healing of ills wherever found, we will be more in line with the glorious plan of our Lord and God. Jesus *always* healed the sick—all of them—who came to Him. So we should *always* expect great miracles of physical healing. We should believe for greater, more astounding healings than have ever been recorded. And God desires entire nations to be healed. So should we!

Let us increase our vision. Let us intercede to see God's desires burst forth on this deeply troubled planet. The Lord made a provision in the heavenly city which shall descend, a provision to cure any illness that could possibly develop in Messiah's domain. He stated, "...the leaves of the tree were for the healing of the nations" (Rev. 22:2).

Greek Words Translated *Heal/Healing* in the *King James Version*

Verbs

Diasozo ("dee-as-odze'-o"), #1295 in *Strong's*—making thoroughly sound or whole.

...and as many as touched (Him) were made perfectly *whole* (diasozo).

Matthew 14:36

Therapeuo ("ther-ap-yoo'-o"), #2323 in *Strong's*—to heal, cure, restore to health.

Jesus went about all Galilee, teaching... preaching...and *healing* (therapeuo) all manner

of sickness and all manner of disease among the people.

Matthew 4:23

Iaomai ("ee-ah'-om-ahee"), #2390 in *Strong's*—to cure, to heal, to make whole.

...by whose stripes ye were *healed* (*iaomai*).

I Peter 2:24

Sozo ("sode-zo"), #4982 in *Strong's*—to make sound or to make whole.

...he had faith to be *healed* (*sozo*).

Acts 14:9

Nouns

Therapeia ("ther-ap-i'-ah"), #2322 in *Strong's*—help a person receive healing; caring for a household.

...he spoke unto them of the kingdom of God, and healed them that had need of *healing* (*tberapeia*).

Luke 9:11

Iama ("ee'-am-ah"), #2386 in *Strong's*—healing or effecting a cure.

...to another the gifts of *healing* (*iama*) by the same Spirit.

1 Corinthians 12:9

Iasis ("ee′-as-is"), #2392 in *Strong's*—the act of healing.

I do *cures* (*iasis*) today and and tomorrow...

Luke 13:32

Health

Soteria ("so-tay-ree′-ah"), #4991 in *Strong's*—health, soundness, safety.

...for this is for your *health* (*soteria*)...

Acts 27:34

Note: Later versions and newer translations use the word *survival* for health.

Hugiaino ("hoog-ee-ah′-ee-no"), #5198 in *Strong's*—to be healthy or hygienically sound.

...that thou mayest prosper and be in health (*hugiano*), even as thy soul prospereth.

3 John 2

Heal—*Therapeuo*

A major word used 44 times for healing in the New Testament is *therapeuo* ("ther-ap-yoo′-o"), #2323 in *Strong's*. Our English words *therapy* and *therapeutic* originate from this word. Using lexical tools and sources going back to antiquity, let us see how a serving word ends associated with miracles.

The classical grammarians and language historians tell us *therapeuo* originally was a servant word. It is defined as caring for, attending to, nurturing, waiting upon, serving in any beneficial capacity, helping, assisting, ministering to, providing for. It is related to *therapon* ("ther-ap'-ohn"), #2324 in *Strong's*, a menial domestic who attends to the needs of a household in a cherishing way.

In a large estate the household staff included all domestic servants and those whose function consisted of household maintenance. Also included were those who manicured the lawns and took care of the animals used for riding or plowing.

Therapeuo progressed to mean giving family members relief in time of sickness. It was associated with curing, healing, mending, restoring, treating medically, and doing the work of a physician.

It is easy for a word with a 2,000-year history to change as the language, customs, idiom, and usage change. Jesus' entry into the world changed *therapeuo* from natural methods of healing to miracles of healing.

Of the 44 times *therapeuo* is used, two are in Revelation 13:2 and 12, describing the Tribulation beast that is healed *(therapeuo)*. In Acts 17:25 the word is used to describe men worshipping idols. The *New International Version* reads, "...**he is not served by human hands.**"

In Luke 4:23 the word *therapeuo* is used of the medical profession: "...**Physician, heal thyself....**" In Luke 8:43, the woman with the issue of blood could not be healed by usual medical methods, but she was healed by Jesus.

Thus 41 out of 44 words refer to miraculous cures bestowed by Jesus and His disciples upon needy people.

Look at the progressive unfolding of the word *therapeuo* from:

(1) serving your fellow man; to

(2) tending sick humanity; to

(3) medically treating the human race; to

(4) miraculously healing sick people.

This sends us three messages:

(1) The Servant of the Lord is fulfilling Old Testament prophecies by His healing miracles. In taking up the cause of the helpless, Jesus

authenticates His being God's suffering servant, as prophesied by Isaiah.

(2)   Giving His followers authority to heal *(thera-peuo)* all diseases demonstrates Jesus' power to break into our suffering world and give Christianity victory over the power of Satan. (Luke 10:9,19.)

(3)   Healings wrought in the name of the Lord in today's churches give evidence that the exalted Lord is actively present with His worshippers. He answers their prayers by demonstrating His power to heal all manner of sickness and all manner of disease.

Two ominous figures—sin and suffering—dogged the footsteps of Adam and Eve as they left the Garden. Jesus took both into focus when He died for our sins and our sicknesses. Psalm 103:3 says that He forgives all our sins and heals all our diseases.

On the Passover the lamb served two purposes for God's people. Its blood covered sin's judgment, and eating the Passover lamb gave the Israelites power and vitality to march out of Egypt. Psalm 105:37 says, **"...and there was not one feeble person among their tribes."** Over two million people left Egypt during the

Exodus! One lamb served two purposes: salvation and healing.

The communion service has two elements: the cup and the wafer. The cup symbolizes the blood of Jesus, which affected the forgiveness of sins. The wafer represents the broken body of Jesus, by Whose stripes we were healed. All who take communion are promised a double cure—forgiveness and healing—for a double curse—sin and sickness.

In the hymn "Rock of Ages," Augustus M. Toplady wrote this line: "Be of sin a double cure, save from wrath [salvation] and make me pure [whole]."[2]

Not only is *therapeuo* a valid word for healing in the New Testament, its potency and vitality is still available today for all believers in Jesus Christ. Don't let theological rationalism or unbelief take from you the blessing of being healed in answer to believing prayer.

Not one verse of Scripture says answers to prayer were meant only for first century believers. Thank God, He still sends His Word and heals today as He did in days of old. We serve a God Whose love, power, and willingness to bless have never changed.

Scriptures

So Abraham prayed to God; and God healed Abimelech, his wife, and his maid servants. Then they bore children.

Genesis 20:17 NKJV

And He said, "If you will give earnest heed to the voice of the Lord your God, and do what is right in His sight, and give ear to His commandments, and keep all His statutes, I will put none of the diseases on you which I have put on the Egyptians; for I, the Lord, am your healer."

Exodus 15:26 NAS

The LORD will keep you free from every disease. He will not inflict on you the horrible diseases you knew in Egypt, but he will inflict them on all who hate you.

Deuteronomy 7:15 NIV

So Naaman went down to the Jordan River and dipped himself seven times, as the prophet had told him to. And his flesh became as healthy as a little child's, and he was healed!

2 Kings 5:14 TLB

[3] The LORD will sustain him on his sickbed and restore him from his bed of illness.

⁴ I said, "O LORD, have mercy on me; heal me, for I have sinned against you."

Psalm 41:3,4 NIV

² Praise the LORD, O my soul, and forget not all his benefits—
³ He forgives all my sins and heals all my diseases,
⁴ He redeems my life from the pit and crowns me with love and compassion,
⁵ He satisfies my desires with good things so that my youth is renewed like the eagle's.

Psalm 103:2-5 NIV

He sent His word and healed them, and delivered them from their destructions.

Psalm 107:20 NIV

⁷ Do not be wise in your own eyes; fear the LORD and shun evil.
⁸ This will bring health to your body and nourishment to your bones.

Proverbs 3:7,8 NIV

²⁰ My son, pay attention to what I say; listen closely to my words.
²¹ Do not let them out of your sight, keep them within your heart;
²² for they are life to those who find them and health to a man's whole body.

Proverbs 4:20-22 NIV

A cheerful heart does good like medicine, but a broken spirit makes one sick.

Proverbs 17:22 TLB

⁴ Surely He has borne our griefs and carried our sorrows; yet we esteemed Him stricken, smitten by God, and afflicted.
⁵ But He was wounded for our transgressions, he was bruised for our iniquities; the chastisement for our peace was upon Him, and by His stripes we are healed.

Isaiah 53:4,5 NKJV

Then your light will break forth like the dawn, and your healing will quickly appear; then your righteousness will go before you, and the glory of the LORD will be your rear guard.

Isaiah 58:8 NIV

But to you who fear My name the Sun of Righteousness shall arise with healing in His wings; and you shall go out and grow fat like stall-fed calves.

Malachi 4:2 NKJV

²³ Jesus went throughout Galilee, teaching in their synagogues, preaching the good news of

the kingdom, and healing every disease and sickness among the people.

[24] News about him spread all over Syria, and people brought to him all who were ill with various diseases, those suffering severe pain, the demon-possessed, the epileptics and the paralytics, and he healed them.

Matthew 4:23,24 NIV

[16] And when evening had come, they brought to Him many who were demon-possessed; and He cast out the spirits with a word, and healed all who were ill

[17] in order that what was spoken through Isaiah the prophet might be fulfilled, saying, "He Himself took our infirmities, and carried away our diseases."

Matthew 8:16,17 NAS

[4] Jesus answered and said to them, "Go and tell John the things which you hear and see:

[5] "The blind see and the lame walk; the lepers are cleansed and the deaf hear; the dead are raised up and the poor have the gospel preached to them."

Matthew 11:4,5 NKJV

Aware of this, Jesus withdrew from that place. Many followed him, and he healed all their sick....

Matthew 12:15 NIV

⁴⁰ And a leper came to him beseeching him, and kneeling said to him, "If you will, you can make me clean."

⁴¹ Moved with pity, he stretched out his hand and touched him, and said to him, "I will; be clean."

⁴² And immediately the leprosy left him, and he was made clean.

Mark 1:40-42 RSV

¹¹ "I say to you, arise, take up your bed, and go your way to your house."

¹² Immediately he arose, took up the bed, and went out in the presence of them all, so that all were amazed and glorified God, saying, "We never saw anything like this!"

Mark 2:11,12 NKJV

¹ Another time he went into the synagogue, and a man with a shriveled hand was there.

² Some of them were looking for a reason to accuse Jesus, so they watched him closely to see if he would heal him on the Sabbath.

³ Jesus said to the man with the shriveled hand, "Stand up in front of everyone."

⁴ Then Jesus asked them, "Which is lawful on the Sabbath: to do good or to do evil, to save life or to kill?" But they remained silent.

⁵ He looked around at them in anger and, deeply distressed at their stubborn hearts, said to the man, "Stretch out your hand." He stretched it out, and his hand was completely restored.

Mark 3:1-5 NIV

¹⁴ Then He appointed twelve, that they might be with Him and that He might send them out to preach,

¹⁵ and to have power to heal sicknesses and to cast out demons.

Mark 3:14,15 NKJV

¹ They went across the lake to the region of the Gerasenes.

² When Jesus got out of the boat, a man with an evil spirit came from the tombs to meet him.

³ This man lived in the tombs, and no one could bind him any more, not even with a chain.

⁴ For he had often been chained hand and foot, but he tore the chains apart and broke the irons on his feet. No one was strong enough to subdue him.

⁵ Night and day among the tombs and in the hills he would cry out and cut himself with stones.

⁶When he saw Jesus from a distance, he ran and fell on his knees in front of him.

⁷He shouted at the top of his voice, "What do you want with me, Jesus, Son of the Most High God? Swear to God that you won't torture me!"

⁸For Jesus was saying to him, "Come out of this man, you evil spirit!"

⁹Then Jesus asked him, "What is your name?" "My name is Legion," he replied, "for we are many."

¹⁰And he begged Jesus again and again not to send them out of the area.

¹¹A large herd of pigs was feeding on the nearby hillside.

¹²The demons begged Jesus, "Send us among the pigs; allow us to go into them."

¹³He gave them permission, and the evil spirits came out and went into the pigs. The herd, about two thousand in number, rushed down the steep bank into the lake and were drowned.

¹⁴Those tending the pigs ran off and reported this in the town and countryside, and the people went out to see what had happened.

¹⁵When they came to Jesus, they saw the man who had been possessed by the legion of demons, sitting there, dressed and in his right mind; and they were afraid.

¹⁶ Those who had seen it told the people what had happened to the demon-possessed man—and told about the pigs as well.

¹⁷ Then the people began to plead with Jesus to leave their region.

¹⁸ As Jesus was getting into the boat, the man who had been demon-possessed begged to go with him.

¹⁹ Jesus did not let him, but said, "Go home to your family and tell them how much the Lord has done for you, and how he has had mercy on you."

²⁰ So the man went away and began to tell in the Decapolis how much Jesus had done for him. And all the people were amazed.

Mark 5:1-20 NIV

²¹ When Jesus had again crossed over by boat to the other side of the lake, a large crowd gathered around him while he was by the lake,

²² one of the synagogue rulers, named Jairus, came there. Seeing Jesus, he fell at his feet

²³ and pleaded earnestly with him, "My little daughter is dying. Please come and put your hands on her so that she will be healed and live."

²⁴ So Jesus went with him. A large crowd followed and pressed around him.

²⁵ And a woman was there who had been subject to bleeding for twelve years.

²⁶ She had suffered a great deal under the care of many doctors and had spent all she had, yet instead of getting better she grew worse.

²⁷ When she heard about Jesus, she came up behind him in the crowd and touched his cloak, ²⁸ because she thought, "If I just touch his clothes, I will be healed."

²⁹ Immediately her bleeding stopped and she felt in her body that she was freed from her suffering.

³⁰ At once Jesus realized that power had gone out from him. He turned around in the crowd and asked, "Who touched my clothes?"

³¹ "You see the people crowding against you," his disciples answered, "and yet you can ask, 'Who touched me?'"

³² But Jesus kept looking around to see who had done it.

³³ Then the woman, knowing what had happened to her, came and fell at his feet and, trembling with fear, told him the whole truth.

³⁴ He said to her, "Daughter, your faith has healed you. Go in peace and be freed from your suffering."

³⁵ While Jesus was still speaking, some men came from the house of Jairus, the synagogue ruler. "Your daughter is dead," they said. "Why bother the teacher any more?"

³⁶ Ignoring what they said, Jesus told the synagogue ruler, "Don't be afraid; just believe."

³⁷ He did not let anyone follow him except Peter, James and John the brother of James.

³⁸ When they came to the home of the synagogue ruler, Jesus saw a commotion, with people crying and wailing loudly.

³⁹ He went in and said to them, "Why all this commotion and wailing? The child is not dead but asleep."

⁴⁰ But they laughed at him. After he put them all out, he took the child's father and mother and the disciples who were with him, and went in where the child was.

⁴¹ He took her by the hand and said to her, "Talitha koum!" (which means, "Little girl, I say to you, get up!").

⁴² Immediately the girl stood up and walked around (she was twelve years old). At this they were completely astonished.

[43] He gave strict orders not to let anyone know about this, and told them to give her something to eat.

Mark 5:21-43 NIV

And they were casting out many demons and were anointing with oil many sick people and healing them.

Mark 6:13 NAS

[15] He said to them, "Go into all the world and preach the good news to all creation.
[16] "Whoever believes and is baptized will be saved, but whoever does not believe will be condemned.
[17] "And these signs will accompany those who believe: In my name they will drive out demons; they will speak in new tongues;
[18] they will pick up snakes with their hands; and when they drink deadly poison, it will not hurt them at all; they will place their hands on sick people, and they will get well."

Mark 16:15-18 NIV

The Spirit of the Lord is upon Me, because He has anointed Me to preach the gospel to the poor; he has sent Me to heal the brokenhearted, to proclaim liberty to the captives and recovery of sight to the blind, to set at liberty those who are oppressed.

Luke 4:18 NKJV

38 And He arose and left the synagogue, and entered Simon's home. Now Simon's mother-in-law was suffering from a high fever; and they made request of Him on her behalf.

39 And standing over her, He rebuked the fever, and it left her; and she immediately arose and waited on them.

40 And while the sun was setting, all who had any sick with various diseases brought them to Him; and laying His hands on every one of them, He was healing them.

Luke 4:38-40 NAS

Heal the sick; and as you heal them, say, "The Kingdom of God is very near you now."

Luke 10:9 TLB

11 He saw a seriously handicapped woman who had been bent double for eighteen years and was unable to straighten herself.

12 Calling her over to him Jesus said, "Woman, you are healed of your sickness!"

13 He touched her, and instantly she could stand straight. How she praised and thanked God!

¹⁴ But the local Jewish leader in charge of the synagogue was very angry about it because Jesus had healed her on the Sabbath day. "There are six days of the week to work," he shouted to the crowd. "Those are the days to come for healing, not on the Sabbath!"

¹⁵ But the Lord replied, "You hypocrite! You work on the Sabbath! Don't you untie your cattle from their stalls on the Sabbath and lead them out for water?

¹⁶ "And is it wrong for me, just because it is the Sabbath day, to free this Jewish woman from the bondage in which Satan has held her for eighteen years?"

¹⁷ This shamed his enemies. And all the people rejoiced at the wonderful things he did.

Luke 13:11-17 TLB

² There in front of him was a man suffering from dropsy.

³ Jesus asked the Pharisees and experts in the law, "Is it lawful to heal on the Sabbath or not?"

⁴ But they remained silent. So taking hold of the man, he healed him and sent him away.

Luke 14:2-4 NIV

¹⁴ He looked at them and said, "Go to the Jewish priest and show him that you are healed!" And as they were going, their leprosy disappeared.

¹⁵ One of them came back to Jesus, shouting, "Glory to God, I'm healed!"

Luke 17:14,15 TLB

¹ One day Peter and John were going up to the temple at the time of prayer—at three in the afternoon.

² Now a man crippled from birth was being carried to the temple gate called Beautiful, where he was put every day to beg from those going into the temple courts.

³ When he saw Peter and John about to enter, he asked them for money.

⁴ Peter looked straight at him, as did John. Then Peter said, "Look at us!"

⁵ So the man gave them his attention, expecting to get something from them.

⁶ Then Peter said, "Silver or gold I do not have, but what I have I give you. In the name of Jesus Christ of Nazareth, walk."

⁷ Taking him by the right hand, he helped him up, and instantly the man's feet and ankles became strong.

[8] He jumped to his feet and began to walk. Then he went with them into the temple courts, walking and jumping, and praising God.

[9] When all the people saw him walking and praising God,

[10] they recognized him as the same man who used to sit begging at the temple gate called Beautiful, and they were filled with wonder and amazement at what had happened to him.

Acts 3:1-10 NIV

[14] Is any one of you sick? He should call the elders of the church to pray over him and anoint him with oil in the name of the Lord.

[15] And the prayer offered in faith will make the sick person well; the Lord will raise him up. If he has sinned, he will be forgiven.

[16] Therefore confess your sins to each other and pray for each other so that you may be healed. The prayer of a righteous man is powerful and effective.

James 5:14-16 NIV

Who Himself bore our sins in His own body on the tree, that we, having died to sins, might live for righteousness—by whose stripes you were healed.

1 Peter 2:24 NKJV

The Healings of Christ

Jesus began His public ministry as a ministry of miracles. Everything about His life involved miracles: His conception birth, life, wisdom and teachings, ministry, death, resurrection, appearances, and ascension—all of these were astounding and undeniable miracles.

Many people have said that miracles were just for the days of the Old and New Testaments, but that is not true. Jesus Christ is as much a miracle-worker now as He ever was; and people need His miracle touch now more than ever.

We are called to walk as the Christians did in the New Testament. To serve the needs of people today, Jesus must be allowed to live in us, His power and His personal presence guiding us. This is true Christianity—walking in the power and presence and wisdom of Jesus. So many religious ceremonies are merely impersonal tradition, offering nothing but lifeless formality. Jesus' ministry brought life and deliverance everywhere He went. He wants us to live aware of His living, miracle-working power.

When people act on God's Word in bold faith, the faith which produces miracles, then multitudes will come from miles away, eager to see Christ's miracle-power in demonstration.

Jesus always attracted the multitudes by His miracles then, and He does so today, wherever miracles are done in His name. He is the same yesterday, today, and forever.

If we preach as the early Church preached, we will get the same results that they got: miracles and healings. It doesn't matter where we are or who we are. If we want to get Bible results, we have to preach what the Bible says: that miracles are a part of the present-day ministry of Jesus Christ.

The Healings of Christ

	Matthew	Mark	Luke	John
1. Nobleman's son healed				4:46-54
2. Healing the demoniac		1:23-28	4:33-37	
3. Healing Peter's mother-in-law	8:14,15	1:29-31	4:38,39	
4. Healing the leper	8:2-4	1:40-42	5:12,13	
5. Healing the paralytic	9:2-8	2:2-12	5:18-26	

	Matthew	Mark	Luke	John
6. Healing the man at the pool				5:2-9
7. Healing the withered hand	12:9-13	3:1-5	6:6-10	
8. Healing many near Galilee	12:15	3:7-12		
9. Healing the centurion's servant	8:5-13		7:2-10	
10. Raising the widow's son		7:12-16		
11. Healing the dumb demoniac man	12:22		11:14	
12. Healing the Gadarene demoniacs	8:28-34	5:1-20	8:26-39	
13. Healing the afflicted woman	9:20-22	5:25-34	8:43-48	
14. Raising Jairus' daughter	9:18,19, 23-26	5:22-24, 35-43	8:41,42, 49-56	

	Matthew	Mark	Luke	John
15. Healing the blind man and the dumb man	9:27-34			
16. Healing the Syrophoenician woman's daughter	15:22-28	7:25-30		
17. Healing the deaf and dumb man	7:32-37			
18. Healing the blind man at Bethsaida		8:22-26		
19. Healing the demoniac son	17:14-21	9:14-29	9:37-42	
20. Healing the ten lepers				17:11-19
21. Healing the blind man				9:1-41
22. Raising Lazarus				11:1-46
23. Healing the woman's infirmity			13:10-17	

	Matthew	Mark	Luke	John
24. Healing the man with dropsy			14:1-6	
25. Healing the two blind men	20:29-34	10:46-52	18:35-43	
26. Healing in the temple	21:14			
27. Healing the servant's ear			20:50,51	

Prayer for
Health and Healing

Father, in the name of Jesus, I confess Your Word concerning healing. As I do this, I believe and say that Your Word will not return to You void, but will accomplish what it says it will. Therefore, I believe in the name of Jesus that I am healed, according to First Peter 2:24. It is written in Your Word that Jesus Himself took our infirmities and bore our sicknesses. Therefore, with great boldness and confidence I say on the authority of that written Word that I am redeemed from the curse of sickness, and I refuse to tolerate its symptoms.

Satan, I speak to you in the name of Jesus and say that your principalities, powers, your spirits who rule the present darkness, and your spiritual wickedness in heavenly places are bound from operating against me in any way. I am the property of Almighty God, and I give you no place in me. I dwell in the secret place of the Most High God. I abide, remain stable and fixed under the shadow of the Almighty, Whose power no foe can withstand.

Now, Father, because I reverence and worship You, I have the assurance of Your Word that the angel of the Lord encamps around about me and delivers me from every evil work. No evil shall befall me; no plague or calamity shall come near my dwelling. I confess the Word of God abides in me and delivers to me perfect soundness of mind and wholeness in body and spirit from the deepest parts of my nature in my immortal spirit even to the joints and marrow of my bones. That Word is medication and life to my flesh, for the law of the Spirit of life operates in me and makes me free from the law of sin and death.

I have on the whole armor of God, and the shield of faith protects me from all the fiery darts of the wicked one. Jesus is the High Priest of my confession, and I hold fast to my confession of faith in Your Word. I stand immovable and fixed in full assurance that I have health and healing now in the name of Jesus.

Once this has been prayed, thank the Father that Satan is bound and continue to confess this healing and thank God for it.

Scripture References

Isaiah 55:11	Psalm 91:1
Galatians 3:13	Ephesians 6:11,16
James 4:7	Psalm 91:10
1 Peter 2:24	Romans 8:2
Ephesians 6:12	Psalm 34:7
Matthew 8:17	Proverbs 4:22
2 Corinthians 10:4	2 Timothy 1:7
Psalm 112:7	Hebrews 4:12,14

---

[1] p. 1187.

[2] Augustus M. Toplady and Thomas Hastings, *Rock of Ages, Cleft for Me* (Nashville: United Methodist Publishing House, 1964, 1966).

VICTORIOUS LIVING

God did not intend for us to barely get along in life. We are to reign as kings in this life. We are to take charge in adverse circumstances and drive the devil away from us. When evil surrounds us the very atmosphere around us can be charged with the power of the name of Jesus.

—John Osteen

Greek and Hebrew Word Studies

OLD TESTAMENT—*PARACH*

Those that be planted in the house of the Lord shall *flourish* (*parach*) in the courts of our God.

Psalm 92:13

NEW TESTAMENT—*HUPERNIKAO*

Nay, in all these things we are more than *conquerors* (hupernikao) through him that loved us.

Romans 8:37

Faith is not a feeling or an emotion. Many people mistake optimism or belief based on natural knowledge or experience for faith. "Natural" faith, or mental belief, leads to false expectations which will bring nothing from the Lord. This kind of faith results in selfish ambitions, wrong motives, and seeking God's promises to satisfy personal desires.

How do you develop faith for a life of victory? First, feed on the Scriptures, then apply them! Agree with people of faith and resist the devil, negative thinking, and condemnation. Be led by the Holy Spirit. (Rom. 8:14,15.)

Faith is an act! Verbal confession is only a place where faith begins. When the Holy Spirit drops faith into your heart to believe on Jesus as Savior, you must act on that in order to be saved. (Rom. 10:10,13.) Inactive faith is useless. Faith must be active to be alive. (James 2:17.)

—Marilyn Hickey
The Word Bible[1]

Victorious Living—*Parach*

The subject of victorious life for God's people reverberates throughout the Old Testament. Aspects of God's victorious designs can be seen in several of the major themes which the Old Testament strongly affirms.

One of the first truths God established after the Creation and Fall of man is that the human race will eventually crush the head of the serpent. (See Genesis 3:15; compare its New Testament reflection in Romans 16:20.)

The major theme of Israel's complete redemption, ultimate exaltation, and honor is interwoven throughout the Bible. To eliminate it from Scripture would rip the Book to shreds!

The Word of God contains other storehouses and treasuries of victory as well. These include the grand truths of God's promised redemption of the nations, the healing of nature and the animal kingdom, the extension of human life, and the ending of war between nations. Each of these subjects is important in God's revelation through the Old Testament. The responsibility for the accomplishing of these majestic victories is divinely laid on the shoulders of the Son of God. (Compare Isaiah 9:6,7 with Luke 1:31-33).

Another great picture of victory can be seen by simply studying the accounts of Israel's military exploits in the books of Joshua and Judges. The Exodus from Egypt presents a stunningly beautiful drama of freedom, triumph, and victorious life.

The Old Testament consistently and steadfastly holds to the view that righteousness will ultimately prevail. The righteous shall overcome, and the wicked will perish. Thus the Old Testament records, promotes, and maintains faith in the Sovereign God Who triumphs over His enemies and causes His people to triumph over theirs!

With all these victory themes to consider, where should one start? Rather than define such standard terms as "victory, power, valor and strength," let us start with the Hebrew word for "flourish."

The word *parach* (pronounced "paw-rakh'"), #6524 in *Strong's*, means to blossom; to bud; to break forth, spring up, grow, flourish, sprout. This word is a vibrant picture of life in action. It describes healthy growth and production.

Parach occurs more than 35 times in the Old Testament. We shall examine a few of those occurrences to understand how this word is used in Scripture.

In several references, *parach* is translated "to bud." One example, Isaiah 27:6, says: **"...Israel shall blossom and bud, and fill the face of the world with fruit."** Another example is Numbers 17:8: **"...and, behold, the rod of Aaron for the house of Levi was** *budded*, **and brought forth buds, and bloomed blossoms...."** The miracle of this verse concerns a dry branch which God rejuvenated, against all natural expectations, and caused to live again.

A similar horticultural picture is seen in Job 14:7-9, which pictures a tree cut down to its stump and evidently dead. There is some hope this tree may sprout again, because **"through the scent of water it will *bud* (*parach*), and bring forth boughs like a plant."**

In a larger number of references *parach* is translated "to blossom." Among these are verses one and two in Isaiah 35, speaking of the time when the desert shall "blossom as the rose" and "blossom abundantly." Two references portray redeemed Israel as a society which blossoms into unparalleled beauty and productiveness in the time of God's renewed favor. Hosea 14:5 declares, **"I will be as the dew unto Israel: he shall *grow* (*parach*, literally "blossom") as the lily, and cast forth his roots as Lebanon."**

The greatest and clearest application to victorious living occurs when *parach* is translated "flourish," as it is in several beloved verses.

Psalm 72:7 speaks of life under Messiah's reign: **"In his days shall the righteous *flourish (parach)*; and abundance of peace so long as the moon endureth."** This means the righteous will grow, spring up, blossom, bloom, and live enriched, peaceful, healthy, vibrant lives. It is as though the Kingdom of our Lord is the natural environment in which unhindered righteousness and lasting peace can thrive!

Notice how Isaiah 66:13,14 portrays the flourishing of health and happiness among God's people as a result of His comfort and favor:

> **As one whom his mother comforteth, so will I comfort you; and ye shall be comforted in Jerusalem.**

> **And when ye see this, your heart shall rejoice, and your bones shall *flourish (parach)* like an herb: and the hand of the Lord shall be known toward his servants, and his indignation toward his enemies.**

In the romantic setting of Song of Solomon 6:11, we read, **"I went down into the garden...to see whether** the vine *flourished (parach)*, and the pomegranates budded."

Finally we see Psalm 92:13,14—our main text:

Those that be planted in the house of the Lord shall *flourish (parach)* in the courts of our God.

They shall still bring forth fruit in old age; they shall be fat and *flourishing (parach)*.

What a picture of health, vitality, happiness, productivity, nourishment, beauty and satisfaction! Jesus stated He came to bring His people life in "all its fullness," as *The New English Bible* translates John 10:10. God desires that His children should live a life that is marked by *flourishing (parach)*.

There is more to life than having food and drink, and living in good health, having monetary prosperity, and being fashionably attired. There is more to life than one's productivity, labor, achievements, talent, and renown. There is more to life than one's ministry! There is more to life than "spiritual" matters.

Many people attempt to find life, worth, self-respect and purpose for living in these fine things. But life can never be measured by such matters. It can be found only in our fellowship with the Lord. Life exists in the Lord Jesus, and His life gives light to the human race. (See John 1:4.) The Lord Himself *has* our life, and the Lord Himself *is* our life. (Col. 3:3,4.)

This is to say, our lives have been deposited in His hands. He will cause our lives to blossom, flourish, and spring forth in all ways for His own increase and pleasure. This begins in the present age and will expand greatly following His glorious appearing.

When believers find the Lord's loving-kindness to be "better than life" (Ps. 63:3), they also find this life to be immeasurably bettered. God causes every facet of their lives to flourish, blossom and grow into full capacity.

We often spend so much energy pursuing a happy life rather than diligently seeking to know God as He truly is. He is so desirous for His people to know Him *deeply* and love Him *knowledgeably*. When His saints indeed make this their great pursuit, God causes the vital life fluid to course through every branch of the tree. *All* parts of one's life—talents, genius, wisdom, soul-contentment, physical needs, ministry, productivity, family—bloom in a flourishing manner.

Ponder carefully these wonderful verses:

Blessed is the man...(whose) delight is in the law of the Lord; and in his law doth he meditate day and night.

And he shall be like a tree planted by the rivers of water, that bringeth forth his fruit in his season; his leaf also shall not wither; and whatsoever he doeth shall prosper.

Psalm 1:1-3

Compare Jeremiah 17:7,8 which says:

Blessed is the man that trusteth in the Lord, and whose hope the Lord is.

For he shall be as a tree planted by the waters, and that spreadeth out her roots by the river, and shall not see when heat cometh, but her leaf shall be green; and shall not be careful in the year of drought, neither shall cease from yielding fruit.

Jeremiah 9:23,24 says:

Thus saith the Lord, Let not the wise man glory in his wisdom, neither let the mighty man glory in his might, let not the rich man glory in his riches:

> **But let him that glorieth glory in this, that he understandeth and knoweth me, that I am the Lord which exercise lovingkindness, judgment, and righteousness, in the earth: for in these things I delight, saith the Lord.**

These verses show that a happy, prosperous, blessed, fruitful, fulfilling, lengthy, flourishing life results from knowing, understanding, delighting in, and trusting the Lord. The victorious life is anchored to one's *relationship* with God. It is the one who is planted in God's house whose life flourishes.

The Old Testament is replete with thrilling examples of spectacular victories Israel was granted through faith in the mighty God. Every child raised in Sunday school has come to love the spine-tingling accounts of deliverance, triumph, conquest, rescue, and power recorded in the Bible.

Each and every time we read it, the eleventh chapter of Hebrews, listing exploits of the Old Testament heroes of faith, has an almost electric effect on us as New Testament believers.

The Scriptures in both old and new covenants are quite emphatic that God wishes us to triumph over our enemy and enjoy a victorious, peaceable, happy life. But sometimes we can think victory entails merely the dramatic deliverances, spectacular battles, and obvious successes which God is pleased to send us. But victory is much more than that.

When Jesus declared He would set His people free, they replied that they had never been in bondage to any man. Jesus' answer is extremely revealing: **"Whoever commits sin is in bondage to sin."** (John 8:31-34.) From this we can immediately draw some pointed conclusions.

Victory must involve deliverance from inner turmoil as well as external distresses. For example, if the Lord delivers you from your enemies, makes them ashamed for afflicting you (according to His promises), sets you conspicuously in His favor and blessings—yet every fiber of your being is still crying out vehemently for revenge—you do not have victory!

We must carefully guard our hearts in these issues of life. When God knows we can handle and accept victories in a Christ-like attitude, meekly and with a pure heart, He will bring us into a level of victory beyond that which we are able to comprehend at present. He has a flourishing, glorious life for us. The saints have spoken about it and longed for it. But it exceeds both our knowledge and our expectations. It is above what we can ask or even think!

The Old Testament records how God gave the Law to Israel so that His people should *live.* (See Leviticus 18:5; Deuteronomy 4:1; 5:33; 30:6,20.) In giving the Law, God's intentions were more than simply causing His people to ride on the high places of the earth, and exalting Israel as His trophy nation for the rest of the world to emulate, and making them to triumph over their enemies. These subjects are eternally important to the Lord Jehovah. But God's great desire was that His people, through their loving relationship with Him, would model the kind of life only He can give and which all the nations could observe with their own eyes! That is why this observation was made: **"*Happy* is that people whose God is the Lord"** (Psalm 144:15). (Compare 1 Kings 10:7-9; contrast Psalm 81:13-16.)

Victorious living involves our having the various parts of our lives balanced, healthy, and under God's supervision and approval! Those who are not walking with the Lord but are rich financially are among the poorest people on earth. Those who have experienced great victories from the Lord and have been mightily used of God but are living in continual turmoil in their own souls are not living the victorious life our Lord Jesus provided in the gospel of peace.

The wonderful life God has provided for us and eagerly yearns for us to experience is *in His Son*. There still remains a rest into which we should enter, and we *shall* obtain it.

The last picture in this study is the description God gives of ideal human life that will exist in the coming age of His direct reign. Notice the elements of human dignity, happiness, ownership of one's garden, industry, and rest. Most particularly, there will be the complete absence of all violence, fear, disquiet, mistreatment, harm and malice from any human being. "**...nation shall not lift up a sword against nation, neither shall they learn war any more. But they shall sit every man under his vine and under his fig tree; and none shall make them afraid: for the mouth of the Lord of hosts hath spoken it**" (Mic. 4:3,4).

**Greek Words Translated *Victory*
In the *King James Version***

Nike—**Noun**

An example of *nike* ("nee'-kay"), #3529 in *Strong's*:

...this is the *victory (nike)* that overcometh the world, even our faith.

1 John 5:4

Nike appears only this one time in the Greek New Testament. Consulting various Greek lexicons, *nike* is defined as victory in battle, having the advantage, conquering, prevailing, overcoming, the power (faith) that confers victory, the means (faith) for winning a victory, and conquering as a means of success.

Dictionaries consulted draw attention to its usage triumphantly connected with our personal faith in God. Faith is the principle, the cause, the ground, and the pledge of victory. One grammarian, J. Dawson (circa 1835 A.D.), traced *nike* to two Greek words: *ne-* ("not") and *eiko-* ("to yield").[2]

We can readily see that *nike* confidence or victorious faith refuses to yield to defeat, despair, discouragement, or doubt. The Christian is not only born for battle but destined to win the victory over the sensual (the flesh), the earthly (the world), and the demonic (the devil's) wisdom with which we contend in our present human existence. (James 3:15.) The message of *nike*—past, present, or future—is: "We win!"

Nikos—Noun

An example of *nikos* ("nee'-kos"), #3534 in *Strong's*:

But thanks be to God, which giveth us the *victory (nikos)* through our Lord Jesus Christ.

1 Corinthians 15:57

Nikos appears four times in the Greek New Testament. Matthew 12:20 quotes it from a prophecy of Isaiah describing the life of Christ. Paul uses *nikos* three times—First Corinthians 15:54,55,57—describing the believer's ultimate triumph over death and the grave.

Nikos is another form of *nike*. This is similar to changing *aeroplane* to *airplane* and ultimately to *plane*. One feature of *nikos* is its conclusion. Definitions include: a triumph, a conquest, success, supremacy, leaving a foe utterly vanquished, to defeat death, overcoming the last foe, and the final conquest over every form of evil.

The setting in First Corinthians 15 shows that *nikos* is a process which is continually going on, giving the believer ongoing victory over sin in the strength imparted by Jesus Christ and His Word.

In First Corinthians 15:54, **"...Death is swallowed up in victory"**—successfully, continually, permanently, and forever! *Nikos* takes on the character of overcoming. The battle has been decided in our favor, even though it is not over yet. This is one fight that is rigged! The praying and interceding believers are not proceeding to a victory. They are proceeding *from* a victory that was won at the Cross.

Nikao—Verb

An example of *nikao* ("nik-ah'-o"), #3528 in *Strong's*:

> ...them that had gotten the victory *(nikao)* over the beast, and over his image, and over his mark....

Revelation 15:2

Nikao appears 28 times in the Greek New Testament. It is a combative word defined as getting the upper hand, gaining the mastery over a foe, conquering, surpassing, overpowering an adversary, being superior in battle, to come off victorious, to subdue, to be invincible, to prevail in conflict, and to win the war. In the Greek Old Testament (LXX), the Septuagint, *nikao* is almost exclusively used for denoting victory over hostile powers.

Nikao was first used in reference to military battle, then transferred to any other type of conflict. It includes winning a race, winning a case at law and, in general, maintaining your cause.

Spoken of Jesus and His followers, *nikao* shows them victorious over the world, over evil, and over all the adversaries of the Kingdom of God.

In Revelation 15:2 *nikao* describes those who preserve themselves pure from idolatry and come through as conquerors after their contest with the Beast.

Hupernikao—More Than Conquerors

Hupernikao ("hoop-er-nik-ah'-o"), #5245 in *Strong's,* appears only once in the Greek New Testament. Paul, describing the surpassing victory of all believers in Christ, uses this word in Romans 8:37: **"...we are more than conquerors."**

Definitions of *hupernikao* include to conquer decisively, to conquer eminently, to achieve a brilliant victory, to triumph victoriously, to be super-victorious, to be overwhelmingly victorious, scoring a heavy victory, winning a most glorious victory, to be hyper-conquerors, to prevail mightily, to gain a surpassing victory and to prevail completely in a transcending total victory.

Martin Luther translated the word as, "we overcome far." H.A.W. Meyer in his commentary stated: *Hupernikao* in the secular sense is a victory that is "envy provoking."[3] There is in it an almost "holy arrogance of victory" that is not of self. It is conscious of the dynamic might that is in our victorious Savior.[4]

By looking at Romans 8:35 you will see seven adversaries blocking the progress of all believers: **"Who shall separate us from the love of Christ? shall tribulation, or distress, or persecution, or famine, or nakedness, or peril, or sword?"**

Paul does not advocate "barely getting by" or "just being able to keep your head above water." So great is the victory secured by the finished work of Christ that Paul finds the word *nikao* insufficient. Using *hupernikao*, he relates that Christ overpowered the Enemy. With His help we overcome *all* adversity. In the fight of faith we are over-victorious!

The Greeks were great at compounding words to give added intensity. One prefix used frequently in New Testament words is *huper*. *Strong's Concordance* lists 28 such words (between #5228 and #5257).

Two English words are based on *huper: super* and *hyper*. The following words and terms can be traced back to the word *huper:* Super Bowl, Superman, Super Tuesday, super-duper, supersonic, supermarket, hyperactive, hyperacidity, hyperbole, being hyper, media hype.

In both usages, *super* and *hyper*, the thought is "over and beyond." *Nikao* is the word for winning in the conflict between good and evil, truth and error, the power of light and the power of darkness. To compound the word and make it *hypernikao* is to expand the victory concept to an awesome greatness.

Followers of Jesus Christ participated in a three-dimensional triumph—past, present, and future.

In the past Jesus Christ triumphed over Satan's domain, defeating once and for all death, hell, sin, and the grave. (1 John 3:8.)

At present all believers have authority from God to overcome the sensual flesh, the humanistic world system, and the destructive power of the kingdom of Satan.

One feature of *hupernikao* is its future tense. In eternity all believers will be triumphant trophies of the Lord Jesus Christ. He admires us, He is magnified in us, and He exults over us. His overwhelming victory at Calvary becomes forever *hupernikao*—forever bringing Him glory and honor.

We triumph in our present life. We triumph at our time of departure. We truimph for all eternity. We are more than conquerors!

Scriptures

[4] Then Joseph said to his brothers, "Come close to me." When they had done so, he said, "I am your brother Joseph, the one you sold into Egypt! [5] And now, do not be distressed and do not be angry with yourselves for selling me here, because it was to save lives that God sent me ahead of you. [6] For two years now there has been famine in the land, and for the next five years there will not be plowing and reaping. [7] But God sent me ahead of you to preserve for you a remnant on earth and to save your lives by a great deliverance. [8] So then, it was not you who sent me here, but God. He made me father to Pharaoh, LORD of his entire household and ruler of all Egypt.

Genesis 45:4-8 NIV

The terror of the Lord shall fall upon all the people whose land you invade, and they will flee before you.

Exodus 23:27 TLB

The Lord God is your leader, and he will fight for you with his mighty miracles, just as you saw him do in Egypt.

Deuteronomy 1:3 TLB

Fear them not; it is the Eternal your God who fights for you.

Deuteronomy 3:22 Moffatt

[22] If you carefully observe all these commands I am giving you to follow—to love the LORD your God, to walk in all his ways and to hold fast to him—

[23] then the LORD will drive out all these nations before you, and you will dispossess nations larger and stronger than you.

[24] Every place where you set your foot will be yours: from the desert to Lebanon, and from the Euphrates River to the western sea.

[25] No man will be able to stand against you. The LORD your God, as he promised you, will put the terror and fear of you on the whole land, wherever you go.

[26] See, I am setting before you today a blessing and a curse—

[27] the blessing if you obey the commands of the LORD your God that I am giving you today;

[28] the curse if you disobey the commands of the LORD your God and turn from the way that I command you today by following other gods, which you have not known.

Deuteronomy 11:22-28 NIV

This book of the law shall not depart out of your mouth, but you shall meditate on it day and night, that you may be careful to do according to all that is written in it; for then you shall make your way prosperous, and then you shall have good success.

Joshua 1:8 RSV

[8] He raises the poor from the dust and lifts the needy from the ash heap; he seats them with princes and has them inherit a throne of honor. For the foundations of the earth are the LORD's; upon them he has set the world.
[9] He will guard the feet of his saints, but the wicked will be silenced in darkness. It is not by strength that one prevails;
[10] those who oppose the LORD will be shattered. He will thunder against them from heaven; the LORD will judge the ends of the earth. He will give strength to his king and exalt the horn of his anointed.

1 Samuel 2:8-10 NIV

[30] By your power I can crush an army; by your strength I leap over a wall.
[31] As for God, his way is perfect; the word of the Lord is true. He shields all who hide behind him.
[32] Our Lord alone is God; we have no other Savior.

³³ God is my strong fortress; he has made me safe.

³⁴ He causes the good to walk a steady tread like mountain goats upon the rocks.

³⁵ He gives me skill in war and strength to bend a bow of bronze.

³⁶ You have given me the shield of your salvation; your gentleness has made me great.

³⁷ You have made wide steps for my feet, to keep them from slipping.

³⁸ I have chased my enemies and destroyed them. I did not stop till all were gone.

³⁹ I have destroyed them so that none can rise again. They have fallen beneath my feet.

⁴⁰ For you have given me strength for the battle and have caused me to subdue all those who rose against me.

⁴¹ You have made my enemies turn and run away; I have destroyed them all.

⁴² They looked in vain for help; they cried to God, but he refused to answer.

⁴³ I beat them into dust; I crushed and scattered them like dust along the streets.

⁴⁴ You have preserved me from the rebels of my people you have preserved me as the head of the nations. Foreigners shall serve me

[45] and shall quickly submit to me when they hear of my power.

[46] They shall lose heart and come, trembling, from their hiding places.

[47] The Lord lives. Blessed be my Rock. Praise to him—the Rock of my salvation.

[48] Blessed be God who destroys those who oppose me

[49] and rescues me from my enemies. Yes, you hold me safe above their heads. You deliver me from violence.

[50] No wonder I give thanks to you, O Lord, among the nations, and sing praises to your name.

2 Samuel 22:30-50 TLB

[38] And you shall not forget the covenant that I have made with you. You shall not fear other gods,

[39] but you shall fear the LORD your God, and he will deliver you out of the hand of all your enemies.

2 Kings 17:38,39 RSV

[2] But they delight in doing everything God wants them to, and day and night are always meditating on his laws and thinking about ways to follow him more closely.

[3] They are like trees along a river bank bearing luscious fruit each season without fail. Their leaves shall never wither, and all they do shall prosper.

Psalm 1:2,3 TLB

⁵ Through you we push back our enemies; through your name we trample our foes.
⁶ I do not trust in my bow, my sword does not bring me victory;
⁷ but you give us victory over our enemies, you put our adversaries to shame.
⁸ In God we make our boast all day long, and we will praise your name forever. Selah.

Psalm 44:5-8 NIV

Oh, clap your hands, all you peoples! Shout to God with the voice of triumph!

Psalm 47:1 NKJV

¹² The righteous flourish like the palm tree, and grow like a cedar in Lebanon.
¹³ They are planted in the house of the LORD, they flourish in the courts of our God.
¹⁴ They still bring forth fruit in old age, they are ever full of sap and green,
¹⁵ to show that the LORD is upright; he is my rock, and there is no unrighteousness in him.

Psalm 92:12-15 RSV

The Eternal intervenes on my behalf: Eternal One, thy kindness never fails, thou wilt not drop the work thou hast begun.

Psalm 138:8 Moffatt

²⁷ He who diligently seeks good seeks [God's] favor, but he who searches after evil, it shall come upon him.

²⁸ He who leans on, trusts and is confident in his riches shall fall, but the [uncompromisingly] righteous shall flourish like a green bough.

Proverbs 11:27,28 AMP

²⁸ Do you not know? Have you not heard? The LORD is the everlasting God, the Creator of the ends of the earth. He will not grow tired or weary, and his understanding no one can fathom.

²⁹ He gives strength to the weary and increases the power of the weak.

³⁰ Even youths grow tired and weary, and young men stumble and fall;

³¹ but those who hope in the LORD will renew their strength. They will soar on wings like eagles; they will run and not grow weary, they will walk and not be faint.

Isaiah 40:28-31 NIV

¹⁰ Fear not, for I am with you; be not dismayed, for I am your God. I will strengthen you, yes, I will help you, I will uphold you with My righteous right hand.

[11] Behold, all those who were incensed against you shall be ashamed and disgraced; they shall be as nothing, and those who strive with you shall perish.

[12] You shall seek them and not find them—those who contended with you. Those who war against you shall be as nothing, as a nonexistent thing.

[13] For I, the LORD your God, will hold your right hand, saying to you, "Fear not, I will help you."

Isaiah 41:10-13 NKJV

I will bring the blind by a way they did not know; I will lead them in paths they have not known. I will make darkness light before them, and crooked places straight. These things I will do for them, and not forsake them.

Isaiah 42:16 NKJV

[2] Enlarge the place of your tent, stretch your tent curtains wide, do not hold back; lengthen your cords, strengthen your stakes.

[3] For you will spread out to the right and to the left; your descendants will dispossess nations and settle in their desolate cities.

[4] Do not be afraid; you will not suffer shame. Do not fear disgrace; you will not be humiliated. You

will forget the shame of your youth and remember no more the reproach of your widowhood.
⁵ For your Maker is your husband—the LORD Almighty is his name—the Holy One of Israel is your Redeemer; he is called the God of all the earth.

Isaiah 54:2-5 NIV

¹⁰ If you extend your soul to the hungry and satisfy the afflicted soul, then your light shall dawn in the darkness, and your darkness shall be as the noonday.
¹¹ The LORD will guide you continually, and satisfy your soul in drought, and strengthen your bones; you shall be like a watered garden, and like a spring of water, whose waters do not fail.

Isaiah 58:10,11 NKJV

Then you shall have delight in the Eternal's favour, for he will let you hold the land in triumph, enjoying your father Jacob's heritage: so the Eternal himself promises.

Isaiah 58:14 Moffatt

²⁵ I will make a covenant of peace with them and rid the land of wild beasts so that they may live in the desert and sleep in the forests in safety.

²⁶ I will bless them and the places surrounding my hill. I will send down showers in season; there will be showers of blessing.

²⁷ The trees of the field will yield their fruit and the ground will yield its crops; the people will be secure in their land. They will know that I am the LORD, when I break the bars of their yoke and rescue them from the hands of those who enslaved them.

²⁸ They will no longer be plundered by the nations, nor will wild animals devour them. They will live in safety, and no one will make them afraid.

²⁹ I will provide for them a land renowned for its crops, and they will no longer be victims of famine in the land or bear the scorn of the nations.

³⁰ Then they will know that I, the LORD their God, am with them and that they, the house of Israel, are my people, declares the Sovereign LORD.

³¹ You my sheep, the sheep of my pasture, are people, and I am your God, declares the Sovereign LORD.

Ezekiel 34:25-31 NIV

²⁴ Then the king issued a command to bring the men who had accused Daniel, and throw them into the den along with their children and

wives, and the lions leaped upon them and tore them apart before they even hit the bottom of the den.

25,26 Afterward King Darius wrote this message addressed to everyone in his empire: "Greetings! I decree that everyone shall tremble and fear before the God of Daniel in every part of my kingdom. For his God is the living, unchanging God whose kingdom shall never be destroyed and whose power shall never end.

27 "He delivers his people, preserving them from harm; he does great miracles in heaven and earth; it is he who delivered Daniel from the power of the lions."

28 So Daniel prospered in the reign of Darius, and in the reign of Cyrus the Persian.

Daniel 6:24-28 TLB

Those who do wickedly against the covenant he shall corrupt with flattery; but the people who know their God shall be strong, and carry out great exploits.

Daniel 11:32 NKJV

1 What shall we say, then? Shall we go on sinning so that grace may increase?

2 By no means! We died to sin; how can we live in it any longer?

³ Or don't you know that all of us who were baptized into Christ Jesus were baptized into his death?

⁴ We were therefore buried with him through baptism into death in order that, just as Christ was raised from the dead through the glory of the Father, we too may live a new life.

⁵ If we have been united with him in his death, we will certainly also be united with him in his resurrection.

⁶ For we know that our old self was crucified with him so that the body of sin might be rendered powerless, that we should no longer be slaves to sin—

⁷ because anyone who has died has been freed from sin.

⁸ Now if we died with Christ, we believe that we will also live with him.

⁹ For we know that since Christ was raised from the dead, he cannot die again; death no longer has mastery over him.

¹⁰ The death he died, he died to sin once for all; but the life he lives, he lives to God.

¹¹ In the same way, count yourselves dead to sin but alive to God in Christ Jesus.

¹² Therefore do not let sin reign in your mortal body so that you obey its evil desires.

[13] Do not offer the parts of your body to sin, as instruments of wickedness, but rather offer yourselves to God, as those who have been brought from death to life; and offer the parts of your body to him as instruments of righteousness. [14] For sin shall not be your master, because you are not under law, but under grace.

Romans 6:1-14 NIV

For the Spirit which God has given us is not a spirit of cowardice, but one of power and of love and of sound judgement.

2 Timothy 1:7 Weymouth

Now if [all these things be true, then be sure] the Lord knows how to rescue the godly out of temptations and trials, and how to keep the ungodly under chastisement until the day of judgement and doom.

2 Peter 2:9 AMP

As for you, dear children, you are God's children, and have successfully resisted them; for greater is He who is in you than he who is in the world.

1 John 4:4 Weymouth

For whatever is born of God overcomes the world. And this is the victory that has overcome the world—our faith.

1 John 5:4 NKJV

Prayer for
Being Equipped for Success

Father, I thank You that the entrance of Your words gives light. I thank You that Your Word which You speak *(and which I speak)* is alive and full of power—making it active, operative, energizing, and effective. I thank You, Father, that [You have given me a spirit] of power, and of love, and of a calm and well-balanced mind, and discipline, and self-control. I have Your power and ability and sufficiency, for You have qualified me (making me to be fit and worthy and sufficient) as a minister and dispenser of a new covenant [of salvation through Christ].

In the name of Jesus, I walk out of the realm of failure into the arena of success, giving thanks to You, Father, for You have qualified and made me fit to share the portion which is the inheritance of the saints (God's holy people) in the light.

Father, You have delivered and drawn me to Yourself out of the control and the dominion of darkness *(failure, doubt, and fear)* and have transferred me into the Kingdom of the Son of Your love, in Whom there is good success [and freedom from fears, agitating passions, and moral conflicts]. I rejoice in

Jesus Who has come that I might have life and have it more abundantly.

Today I am a new creation, for I am (engrafted) in Christ the Messiah. The old (previous moral and spiritual condition) has passed away. Behold, the fresh and new has come! I forget those things which are behind me and reach forth unto those things which are before me. I am crucified with Christ: nevertheless I live; yet not I, but Christ lives in me: and the life which I now live in the flesh I live by the faith of the Son of God, Who loved me, and gave Himself for me.

Today I attend to the Word of God. I consent and submit to Your sayings, Father. Your words shall not depart from my sight; I will keep them in the midst of my heart. For they are life (success) to me, healing and health to all my flesh. I keep my heart with all vigilance and above all that I guard, for out of it flow the springs of life.

Today I will not let mercy and kindness and truth forsake me. I bind them about my neck; I write them upon the tablet of my heart. So therefore I will find favor, good understanding, and high esteem in the sight [or judgment] of God and man.

Today my delight and desire are in the Law of the Lord, and on His Law I habitually meditate (ponder and study) by day and by night. Therefore I am like a tree firmly planted [and tended] by the streams of water, ready to bring forth my fruit in my season; my leaf also shall not fade or wither, and everything I do shall prosper [and come to maturity].

Now thanks be to God, Who always causes me to triumph in Christ!

Scripture References

Psalm 119:130	*John 10:10b* AMP
Hebrews 4:12a AMP	*Philippians 3:13b*
2 Timothy 1:7b AMP	*Galatians 2:20*
2 Corinthians 3:5b-6a AMP	*Proverbs 4:20-23* AMP
Colossians 1:12,13 AMP	*Proverbs 3:3,4* AMP
2 Corinthians 1:12,13 AMP	*Psalm 1:2,3* AMP
2 Corinthians 5:17 AMP	*2 Corinthians 2:14*

[1] p. 1196.

[2] John Dawson, *A Greek-English Lexicon to the New Testament* (London: Longman and Co., 1861).

[3] Heinrich A. W. Meyer, *Critical and Exegetical Hard-Book to the Epistle to the Romans* (Indiana: Alpha Publications, 1884), p. 343.

[4] Nigel Turner, *Christian Words* (Nashville: Thomas Nelson Publishers, 1981), p. 304.

CONFESSION

Christianity is called the Great Confession, but most Christians who are defeated in life are defeated because they believe and confess the wrong things. Faith-filled words will put you over. Fear-filled words will defeat you. Words are the most powerful thing in the universe.

—Charles Capps

Greek and Hebrew Word Studies

OLD TESTAMENT—'AMAR

I will *say ('amar)* of the Lord, He is my refuge and my fortress: my God; in him will I trust.

Psalm 91:2

NEW TESTAMENT—HOMOLOGEO

For with the heart man believeth unto righteousness; and with the mouth *confession (homologeo)* is made unto salvation.

Romans 10:10

Most people have used the words of their mouth to hold themselves in bondage. But as you begin to speak the Word of God from the heart, it will produce liberty. It will produce the health and healing the Word said it would.

If we will begin to *establish the things God said*, and *establish His Word on this earth*, then, thank God, we will rise to a new level of faith.

We will walk in the level of life where we release the ability of God *by the words of our mouth*. We can release the ability of God within ourselves by the words of our mouth and cause His Word and His power to become available to us.

Charles Capps
The Word Bible[1]

'Amar

The issues of words, speech, speaking and declaring are of great importance in the Old Testament, commencing with the Creator's speaking the universe into ordered existence. The naming of the animals by Adam was a continuation of the divine principle of assigning a character designation to something created.

First, we read, **"God called the light Day, and the darkness he called Night"** (Gen. 1:5). Later we read

"...whatsoever Adam called every living creature, that was the name thereof" (Gen. 2:19).

Notice that the covenants were first spoken words. (See Genesis 17:1-8; Exodus 20:1-22; Second Samuel 7:8-29.) Later they became written words. (Compare these former references, in sequence, with Psalm 105:5-11; Exodus 31:18; Psalm 89:20-37.)

The Law was spoken by God and written down by Moses. (Ex. 34:27.) The Word of the Lord to the prophets was introduced by phrases such as *Thus saith the Lord* and *Hear the word of the Lord*. Next, God commanded the prophets to write down His words. (See Jeremiah 36:1-10; Habakkuk 2:2,3.)

The subject of words and their importance is vast, perhaps inexhaustible. Let us look briefly at a few Hebrew words for "say," "speak," "declare," and "confess."

The main Hebrew word here is the verb *'amar* ("aw'mar'"), #559 in *Strong's*. In general, *'amar* means to say, but in various contexts it may suggest speaking, telling, commanding, or promising.

'Amar occurs about 5,000 times in the Old Testament. From this verb is formed the noun *'imrah* ("im-raw'"), #565 in *Strong's*, which means "word, utterance,

speech, saying." This word occurs in the prophetic phrase *the word of the Lord*.

The secondary Hebrew verb for "speak" is *dabar* ("daw-bar'"), and its derivative is the noun *dabar* ("daw-bawr'"), #1697 in *Strong's*, meaning "word, speech, matter." In Hebrew, the *Ten Commandments* is literally the "ten words," as though each commandment was a word or a matter the Lord desired to present.

In its verb and noun forms, *dabar* occurs more than 2,500 times in Old Testament writings. The noun *dabar* ("speech") is translated in the *King James Version* by more than 80 different English words, showing the great variety of application the word conveys. *Dabar* is thus quite similar to the Greek word *logos*, which also means word, matter, subject, issue, thing.

One Hebrew word which deserves special note is the verbs *yadah* ("yaw-daw'"), #3034 in *Strong's*, translated confess, give thanks, praise, thank. This verb comes from *yad* ("yawd"), #3027 in *Strong's*, a noun meaning hand. *Yadah* thus means to confess, speak, thank, or praise with one's hand extended. When it is translated "confess," it is often in context of confessing one's sins, as in Nehemiah 9:2, Proverbs 28:13 and Daniel 9:20. In other references, it refers to confessing the name of the Lord. (1 Kings 8:33,35; 2 Chron. 6:24-27.)

In the vast majority of references, though, it has to do with thanking and praising God. In Hebrew thought, all these—intense prayer, praise, confession and thanks—are accompanied by the extension or lifting of one's hands. It is clearly described in Lamentations 3:41: **"Let us lift our heart with our hands unto God in the heavens."**

This is reflected also in the famous New Testament command of First Timothy 2:8. Again, the inner attitude of the heart is yoked to the external act of lifting one's hands in prayer and worship. **"I will therefore that men pray every where, *lifting up holy hands*, without wrath and doubting."**

Returning to our main word '*amar*, we see it put to magnificent use in Psalm 91:2: **"I will *say* of the Lord, He is my refuge and my fortress: my God; in him will I trust."**

God is our fortress. This is an absolute certainty which will remain as true whether we speak it or believe it silently. But we are to *say* it—to declare it aloud—for it is worthy of our constant affirmation. "The Lord is my refuge and my fortress!" Such a confession electrifies the inner man and terrifies the Enemy.

Please compare Psalm 107:2 and 118:2-4. In the first reference, those the Lord has redeemed are told to speak up and say God has redeemed them. In the latter reference, three groups—Israel, the house of Aaron, then all who fear the Lord—are each, in turn, instructed to say, "His mercy endures forever!"

In conclusion, we see that the Old Testament introduces God's spoken Word as the vehicle of Creation. It goes on to present the teaching of God's laws to one's children as a verbal matter. (Deut. 6:6-9.) It portrays prayer, confession, praise, thanks, and affirmation as spiritual issues with verbal components.

As a final thought, notice how God's great works produce an instant response of affirmation in the mouths of His people, and even of unbelievers! Psalm 126:1-3 says:

When the Lord turned again the captivity of Zion, we were like them that dream.

Then was our mouth filled with laughter, and our tongue with singing: then said they among the heathen, The Lord hath done great things for them.

The Lord hath done great things for us, whereof we are glad.

Homologeo—The Verb "To Confess" and *Homologia*—The Noun "The Confession"

Here is a list of *homologeo* definitions from many scholastic sources. Scholars consulted range between 1700 A.D. and 1990 A.D. They represent many religious persuasions, but there is a conspicuous uniformity in all their definitions.

1. To say openly and not keep silence.

2. To make a statement. In a legal sense, to bear witness. To make a proclamation.

3. To say the same thing.

4. To use the same language.

5. To agree with, to acknowledge, to admit.

6. To assent, accord, avow, aver, affirm, to assure.

7. To speak out freely and plainly.

8. Public acknowledgement.

9. Speaking that of which you are convinced and that of which you know is true.

10. Speaking words that are the result of deep conviction of facts.

One theologian stated in his dictionary: *Homologeo* is putting belief and confession together. When "heart and mouth are in unison, there is a promise of justification and salvation for eternity (Rom. 10:8.)."[2]

Scriptures

Teach them to your children. Talk about them when you are sitting at home, when you are out walking, at bedtime, and before breakfast!

Deuteronomy 11:19 TLB

Do not let this Book of the Law depart from your mouth; meditate on it day and night, so that you may be careful to do everything written in it. Then you will be prosperous and successful.

Joshua 1:8 NIV

Sing to Him, sing praises to Him; speak of all His wonders.

1 Chronicles 16:9 NAS

How long will you go on like this, Job, blowing words around like wind?

Job 8:2 TLB

You will also decree a thing, and it will be established for you; and light will shine on your ways.

Job 22:28 NAS

¹ Lord, who may go and find refuge and shelter in your tabernacle up on your holy hill?
² Anyone who leads a blameless life and is truly sincere.
³ Anyone who refuses to slander others, does not listen to gossip, never harms his neighbor,
⁴ speaks out against sin, criticizes those committing it, commends the faithful followers of the Lord, keeps a promise even if it ruins him.

Psalm 15:1-4 TLB

³ Though you probe my heart and examine me at night, though you test me, you will find nothing; I have resolved that my mouth will not sin.
⁴ As for the deeds of men—by the word of your lips I have kept myself from the ways of the violent.

Psalm 17:3,4 NIV

May my spoken words and unspoken thoughts be pleasing even to you, O Lord my Rock and my Redeemer.

Psalm 19:14 TLB

I will praise the Lord no matter what happens. I will constantly speak of his glories and grace.

Psalm 34:1 TLB

¹² Who is the man who desires life, and loves length of days that he may see good?

[13] Keep your tongue from evil, and your lips from speaking deceit.

Psalm 34:12,13 NAS

The mouth of the [uncompromisingly] righteous utters wisdom, and his tongue speaks with justice.

Psalm 37:30 AMP

[1] My heart is stirred by a noble theme as I recite my verses for the king; my tongue is the pen of a skillful writer.
[2] You are the most excellent of men and your lips have been anointed with grace, since God has blessed you forever.

Psalm 45:1,2 NIV

[15] My mouth shall tell of Your righteousness and Your salvation all the day, for I do not know their limits.
[16] I will go in the strength of the Lord GOD; I will make mention of Your righteousness, of Yours only.
[17] O God, You have taught me from my youth; and to this day I declare Your wondrous works.

Psalm 71:15-17 NKJV

My tongue shall speak of Your word, for all Your commandments are righteousness.

Psalm 119:172 NKJV

Put away from you a deceitful mouth, and put devious lips far from you.

Proverbs 4:24 NAS

You are snared by the words of your own mouth; you are taken by the words of your mouth.

Proverbs 6:2 NKJV

To fear the LORD is to hate evil; I hate pride and arrogance, evil behavior and perverse speech.

Proverbs 8:13 NIV

Blessings crown the head of the righteous, but violence overwhelms the mouth of the wicked.

Proverbs 10:6 NIV

[11] The mouth of the righteous is a fountain of life, but violence overwhelms the mouth of the wicked.
[12] Hatred stirs up dissension, but love covers over all wrongs.
[13] Wisdom is found on the lips of the discerning, but a rod is for the back of him who lacks judgment.
[14] Wise men store up knowledge, but the mouth of a fool invites ruin.

Proverbs 10:11-14 NIV

[18] He who conceals hatred has lying lips, and he who spreads slander is a fool.

[19] When there are many words, transgression is unavoidable, but he who restrains his lips is wise. [20] The tongue of the righteous is as choice silver, the heart of the wicked is worth little. [21] The lips of the righteous feed many, but fools die for lack of understanding.

Proverbs 10:18-21 NAS

[31] The mouth of the righteous brings forth wisdom, but a perverse tongue will be cut out. [32] The lips of the righteous know what is fitting, but the mouth of the wicked only what is perverse.

Proverbs 10:31,32 NIV

[13] The wicked is ensnared by the transgression of his lips, but the righteous will come through trouble. [14] A man will be satisfied with good by the fruit of his mouth, and the recompense of a man's hands will be rendered to him. [15] The way of a fool is right in his own eyes, but he who heeds counsel is wise. [16] A fool's wrath is known at once, but a prudent man covers shame. [17] He who speaks truth declares righteousness, but a false witness, deceit. [18] There is one who speaks like the piercings of a sword, but the tongue of the wise promotes health.

¹⁹ The truthful lip shall be established forever, but a lying tongue is but for a moment.

Proverbs 12:13-19 NKJV

² From the fruit of a man's mouth he enjoys good, but the desire of the treacherous is violence.
³ The one who guards his mouth preserves his life; the one who opens wide his lips comes to ruin.

Proverbs 13:2,3 NAS

In the mouth of the foolish is a rod for his back, but the lips of the wise will preserve them.

Proverbs 14:3 NAS

¹ A gentle answer turns away wrath, but a harsh word stirs up anger.
² The tongue of the wise commends knowledge, but the mouth of the fool gushes folly.
³ The eyes of the LORD are everywhere, keeping watch on the wicked and the good.
⁴ The tongue that brings healing is a tree of life, but a deceitful tongue crushes the spirit.

Proverbs 15:1-4 NIV

²³ The heart of the wise teaches his mouth, and adds persuasiveness to his lips.
²⁴ Pleasant words are a honeycomb, sweet to the soul and healing to the bones.

Proverbs 16:23,24 NAS

[20] From the fruit of his mouth a man's stomach is filled; with the harvest from his lips he is satisfied.
[21] The tongue has the power of life and death, and those who love it will eat its fruit.

Proverbs 18:20,21 NIV

[17] Do you not understand that everything that goes into the mouth passes into the stomach, and is eliminated?
[18] But the things that proceed out of the mouth come from the heart, and those defile the man.

Matthew 15:17,18 NAS

Truly, I tell you, whoever says to this mountain, Be lifted up and thrown into the sea! and does not doubt at all in his heart, but believes that what he says will take place, it will be done for him.

Mark 11:23 AMP

Let us hold firmly to an unflinching avowal of our hope, for He is faithful who gave us the promises.

Hebrews 10:23 Weymouth

Prayer To Watch What You Say

Father, today I make a commitment to You in the name of Jesus. I turn from idle words and foolishly talking things that are contrary to my true desire to myself and toward others. Your Word says that the tongue defiles; that the tongue sets on fire the course of nature; that the tongue is set on fire of hell.

In the name of Jesus, I am determined to take control of my tongue. I am determined that hell will not set my tongue on fire. I renounce, reject, and repent of every word that has ever proceeded out of my mouth against You, God, and Your operation. I cancel its power and dedicate my mouth to speak excellent and right things. My mouth shall utter truth.

I am the righteousness of God. I set the course of my life for obedience, for abundance, for wisdom, for health, and for joy. Everything I speak is becoming to God. I refuse to compromise or err from pure and sound words. My words and my deeds shall show forth Your righteousness and Your salvation all of my days. I guard my mouth and my heart with all diligence. I refuse to give Satan any place in me.

Father, Your Words are top priority to me. They are spirit and life. I let the Word dwell in me richly in all wisdom. The ability of God is released within me by the words of my mouth and by the Word of God. I speak Your words out of my mouth. They are alive in me. You are alive and working in me. So, I can boldly say that my words are words of faith, words of power, words of love, and words of life. They produce good things in my life and in the lives of others. Because I choose Your words for my lips, I choose Your will for my life, and I go forth in the power of those words to perform them in Jesus' name.

Scripture References

Ephesians 5:4	*Proverbs 21:23*
2 Timothy 2:16	*Ephesians 4:27*
James 3:6	*James 1:6*
Proverbs 8:6,7	*John 6:63*
2 Corinthians 5:21	*Colossians 3:16*
Proverbs 4:23	*Philemon 6*

[1] pp. 1204, 1205.

[2] Colin Brown, *New Testament Theology,* Vol. 1: A-F (Paternoster Press, 1975), p. 347.

PROSPERITY

True prosperity is the ability to meet the need of mankind in any realm of life. When you are walking in the Word of God, you will prosper and be in health. It is His will for us to be made whole—spirit, soul and body—and to be kept that way until the return of our Lord Christ.

Kenneth Copeland

Greek and Hebrew Word Studies

OLD TESTAMENT—*TSALEACH*

And he shall be like a tree planted by the rivers of water, that bringeth forth his fruit in his season; his leaf also shall not wither; and whatsoever he doeth shall *prosper (tsaleach)*.

Psalm 1:3

NEW TESTAMENT—*EUODOO*

Beloved, I wish above all things that thou mayest *prosper (euodoo)* and be in health, even as thy soul *prospereth (euodoo)*.

3 John 2

Establishing God's covenant on the earth and giving to those in need—these are God's purposes for prosperity.

I've actually heard people say: "I don't need much prosperity. I'm a simple person with a simple life. So I just ask for enough to meet my needs."

They think that's humility, but it's not. It's selfishness! Without realizing it, what these people are actually saying is: "All I care about is meeting my own needs. I have no ambition to meet anyone else's."

How dare we be so sloppy spiritually earning just enough to get by on. How dare we ignore God's promises of prosperity when people all around us are spiritually starving.

It's wrong for you not to want to prosper when that prosperity can mean the difference

between heaven and hell for millions of
people!

—Kenneth Copeland
The Word Bible[1]

Prosper—*Tsaleach*

And he shall be like a tree planted by the
rivers of water, that bringeth forth his fruit in
his season; his leaf also shall not wither; and
whatsoever he doeth shall *prosper (tsaleach)*.

Psalm 1:3

The English word *prosper* means to succeed, to flourish, to thrive, and especially to have economic success.

In Hebrew, the word most often translated "prosperity" or "success" is *tsaleach* (pronounced "tsaw-lay'-
akh"), #6743 in *Strong's*. The *King James Version*
translates this word in 15 different ways, among
which are the following: come mightily, be profitable,
break out, be good, prosper, make prosperous. The
main idea of this verb is to accomplish, finish,
complete and succeed. Thus, the primary meaning of
tsaleach has to do with pushing forward; that is,
achieving some goal. There are several tenses of
tsaleach, and they can be used to convey a variety of
concepts.

In its standard usage, *tsaleach* is translated "prosper," as in Ezekiel 16:13b, which speaks of Jerusalem: "...thou wast exceeding beautiful, and thou didst *prosper* into a kingdom."

It also is translated "came upon" or "came mightily upon" in several references, including Judges 14:6,19 and 15:14. These references describe the way the Spirit of the Lord came mightily upon Samson; that is to say, God's Spirit achieved the goal, accomplished His plans, and had success in and through Samson.

The future tense is used in Joshua 1:8. Through meditating in and following God's Word, Joshua would "make his way prosperous," that is, succeed in his God-given task of conquering the land of Canaan.

The causative form of *tsaleach* is found in such verses as Genesis 24:21,56; Second Chronicles 26:5; 31:21; and Isaiah 55:11. These verses speak of God causing one's way or journey to prosper, causing the man who sought Him to prosper, and causing His own Word to prosper (succeed, reach its goal, complete its purpose).

This causative form is also found in Daniel 8:24,25, speaking of the dreadful king of fierce countenance who shall destroy the holy people, stand against the Prince of Princes, and through his policy cause craft (deceit, treachery, falsehood, in the original Hebrew) to prosper in his hand. It could be paraphrased, "He will cause falsehood and deceit to be *successful* as a matter of policy."

A further shade of meaning is found in the participle form of the causative case. This roughly translates into "one who is caused to be a prosperer," or an achiever, a success, a person of accomplishment. Genesis 39:2 says, **"The Lord was with Joseph, and he was a prosperous man"** (that is, one caused to prosper). The same basic form of *tsaleach* occurs in verses 3 and 23 of Genesis 39, and in Psalm 37:7.

The final example of *tsaleach* will be Isaiah 53:10. Of God's redeeming Servant it is stated, **"...the pleasure of the Lord shall prosper in his hand."** In other words, under the rulership of King Jesus, everything God desires shall be accomplished.

In addition to *tsaleach*, there are other Hebrew words relevant to prosperity. Briefly, we will examine three words: *osher*, *chayil* and *hown*.

Osher

Osher (pronounced "o'-sher"), #6239 in *Strong's*, is always translated "riches" in the *King James Version*. It comes from a verb which means "to accumulate." *Osher* occurs nearly 40 times in the Old Testament.

The Scripture records that Solomon surpassed all the kings of the earth in riches and wisdom. (1 Kings 10:23.)

Two godly kings, Jehoshaphat and Hezekiah, possessed abundant riches. (2 Chron. 18:1; 32:27.)

David stated that riches *(osher)* and honor come from God. (1 Chron. 29:12; note its occurrence again in v. 28.)

Psalm 112:3, speaking of the man who fears the Lord, states wealth and riches *(osher)* are in his house. *Osher* is also used positively in Proverbs 8:18 and 14:24. It occurs in a somewhat neutral sense in Proverbs 30:8 and Jeremiah 9:23. It occurs in a negative sense in such verses as Psalm 52:7 and Ecclesiastes 5:13.

Chayil

The next word *chayil* (pronounced "khah'-yil"), #2428 in *Strong's,* is frequently translated "wealth." Sometimes translated "substance," "power," or "strength," it also is translated "army." Other English words used by the *King James* translators for *chayil* are "strong," "valiant," and "host."

The root from which this word is derived is *chuwl* (pronounced "khool"), #2342 in *Strong's*, meaning "to prosper, be firm, be strong, be mighty, be enduring."

Chayil occurs almost 250 times in the Old Testament and, like *osher*, can be used either with a positive or a negative thrust. For a positive example, see Proverbs 13:22: "...the *wealth* of the sinner is laid up for the just." Its use in Psalm 62:10 is cautionary; and in Ezekiel 28:5, it is jolting.

Hown

The word *hown*, #1952 in *Strong's*, occurs about 25 times in the Old Testament and is translated "wealth, riches, substance." Like the preceding two words, it is used in a positive sense and in negative and warning references.

All but eight of its occurrences are in the book of Proverbs. A delightful study of its scope would be to observe its usages in that book. See Proverbs 1:13; 3:9; 6:31; 8:18; 10:15; 11:4; 12:27; 13:7,11; 18:11; 19:4,14; 24:4; 28:8,22; 29:3; and 30:15,16 (in which the *King James Version* translates it as "enough").

At this point it should be noted that Psalm 35:27 states how the Lord takes pleasure in the "prosperity" of His servant. The Hebrew word in this case is *shalom*, #7965 in *Strong's*, meaning peace, wholeness, completeness, perfection, well-being, welfare, happiness. The three words—*wholeness*, *well-being* and *peace*—come closest to what is being presented to us in this verse.

God really takes pleasure in, and is gladdened by, finding His servants with peace and well-being in their hearts. There are numerous verses which stress God's desire to bless His people with financial and material blessings. But Psalm 35:27 shows God's desire to prosper you with inner *contentment* in your soul, which no amount of money can buy. This kind of contentment is called in Scripture *great gain* (1 Tim. 6:6).

Far from being a well-kept secret is how the subject of prosperity has provoked controversy in the Body of Christ. However, a balanced examination of everything the Scripture says on this subject—or any subject—will produce the peace and harmony God desires. It should be noted here that God has amply stated, through numerous Scripture verses, that His desire is to meet all His people's needs—spiritually, emotionally, physically, nutritionally, financially, materially, and in every way.

The Law of Moses demonstrates it was God's own wish to bless His beloved nation above all nations upon the earth. Although the people initially may have lacked the skills necessary to succeed financially, God declared He would give them the power to get wealth. (Deut. 8:18.) That is to say, He Himself would teach them how to prosper materially.

This was not some scheme that resulted from a human request for prosperity; rather, it was entirely God's idea! The notion that prosperity is evil and poverty is good cannot be found in Scripture.

Those believers who have feared being wealthy have generally reacted to the Scripture verses which warn about the ways financial wealth can corrupt the heart of man in a most despicable way. And they have not been willing to respond to the full counsel of God on this subject.

Some Christians have reasoned that as long as they remain poor, they will never succumb to these hideous side effects of wealth described in the Bible. However, this makes no more sense than amputating a perfectly healthy foot on the grounds that by doing so one will never experience the horrors of gangrene in that foot! Anyone who knows God will certainly realize it is not His will to amputate a limb to prevent a deadly illness that has not even occurred. Neither is it His will that we remain in poverty to avoid the diseases of the rich.

Rather than cut ourselves off, let us avoid the pitfalls which may attend great wealth. A person who chooses to remain poor (out of fear) has not conquered the relevant sin tendencies; he has only circumnavigated them. He has not submitted his heart to God's testing processes.

Abraham was greatly and abundantly rich. Listen to what God said of His friend: "I know him (the Hebrew reads, *I have known him*), that he will command his children and his household after him, and they shall keep the way of the Lord, to do justice and judgment; that the Lord may bring upon Abraham that which he hath spoken of him" (Gen. 18:19).

God had so thoroughly known the inner corridors of Abraham's heart that he was confident of his faithfulness in any circumstance, and of his ability to instruct his descendants in that same kind of faithful adherence to all of God's ways.

Even faced with choices available to the very rich, Abraham never staggered, never swerved from serving God. Faced with the opposite circumstance—famine—Abraham was equally steadfast. He had realistic concerns in that time of testing, and he had to make certain decisions based on worldly facts.

But Abraham's walk with God was not the slightest bit affected by either wealth or famine in the land. So many believers can serve God in hard times but not good times, while others can serve Him in the land of plenty but forsake Him during times of hardship.

When the Scripture tells us that riches are uncertain—that is, subject to change—and that we must not put our trust in them but rather in the Living God, beautiful truths are being laid down for our benefit.

Notice how Abraham did not waver because of any of life's vicissitudes. (Compare Philippians 4:11-13.). Wealth, national famine, family strife, a long delay in God's promise, the request to sacrifice Isaac—none of these things moved Abraham. His eyes were fixed on his Friend and God.

Abraham had more wealth than most men dream of, but it was not his wealth that motivated him. The thing that drove him ever onward was his vision of the day of Messiah's glory (John 8:56), the coming down of the City which God built (Heb. 11:8-10), and the promises of those things he and his children would inherit as an everlasting possession. (Ps. 105:8-12; Rom. 4:13.)

As new covenant believers, let us not emphasize only those verses which warn of sinful attitudes that often plague rich people, the evils of covetousness, and the terrible anguish of those who desire to be wealthy. (And there are enough verses pointing out these truths that no honest Christian can deny God's concern that we have understanding in these matters.)

Neither let us emphasize only those verses which state God's desire to materially bless His people. (And there are enough verses which stress this truth that no honest Christian can deny God's desire that we believe Him in this matter.)

Let us stress that *those who seek God* shall not lack any good thing! (Ps. 34:10.) God-seekers do *not* live a life of deprivation.

It is with good reason that the Scripture warns us how perverted and corrupt minds, destitute of the truth, will suppose godliness is a means of making money. From these persons we are commanded to withdraw ourselves. (1 Tim. 6:5-10.)

A true teacher of biblically sound prosperity will always be in agreement with the teaching of our Lord Jesus: that we are to seek God's Kingdom and God's righteousness—a pursuit with which our hearts are to be consumed. And then prosperity will be one of the *many* blessings which shall follow. (Matt. 6:24-33.)

Prosper—*Euodoo*

As the only Greek word translated "prosper" in the *King James Version*, *euodoo* ("yoo-odd-ah'-oh"), #2137 in *Strong's*, has an interesting history. It falls in the category of the words *adios, adieu, au revoir, bon voyage, farewell* and *goodbye*.

Eu equals good or well as in eugenics, eulogy or euphoria. *Hodos* equals a roadway, a trip or travel, as in odometer or odograph, a device used for measuring distance.

Euodoo originally meant to be on the right road, to grant an expeditious or unhindered journey, to successfully reach the destination safe and sound, to be led along a good road, receiving help on the way, or being on a road that is easy to travel.

Euodoo appears only four times in three verses: Romans 1:10, First Corinthians 16:2, and twice in Third John 2.

In Romans 1:10 Paul states, **"Making request, if by any means now at length I might have a prosperous *journey* (euodoo) by the will of God to come unto you."**

The desire Paul expresses in this verse consists of two kinds of prosperity blessings: (1) that the Lord will allow him after many hindrances to finally make the trip, and (2) that the trip will be a successful one.

Euodoo joins other words used with parting utterances when friends, acquaintances, and loved ones say goodbye. Here is a list of some familiar parting words and their meanings:

Goodbye—"God be with you."

Adieu—"I commend you to God for His safekeeping and blessing."

Godspeed—"May God give you a prosperous journey."

Bon Voyage—"Be blessed with good travel conditions."

Farewell—"May all things go well with you and may you be favored on your journey." (Twice in *King James:* Acts 15:29 and 23:30.)

According to *Christopher Wordsworth's Greek New Testament,*[2] *euodoo* is used today by Greek-speaking people in the same way these other "goodbye" words are used to wish God's blessing on a traveller.

The modern Greek word at parting is *kalon kateuodion.* In English this would be: "May your journey be pleasant, delightful and profitable. May your trip bring you prosperity and good success." It is easy to see that a good, safe, and successful trip is the main thought in the word *euodoo*.

Words change with usage, and in time *euodoo* evolved into a word for material or financial prosperity. It had in it an element of profitable and successful work ethic.

In First Corinthians 16:2 Paul says to that church concerning an offering they were preparing for him: **"Upon the first day of the week let every one of you lay by him in store, as God hath *prospered* (euodoo) him, that there be no gatherings when I come."** He is encouraging them to give as the Lord has given to them. This is an equitable stewardship. Those who have little to give are not overloaded, and those with much can and should give proportionately.

One Anglican rector said his church turned the corner when they broke the "two-shilling syndrome," which had been the norm for decades in that church. He not only related how everyone, regardless of their station in life, would automatically give two shillings every week, but he said some givers squeezed the shilling so tightly the queen yelled, *Ouch!*

First Corinthians 16:2 is the biblical way of giving: Give as you have prospered. Paul succinctly adds a promise to this kind of giving in Second Corinthians 9:11: **"The more you are enriched the more scope will there be for generous giving..."** (Phillips).

Third John 2 relates *euodoo* to spiritual prosperity: **"My prayer for you, my very dear friend, is that you may be as healthy and prosperous in every way as you are in soul"** (Phillips).

The full blessings of redemption include: *Soul prosperity*—forgiveness of sin, peace of mind, and a joyful, intimate relationship with our Lord and Savior.

Physical prosperity—health, stamina, divine life that quickens the mortal body, and robust physical vitality.

Financial prosperity—roof over the head, food on the table, shoes on the feet, bills met, adequate transportation, cash flow to meet the needs; but, most of all, a generous nature that gives freely to gospel and humanitarian causes.

You may have heard someone say this: "We don't have a lot of money, but, thank God, we've all been healthy." Or someone else say this: "We've had a lot of sickness in the family, but we praise the Lord that all our bills are paid and we've got money in the bank."

Third John 2 is not an either/or verse. It is not the best one out of three, or two out of three—it's three out of three! Being blessed spiritually, physically and financially is normal New Testament life. *Euodoo* is having the Lord bless every area of your life: spirit, soul and body.

Some people look at believers who are contending for the full *euodoo* blessings promised in God's Word and accuse them of being a "health and wealth" cult. This term is contradictory to the reality of New Testament living. For Bible believers the "health and wealth" cult is an inapplicable title.

A cult is any religious group that denies the following: the pre-existence of Christ, His Virgin Birth, His sinless life, His atoning death for man's sins and sufferings, His victorious resurrection and post-resurrection appearances for 40 days, His ascension to the Father's throne, His sending of the Holy Spirit on the day of Pentecost to the awaiting first-century Church, His intercession today for all believers, and His soon return to rule the world in righteousness. These are the orthodox beliefs of all born-again Christians. All cults deny one or more of these beliefs.

The "health and wealth cult" is a misnomer for Bible believers. Health is promised in both the Old and the New Testaments. (Is. 58:8; Jer. 30:17; Acts 27:34; 3 John 2.) Wealth is promised on the condition of humble obedience to the Lord's commands and a love for His Word. (Ps. 112:1-3; Deut. 8:18.)

To deny Bible believers the full blessings of redemption is to take away from them promised benefits related to serving the Lord. Have you ever met a dedicated Christian who wanted to prosper to heap it on his lusts? No. Real Christians will want to prosper so they can further the gospel proclamation. One minister accurately proclaimed: "I don't just give in order to get. I give in order to get so that I may give."

We don't hassle with those who accuse Bible believers of being a "health and wealth" cult. The other alternative would be to accept sickness and poverty as God's gifts. This would contradict Proverbs 10:22: **"The blessing of the Lord, it maketh rich, and he addeth no sorrow with it."**

Scriptures

You shall serve the Lord your God; He shall bless your bread and water, and I will take sickness from your midst.

Exodus 23:25 AMP

³ If you follow my decrees and are careful to obey my commands,

⁴ I will send you rain in its season, and the ground will yield its crops and the trees of the field their fruit.

⁵ Your threshing will continue until grape harvest and the grape harvest will continue until planting, and you will eat all the food you want and live in safety in your land.

⁶ I will grant peace in the land, and you will lie down and no one will make you afraid. I will remove savage beasts from the land, and the sword will not pass through your country.

⁷ You will pursue your enemies, and they will fall by the sword before you.

⁸ Five of you will chase a hundred, and a hundred of you will chase ten thousand, and your enemies will fall by the sword before you.

⁹ I will look on you with favor and make you fruitful and increase your numbers, and I will keep my covenant with you.

¹⁰ You will still be eating last year's harvest when you will have to move it out to make room for the new.

¹¹ I will put my dwelling place among you, and I will not abhor you.

[12] I will walk among you and be your God, and you will be my people.

[13] I am the LORD your God, who brought you out of Egypt so that you would no longer be slaves to the Egyptians; I broke the bars of your yoke and enabled you to walk with heads held high.

Leviticus 26:3-13 NIV

If the Eternal be pleased with us, he will bring us to this land and give it to us, a land abounding in milk and honey.

Numbers 14:8 Moffatt

[13] And He will love you and bless you and multiply you; He will also bless the fruit of your womb and the fruit of your land, your grain and your new wine and your oil, the increase of your cattle and the offspring of your flock, in the land of which He swore to your fathers to give you.

[14] You shall be blessed above all peoples; there shall not be a male or female barren among you or among your livestock.

Deuteronomy 7:13,14 NKJV

[6] Observe the commands of the LORD your God, walking in his ways and revering him.

[7] For the LORD your God is bringing you into a good land—a land with streams and pools of water, with springs flowing in the valleys and hills; [8] a land with wheat and barley, vines and fig trees, pomegranates, olive oil and honey; [9] a land where bread will not be scarce and you will lack nothing; a land where the rocks are iron and you can dig copper out of the hills. [10] When you have eaten and are satisfied, praise the LORD your God for the good land he has given you.

Deuteronomy 8:6-10 NIV

And there you shall eat before the LORD your God, and you shall rejoice, you and your households, in all that you undertake, in which the LORD your God has blessed you.

Deuteronomy 12:7 RSV

[1] If you fully obey all of these commandments of the Lord your God, the laws I am declaring to you today, God will transform you into the greatest nation in the world.

[2-6] These are the blessings that will come upon you: Blessings in the city, blessings in the field; many children, ample crops, large flocks and herds; blessings of fruit and bread; blessings when you come in, blessings when you go out.

[7] The Lord will defeat your enemies before you; they will march out together against you but scatter before you in seven directions!

[8] The Lord will bless you with good crops and healthy cattle, and prosper everything you do when you arrive in the land the Lord your God is giving you.

[9] He will change you into a holy people dedicated to himself; this he has promised to do if you will only obey him and walk in his ways.

[10] All the nations in the world shall see that you belong to the Lord, and they will stand in awe.

[11] The Lord will give you an abundance of good things in the land, just as he promised: many children, many cattle, and abundant crops.

[12] He will open to you his wonderful treasury of rain in the heavens, to give you fine crops every season. He will bless everything you do; and you shall lend to many nations, but shall not borrow from them.

[13] If you will only listen and obey the commandments of the Lord your God that I am giving you today, he will make you the head and not the tail, and you shall always have the upper hand.

¹⁴ But each of these blessings depends on your not turning aside in any way from the laws I have given you; and you must never worship other gods.

Deuteronomy 28:1-14 TLB

Then the Lord your God will prosper you abundantly in all the work of your hand, in the offspring of your body and in the offspring of your cattle and in the produce of your ground, for the Lord will again rejoice over you for good, just as He rejoiced over your fathers....

Deuteronomy 30:9 NAS

And they rose early in the morning and went out into the Wilderness of Tekoa; and as they went out, Jehoshaphat stood and said, "Hear me, O Judah and you inhabitants of Jerusalem: Believe in the LORD your God, and you shall be established; believe His prophets, and you shall prosper."

2 Chronicles 20:20 NKJV

If they will hear him and submit, they spend a life of prosperous days and pleasant years.

Job 36:11 Moffatt

¹ Oh, the joys of those who do not follow evil men's advice, who do not hang around with sinners, scoffing at the things of God:

[2] But they delight in doing everything God wants them to, and day and night are always meditating on his laws and thinking about ways to follow him more closely.

[3] They are like trees along a river bank bearing luscious fruit each season without fail. Their leaves shall never wither, and all they do shall prosper.

Psalm 1:1-3 TLB

The young lions do lack and suffer hunger; but they who seek the Lord shall not be in want of any good thing.

Psalm 34:10 NAS

[25] I have been young and now I am old. And in all my years I have never seen the Lord forsake a man who loves him; nor have I seen the children of the godly go hungry.

[26] Instead, the godly are able to be generous with their gifts and loans to others, and their children are a blessing.

Psalm 37:25,26 TLB

Your flock found a dwelling place in it; You, O God, in Your goodness did provide for the poor and needy.

Psalm 68:10 AMP

¹ Praise the Lord! For all who fear God and trust in him are blessed beyond expression. Yes, happy is the man who delights in doing his commands.
² His children shall be honored everywhere, for good men's sons have a special heritage.
³ He himself shall be wealthy, and his good deeds will never be forgotten.
⁴ When darkness overtakes him, light will come bursting in. He is kind and merciful—
⁵ and all goes well for the generous man who conducts his business fairly.

Psalm 112:1-5 TLB

In the house of the [uncompromisingly] righteous is great [priceless] treasure, but with the income of the wicked is trouble and vexation.

Proverbs 15:6 AMP

True humility and respect for the Lord lead a man to riches, honor, and long life.

Proverbs 22:4 TLB

Every man also to whom God has given wealth and possessions and power to enjoy them, and to accept his lot and find enjoyment in his toil—this is the gift of God.

Ecclesiastes 5:19 RSV

If you will only let me help you, if you will only obey, then I will make you rich!

Isaiah 1:19 TLB

Thus says the LORD, your Redeemer, the Holy One of Israel: "I am the LORD your God, who teaches you to profit, who leads you in the way you should go."

Isaiah 48:17 RSV

22 No longer will they build houses and others live in them, or plant and others eat. For as the days of a tree, so will be the days of my people; my chosen ones will long enjoy the works of their hands.
23 They will not toil in vain or bear children doomed to misfortune; for they will be a people blessed by the LORD, they and their descendants with them.
24 Before they call I will answer; while they are still speaking I will hear.

Isaiah 65:22-24 NIV

7 But blessed is the man who trusts in the Lord and has made the Lord his hope and confidence.
8 He is like a tree planted along a riverbank, with its roots reaching deep into the water—a tree not bothered by the heat nor worried by the long

months of drought. Its leaves stay green, and it goes right on producing all its luscious fruit.

Jeremiah 17:7,8 TLB

²¹ Fear not, O land; be glad and rejoice, for the LORD has done marvelous things!
²² Do not be afraid, you beasts of the field; for the open pastures are springing up, and the tree bears its fruit; the fig tree and the vine yield their strength.
²³ Be glad then, you children of Zion, and rejoice in the LORD your God; for He has given you the former rain faithfully, and He will cause the rain to come down for you—the former rain, and the latter rain in the first month.
²⁴ The threshing floors shall be full of wheat, and the vats shall overflow with new wine and oil.
²⁵ So I will restore to you the years that the swarming locust has eaten, the crawling locust, the consuming locust, and the chewing locust, my great army which I sent among you.
²⁶ You shall eat in plenty and be satisfied, and praise the name of the LORD your God, who has dealt wondrously with you; and My people shall never be put to shame.

Joel 2:21-26 NKJV

¹⁰ Bring all the tithes into the storehouse so that there will be food enough in my Temple; if you do, I will open up the windows of heaven for you and pour out a blessing so great you won't have room enough to take it in! Try it! Let me prove it to you!

¹¹ Your crops will be large, for I will guard them from insects and plagues. Your grapes won't shrivel away before they ripen, says the Lord of Hosts.

¹² And all nations will call you blessed, for you will be a land sparkling with happiness. These are the promises of the Lord of Hosts.

Malachi 3:10-12 TLB

...give, and gifts shall be bestowed on you. Full measure, pressed, shaken down, and running over, shall they pour into your laps: for with the same measure that you use they shall measure to you in return.

Luke 6:38 Weymouth

For you know the grace of our Lord Jesus Christ, that though He was rich, yet for your sakes He became poor, that you through His poverty might become rich.

2 Corinthians 8:9 NKJV

⁶ But remember this—if you give little, you will get little. A farmer who plants just a few seeds will get only a small crop, but if he plants much, he will reap much.

⁷ Every one must make up his own mind as to how much he should give. Don't force anyone to give more than he really wants to, for cheerful givers are the ones God prizes.

⁸ God is able to make it up to you by giving you everything you need and more, so that there will not only be enough for your own needs, but plenty left over to give joyfully to others.

⁹ It is as the Scriptures say: "The godly man gives generously to the poor. His good deeds will be an honor to him forever."

¹⁰ For God, who gives seed to the farmer to plant, and later on, good crops to harvest and eat, will give you more and more seed to plant and will make it grow so that you can give away more and more fruit from your harvest.

¹¹ Yes, God will give you much so that you can give away much, and when we take your gifts to those who need them they will break out into thanksgiving and praise to God for your help.

¹² So, two good things happen as a result of your gifts—those in need are helped, and they overflow with thanks to God.

2 Corinthians 9:6-12 TLB

So then those who are of faith are blessed with Abraham, the believer.

Galatians 3:9 NAS

And my God will liberally supply (fill to the full) your every need according to His riches in glory in Christ Jesus.

Philippians 4:19 AMP

Beloved, I pray that you may prosper in all things and be in health, just as your soul prospers.

3 John 2 NKJV

Prayer for Prosperity

Father, in the name of Your Son, Jesus, I confess Your Word over my finances this day. As I do this, I say it with my mouth and believe it in my heart and know that Your Word will not return to You void, but will accomplish what it says it will do.

Therefore, I believe in the name of Jesus that all my needs are met, according to Philippians 4:19. I believe that because I have given tithes and offerings to further Your cause, Father, gifts will be given to me, good measure, pressed down, shaken together, and running over will they pour into my bosom. For with the measure I deal out, it will be measured back to me.

Father, You have delivered me out of the authority of darkness into the Kingdom of Your dear Son. Father, I have taken my place as Your child. I thank

You that You have assumed Your place as my Father and have made Your home with me. You are taking care of me and even now are enabling me to walk in love and in wisdom, and to walk in the fullness of fellowship with Your Son.

Satan, I bind you from my finances, according to Matthew 18:18, and loose you from your assignment against me, in the name of Jesus.

Father, I thank You that Your ministering spirits are now free to minister for me and bring in the necessary finances.

Father, I confess You are a very present help in trouble, and You are more than enough. I confess, God, You are able to make all grace—every favor and earthly blessing—come to me in abundance, so that I am always, and in all circumstances furnished in abundance for every good work and charitable donation.

Scripture References

Isaiah 55:11	*2 Corinthians 6:16,18*
Philippians 4:19	*Matthew 18:18*
Luke 6:38	*Hebrews 1:14*
Mark 10:29,30	*2 Corinthians 9:8*
Colossians 1:13	*Psalm 46:1*

[1] pp. 1133-1135.

[2] London: Rivington's Press, 1864 A.D., out of print.

PROTECTION—SAFETY

I can say with Joshua, in all the promises the Lord has made, He has never failed in one, but He has been with me in every trial and given grace and glory. He has conquered all my enemies and glorified His name again and again. What He has done in the past He will do in the future.

—Maria Woodworth-Etter

Greek and Hebrew Word Studies

OLD TESTAMENT—*SHAMAR*
   The Lord shall *preserve (shamar)* thee from all evil: he shall *preserve (shamar)* thy soul.

Psalm 121:7

NEW TESTAMENT—*KAKOO*
   For I am with thee, and no man shall set on thee to *hurt (kakoo)* thee...

Acts 18:10

The "strong tower" is not a geographical place; it is the name of the Lord, the name of Jesus. When fear or terror tries to come against us, when all kinds of insecurity try to come and steal our peace and our security, when Satan rumbles and enemies try to come and destroy us, we must use the name of Jesus. We must say, "God, the name of Jesus is my strong tower; I run into it." Use the name of Jesus against fear. Fear is an enemy. The name of the Lord is a strong tower for us to run into.

—Happy Caldwell
The Word Bible[1]

Protection—*Shamar*

The Lord shall *preserve (shamar)* thee from all evil: he shall *preserve (shamar)* thy soul.

Psalm 121:7

The Old Testament is an unparalleled account of the Lord's ongoing protection, preservation, safekeeping, and guardianship. He demonstrated it repeatedly in regards to the earth; the animal species; the written records of His dealings; the human race, in general; and, most specifically and dramatically, the nation of Israel.

Several dynamic Hebrew words convey the concept of protection, preservation, or keeping safely. We will examine a few such words in this study.

First, there is *shamar* (pronounced "shaw-mar'"), #8104 in *Strong's*, which means to keep, guard, watch, preserve, protect, and carefully observe. This verb occurs more than 470 times in the Old Testament. In more than half these references, the *King James Version* translates it *keep*.

There are more than 25 English words used to translate *shamar* in all its other occurrences. The most frequent of these is *observe* (45 references) and *preserve* (19 references). *Shamar* is the verb used in the commands to *keep* the Sabbath, the charge of the tabernacle, the statutes of the Lord, and the words of the Law. In other words, these things were to be kept, guarded, watched, preserved, cared for and protected. (See Deuteronomy 5:12, 6:2, 17:9, Numbers 18:4.)

The participle form of *shamar* means "one who guards and keeps, guardian, watchman." In three wonderful verses, God is called the *shamer*—the one who guards. First, Psalm 121:4 is phrased literally as, "The one who is guarding Israel neither slumbers nor sleeps." Secondly, in Psalm 97:10, this word is used of God in a beautiful manner saying He is guarding the

THE SPIRIT-FILLED BELIEVER'S TOPICAL BIBLE

souls of His saints. Finally, in Nehemiah 1:5, God is
said to "keep," or "be the Guardian," of His covenant
and mercy for all who love Him.

Several other Hebrew words strongly portray the
concept of protection. One such verb is *ganan* ("gaw-
nan'"), #1598 in *Strong's,* which occurs eight times in
the Old Testament, and is translated *defend* each time.

The literal meaning of this verb *ganan* is to put a
hedge about or to put a shield about. In fact, the
following Hebrew words are derived from *ganan: gan,*
#1588 in *Strong's,* meaning "enclosed garden"; *magan*
("maw-gan'"), #4042 in *Strong's,* meaning to shield;
and *meginnah* ("meg-innaw'"), #4043 in *Strong's,*
meaning "shield" or "buckler." The sense of shelter-
ing, covering, shielding, and protecting is unmistakable in these words.

A good example of *ganan* is found in Second Kings
19:34: **"I will *defend* this city, to save it, for mine
own sake, and for my servant David's sake."**
(Compare its similar use in Isaiah 31:5.)

There are other verbs which mean to cover protect-
ingly, such as *cakak* ("saw-kak'"), #5526 in *Strong's,*
fitly illustrated by Psalm 5:11: **"Let all those that put
their trust in thee rejoice: let them ever shout for
joy, because thou defendest them** (literally, covering

them over, protecting them): **let them also that love thy name be joyful in thee."**

The verb *natzar* ("naw-tsar'"), #5341 in *Strong's*,— to keep, to preserve—found about 60 times in the Old Testament, is a most beautiful word. Deuteronomy 32:10 describes how God, finding Jacob in a desert land, led him, instructed him, and "kept" him as the apple of His eye. In Isaiah 26:3, we see how God's steadfast followers are "kept" in perfect peace.

In Isaiah 27:3 *natzar* occurs twice, describing the manner in which God will keep His people. He calls them His vineyard and says, **"I the Lord do keep it; I will water it every moment: lest any hurt it, I will keep it night and day."** This shows a continual and complete protection.

Many other examples of this verb could be cited. See Psalm 32:7, Exodus 34:7, and Isaiah 49:8. In this last reference, God the Father pledges to the Messiah: **"I will preserve thee, and give thee for a covenant of the people...."**

This should greatly encourage us, for it was God Who preserved the Child Jesus from a maniacal, bloodthirsty tyrant. He kept Him safe through continual satanic opposition, human onslaught, religious trickery of all types, and angry crowds attempting to stone Him, arrest Him, embarrass Him, and discourage Him. But the Messiah was kept through all of this by God's power—and so shall we be!

A final note about the word *natzar:* it is the root of the word *Nazareth.* The mysterious sentence in Matthew 2:23 states that the prophets said, **"He shall be called a Nazarene."** This has puzzled scholars for centuries. However, in Hebrew it becomes beautifully clear. "He shall be called *ha-notzri,*" which can be translated, the Nazarethite. But it also means the Guardian, Keeper, Protector. Jesus is the Guardian of His people, and He gives perfect protection to those who trust Him.

The last Hebrew word we will mention relating to protection is *betach* (beh'-takh), #983 in *Strong's,* which means safety, security, fearlessness, quietness, assurance, trust, confidence, peacefulness. It occurs in such verses as Psalm 4:8, Isaiah 32:17, Hosea 2:18, and Zechariah 14:11.

An excellent example of *betach* is found in Deuteronomy 33:12: **"...The beloved of the Lord shall dwell in safety by him; and the Lord shall cover him all the day long...."**

In conclusion, the Hebrew Bible displays continual examples of the safety, protection, and preservation which God delights in providing for His people. He preserves us now and forever. May God be praised!

The Greek Words for *Hurt* in the *King James Version*

Hubris

Hubris ("hoo'-bris") is #5196 in *Strong's*. It is used three times to describe reproach and injury; overbearing insolence; insulting, disgracing and dishonoring violence; serious injury done to a person; and losses at sea.

An example of *hubris* is found twice in Acts 27:10. Speaking a warning, Paul says, **"...I perceive that this voyage will be with** *hurt (hubris)* **and much damage...."** In Acts 27:21 Paul says, **"...ye should have hearkened unto me, and not have loosed from Crete, and to have gained this** *harm (hubris)* **and loss."**

Adikeo

Adikeo ("ad-ee-key'-o"), #91 in *Strong's,* is used 27 times. It is a word that describes wronging, insulting, to do ill or treat ill a person or thing, to violate a privilege, to commit the highest injustice against anyone.

All believers are promised protection against *adikeo* by Jesus. He says, **"Behold, I give unto you** *power* (*exousia*)... **over all the** *power* (*dunamis*) **of the enemy: and nothing shall by any means** *hurt* (*adikeo*) **you"** (Luke 10:19).

Blapto

Blapto ("blap'-to"), #984 in *Strong's,* is used two times. It is a word describing anything that would slow down, hinder your progress, retard your running, impede, obstruct, or stop you in any way.

A good promise to help us spread the gospel without the Enemy trying to *blapto* our travel is found in Mark 16:18: **"They shall take up serpents; and if they drink any deadly thing, it shall not** *hurt* (*blapto*) **them...."** The Lord is telling us to get on with His work. The Enemy cannot disable us or *slow us down* (*blapto*) because we have a job to do. God will help us pass all of Satan's obstacle courses.

Blaberos

Blaberos ("blab-er-os'"), #983 in *Strong's,* is used only one time: First Timothy 6:9. It describes **"foolish and** *hurtful* (*blaberos*) **lusts"** that come upon men driven by greed.

Blaberos is any action that will produce pernicious disadvantaging, damaging, injurious, and hurtful results.

Greed will certainly prove hurtful *(blaberos)* to anyone afflicted by it.

Kakoo

Kakoo ("kak-o'-o"), #2559 in *Strong's*, is used six times and means to hurt or injure. One example of the use of *kakoo* can be found in Acts 18:10: **"...no man shall set on thee to *hurt (kakoo)* thee."**

Kakoo has a wide range of definitions. If you make lists of Bible definitions for your own word studies, you can list *kakoo* as to injure, exasperate, harm, do evil to, cause damage, handle badly, persecute, disaffect, mistreat, maltreat, oppress, vex, destroy; poison the minds of people against you; to degrade, distress, afflict, paralyze, spoil, or ruin you.

First Peter 3:13 assures us that where there is zeal for what is right, no true *harm (kakoo)* can come to us.

Synopsis

All the verses about safety and protection are there for us to read, acknowledge, confess, claim, and appropriate for our personal walk with the Lord.

They are not a license for us to do foolish things (like walk through Central Park at 2:00 A.M. when you should be in bed asleep!). They are there to let us know we do not have to live in the fear and dread of evil calamity coming our way.

We know that those living in rebellion have nothing going for them. We know sinners are in for tough times. But *their* fears do not have to be *our* fears; *their* calamities do not have to be *our* calamities.

Be not afraid of sudden fear, neither of the desolation of the wicked, when it cometh.

For the Lord shall be thy confidence, and shall keep thy foot from being taken.

Proverbs 3:25

We are not better than anyone else. God loves all equally. However, we are better protected than anyone who functions in this world without making the Lord and His promises their refuge and place of safety.

We should be totally dependent upon the Lord for the safety and protection He gives us daily. His promises are our support system, and we should claim them every day of our lives! Again, look at First Peter 3:13. It says, **"And who is he that will harm you, if ye be followers of that which is good?"**

The old song says it best: "If Jesus goes with me, I'll go *anywhere!*"[2]

He is our Great Protection!

Scriptures

Afterwards Jehovah spoke to Abram in a vision, and this is what he told him: "Don't be fearful, Abram, for I will defend you. And I will give you great blessings."

Genesis 15:1 TLB

29 Then I said to you, "Do not be in dread or afraid of them.

30 "The LORD your God who goes before you will himself fight for you, just as he did for you in Egypt before your eyes,

31 and in the wilderness, where you have seen how the LORD your God bore you, as a man bears his son, in all the way that you went until you came to this place."

Deuteronomy 1:29-31 RSV

27 The eternal God is your dwelling place, and underneath are the everlasting arms. And he thrust out the enemy before you, and said, Destroy.

28 So Israel dwelt in safety, the fountain of Jacob alone, in a land of grain and wine; yea, his heavens drop down dew.

[29] Happy are you, O Israel! Who is like you, a people saved by the LORD, the shield of your help, and the sword of your triumph! Your enemies shall come fawning to you; and you shall tread upon their high places.

Deuteronomy 33:27-29 RSV

[2] He said: "The LORD is my rock, my fortress and my deliverer;
[3] my God is my rock, in whom I take refuge, my shield and the horn of my salvation. He is my stronghold, my refuge and my savior—from violent men you save me.
[4] "I call to the LORD, who is worthy of praise, and I am saved from my enemies."

2 Samuel 22:2-4 NIV

[15] When the prophet's servant got up early the next morning and went outside, there were troops, horses, and chariots everywhere. "Alas, my master, what shall we do now?" he cried out to Elisha.
[16] "Don't be afraid!" Elisha told him. "For our army is bigger than theirs!"

2 Kings 6:15,16 TLB

[3] But You, O LORD, are a shield for me, my glory and the One who lifts up my head.

⁴ I cried to the LORD with my voice, and He heard me from His holy hill. Selah.

⁵ I lay down and slept; I awoke, for the LORD sustained me.

⁶ I will not be afraid of ten thousands of people who have set themselves against me all around.

⁷ Arise, O LORD; save me, O my God! For You have struck all my enemies on the cheekbone; you have broken the teeth of the ungodly.

Psalm 3:3-7 NKJV

In peace I will both lie down and sleep, for You, Lord, alone make me dwell in safety and confident trust.

Psalm 4:8 AMP

The LORD is a stronghold for the oppressed, a stronghold in times of trouble.

Psalm 9:9 RSV

²⁷ You save the humble but bring low those whose eyes are haughty.

²⁸ You, O LORD, keep my lamp burning; my God turns my darkness into light.

²⁹ With your help I can advance against a troop; with my God I can scale a wall.

[30] As for God, his way is perfect; the word of the LORD is flawless. He is a shield for all who take refuge in him.

[31] For who is God besides the LORD? And who is the Rock except our God?

[32] It is God who arms me with strength and makes my way perfect.

[33] He makes my feet like the feet of a deer; he enables me to stand on the heights.

[34] He trains my hands for battle; my arms can bend a bow of bronze.

[35] You give me your shield of victory, and your right hand sustains me; you stoop down to make me great.

[36] You broaden the path beneath me, so that my ankles do not turn.

Psalm 18:27-36 NIV

[1] Because the Lord is my Shepherd, I have everything I need!

[2,3] He lets me rest in the meadow grass and leads me beside the quiet streams. He restores my failing health. He helps me do what honors him the most.

[4] Even when walking through the dark valley of death I will not be afraid, for you are close beside me, guarding, guiding all the way.

⁵ You provide delicious food for me in the presence of my enemies. You have welcomed me as your guest; blessings overflow!

⁶ Your goodness and unfailing kindness shall be with me all of my life, and afterwards I will live with you forever in your home.

Psalm 23:1-6 TLB

¹ The LORD is my light and my salvation—whom shall I fear? The LORD is the stronghold of my life—of whom shall I be afraid?

² When evil men advance against me to devour my flesh, when my enemies and my foes attack me, they will stumble and fall.

³ Though an army besiege me, my heart will not fear; though war break out against me, even then will I be confident.

⁴ One thing I ask of the LORD, this is what I seek: that I may dwell in the house of the LORD all the days of my life, to gaze upon the beauty of the LORD and to seek him in his temple.

⁵ For in the day of trouble he will keep me safe in his dwelling; he will hide me in the shelter of his tabernacle and set me high upon a rock.

Psalm 27:1-5 NIV

⁶ This poor man cried out, and the LORD heard him, and saved him out of all his troubles.

⁷ The angel of the LORD encamps all around those who fear Him, and delivers them.

Psalm 34:6,7 NKJV

²³ The steps of a man are from the LORD, and he establishes him in whose way he delights;
²⁴ though he fall, he shall not be cast headlong, for the LORD is the stay of his hand.

Psalm 37:23,24 RSV

⁷ The LORD Almighty is with us; the God of Jacob is our fortress. Selah.
⁸ Come and see the works of the LORD, the desolations he has brought on the earth.
⁹ He makes wars cease to the ends of the earth; he breaks the bow and shatters the spear, he burns the shields with fire.
¹⁰ "Be still, and know that I am God; I will be exalted among the nations, I will be exalted in the earth."
¹¹ The LORD Almighty is with us; the God of Jacob is our fortress. Selah.

Psalm 46:7-11 NIV

Give your burdens to the Lord. He will carry them. He will not permit the godly to slip or fall.

Psalm 55:22 TLB

³ When I am afraid, I will trust in you.

⁴ In God, whose word I praise, in God I trust; I will not be afraid. What can mortal man do to me?

Psalm 56:3 NIV

⁹ Look upon our shield, O God; look with favor on your anointed one.

¹⁰ Better is one day in your courts than a thousand elsewhere; I would rather be a doorkeeper in the house of my God than dwell in the tents of the wicked.

¹¹ For the LORD God is a sun and shield; the LORD bestows favor and honor; no good thing does he withhold from those whose walk is blameless.

Psalm 84:9-11 NIV

¹ We live within the shadow of the Almighty, sheltered by the God who is above all gods.

² This I declare, that he alone is my refuge, my place of safety; he is my God, and I am trusting him.

³ For he rescues you from every trap and protects you from the fatal plague.

⁴ He will shield you with his wings! They will shelter you. His faithful promises are your armor.

⁵ Now you don't need to be afraid of the dark any more, nor fear the dangers of the day;

⁶ nor dread the plagues of darkness, nor disasters in the morning.

⁷Though a thousand fall at my side, though ten thousand are dying around me, the evil will not touch me.

⁸I will see how the wicked are punished but I will not share it.

⁹For Jehovah is my refuge! I choose the God above all gods to shelter me.

¹⁰How then can evil overtake me or any plague come near?

¹¹For he orders his angels to protect you wherever you go.

¹²They will steady you with their hands to keep you from stumbling against the rocks on the trail.

¹³You can safely meet a lion or step on poisonous snakes, yes, even trample them beneath your feet!

¹⁴For the Lord says, "Because he loves me, I will rescue him; I will make him great because he trusts in my name.

¹⁵"When he calls on me I will answer; I will be with him in trouble, and rescue him and honor him.

¹⁶I will satisfy him with a full life and give him my salvation."

Psalm 91:1-16 TLB

⁵In my anguish I cried to the LORD, and he answered by setting me free.

⁶ The LORD is with me; I will not be afraid. What can man do to me?

⁷ The LORD is with me; he is my helper. I will look in triumph on my enemies.

⁸ It is better to take refuge in the LORD than to trust in man.

⁹ It is better to take refuge in the LORD than to trust in princes.

¹⁰ All the nations surrounded me, but in the name of the LORD I cut them off.

¹¹ They surrounded me on every side, but in the name of the LORD I cut them off.

¹² They swarmed around me like bees, but they died out as quickly as burning thorns; in the name of the LORD I cut them off.

¹³ I was pushed back and about to fall, but the LORD helped me.

¹⁴ The LORD is my strength and my song; he has become my salvation.

¹⁵ Shouts of joy and victory resound in the tents of the righteous: "The LORD's right hand has done mighty things!

¹⁶ "The LORD's right hand is lifted high; the LORD's right hand has done mighty things!"

Psalm 118:5-16 NIV

[2] My help comes from the LORD, the Maker of heaven and earth.

[3] He will not let your foot slip—he who watches over you will not slumber;

[4] indeed, he who watches over Israel will neither slumber nor sleep.

[5] The LORD watches over you—the LORD is your shade at your right hand;

[6] the sun will not harm you by day, nor the moon by night.

[7] The LORD will keep you from all harm—he will watch over your life;

[8] the LORD will watch over your coming and going both now and forevermore.

Psalm 121:2-8 NIV

[19] He will fulfill the desire of those who fear Him; he also will hear their cry and save them.
[20] The LORD preserves all who love Him, but all the wicked He will destroy.

Psalm 145:19,20 NKJV

But whoso hearkens to me [Wisdom], shall dwell securely and in confident trust, and shall be quiet without fear or dread of evil.

Proverbs 1:33 AMP

²¹ Have two goals: wisdom—that is, knowing and doing right—and common sense. Don't let them slip away,

²² for they fill you with living energy, and are a feather in your cap.

²³ They keep you safe from defeat and disaster and from stumbling off the trail.

²⁴⁻²⁶ With them on guard you can sleep without fear; you need not be afraid of disaster or the plots of wicked men, for the Lord is with you; he protects you.

²⁷,²⁸ Don't withhold repayment of your debts. Don't say "some other time," if you can pay now.

²⁹ Don't plot against your neighbor; he is trusting you.

Proverbs 3:21-29 TLB

The name of the Lord is a strong tower; the righteous runs into it and is safe.

Proverbs 18:10 NAS

¹⁰ Behold, the Lord GOD shall come with a strong hand, and His arm shall rule for Him; behold, His reward is with Him, and His work before Him.

¹¹ He will feed His flock like a shepherd; he will gather the lambs with His arm, and carry them

in His bosom, and gently lead those who are with young.

Isaiah 40:10,11 NKJV

[1] But now, this is what the LORD says—he who created you, O Jacob, he who formed you, O Israel: "Fear not, for I have redeemed you; I have called you by name; you are mine.
[2] "When you pass through the waters, I will be with you; and when you pass through the rivers, they will not sweep over you. When you walk through the fire, you will not be burned; the flames will not set you ablaze."

Isaiah 43:1,2 NIV

"No weapon forged against you will prevail, and you will refute every tongue that accuses you. This is the heritage of the servants of the LORD, and this is their vindication from me," declares the LORD.

Isaiah 54:17 NIV

[16] Above all, take faith as your shield, to enable you to quench all the fire-tipped darts flung by the evil one,
[17] put on salvation as your helmet, and take the Spirit as your sword (that is, the Word of God).

Ephesians 6:16,17 Moffatt

Prayer for
Hedge of Protection

Father, in the name of Jesus, we lift up _____ to You and pray a hedge of protection around him/her. We thank You, Father, that You are a wall of fire round about _____ and that you set Your angels round about him/her.

We thank You, Father, that _____ dwells in the secret place of the Most High and abides under the shadow of the Almighty. We say of You, Lord, You are his/her refuge and fortress, in You will he/she trust. You cover _____ with Your feathers, and under Your wings shall he/she trust. _____ shall not be afraid of the terror by night or the fiery dart that flies by day. Only with his/her eyes will _____ behold and see the reward of the wicked.

Because _____ has made You, Lord, his/her refuge and fortress, no evil shall befall him/her—no accident will overtake him/her—neither shall any plague or calamity come near him/her. For you give Your angels charge over _____, to keep him/her in all Your ways.

Father, because You have set your love upon _____, therefore will You deliver him/her. _____ shall call upon You, and You will answer him/her. You will be with him/her in trouble, and will satisfy _____ with long life and show him/her Your salvation. Not a hair of his/her head shall perish.

Scripture References

Zechariah 2:5   Psalm 91:8-11

Psalm 34:7   Psalm 91:14-16

Psalm 91:1,2   Luke 21:18

Psalm 91:4,5

---

[1] p. 1211.

[2] C. Austin Miles, "If Jesus Goes With Me," *Redemption Hymnal* (London: Elim Publishing House), p. 465.

PART III

"In-Christ" Realities

WHO YOU ARE IN CHRIST

In Revelation 12:11, the Word says the saints overcame the accuser by the blood of Jesus and the *word of their testimony*. That is true not only for end-time martyrs, but it is true for born-again children of God living everyday lives in any generation.

However, you cannot have a "testimony" unless you know the "rights" of a born-again child of God, the things you inherited in, through, and with Jesus because of His work on the cross.

You must know who you are *in Christ*. Then, to bring those things *that you already possess* into manifestation, you must begin to believe them. To be born again, you must have faith that God exists and that He sent His only begotten Son to die for your sins because He loves you. (John 3:16.) Salvation is a free gift for you, purchased by Jesus, but unless you believe that and *confess* it with your mouth, salvation is not manifested in you. It is not a reality for you. (Rom. 10:9,10.)

First, find out from the Word what things are already yours because of Jesus. Then, if you want to build faith for those things to become real in your life, begin to speak out the good things God has done and the things you are believing for Him to do.

Faith without works is dead. (James 2:17.) Faith grows stronger by telling testimonies of Jesus, by continual confession of what you believe God will do.

A weak confession is one full of doubt and is a confession of defeat. As long as people talk defeat, they will not overcome. They have the blood of the Lamb, but the true "word of their testimony" is missing.

What *is* the confession, the word of our testimony, to which we are told in Hebrews 4:14 to "hold fast"? It is the positive things God has done *in* our lives and *for* us. The word of our testimony is speaking out who we are *in Christ*, not just what He has done for us in our natural lives.

From God's viewpoint, everything His Word says you are, or that you have, is true. Those things already are done! The Bible is a legal document setting forth the story, the description, and the provisions of the

Blood Covenant, of which the Abrahamic Covenant (the old covenant) was a forerunner.

There are more than 100 expressions such as "in Christ," "in Him," "in Whom," "through Whom," and so forth in the New Testament that set forth all the things Jesus provided for us by His blood on the cross of Calvary.

Start with Second Corinthians 5:17:

> **Therefore if any man be in Christ he is a new creature: old things are passed away; behold, all things are become new.**

Then go on and memorize as many others as you can, confessing them often, so that the "word of your testimony" is in line with the Word of God. Finding out the reality of who you are *in Christ* will change your life!

"In-Christ" Scriptures

By Me [Jesus]: John 6:57; 14:6.

In Me: John 6:56; 14:20; 15:4,5,7; 16:33.

In My Love: John 15:9.

By Him: 1 Cor. 1:5; 8:6; Col. 1:16,17,20; 3:17; Heb. 7:25; 13:15; 1 Pet. 1:21.

In Him: John 1:4; 3:15,16; Acts 17:28; 2 Cor. 1:20; 5:21; Eph. 1:4,10; Phil. 3:9; Col. 2:6,7,9,10; 1 John 2:6,8,27,28; 3:3,5,6,24; 4:13; 5:14,20.

Of Him: 1 John 1:5; 5:15.

Through Him: Rom. 5:9; 8:37; 1 John 4:9.

With Him: Rom. 6:4,6,8; 8:32; 2 Cor. 13:4; Col. 2:12,13; 3:4; 2 Tim. 2:11,12.

By Himself: Heb. 1:3.

By Christ: Rom. 3:22; 5:15,17; 1 Cor. 1:4; 2 Cor. 5:18; Gal. 2:16; Eph. 1:5; Phil. 1:11, 4:19; 1 Pet. 2:5; 5:10.

In Christ: Rom. 3:24; 8:1,2; 12:5; 1 Cor. 1:2,30; 15:22; 2 Cor. 1:21, 2:14, 3:14; 5:17,19; Gal. 2:4; 3:26,28; 5:6; 6:15; Eph. 1:3,10; 2:6,10,13; 3:6; Phil. 3:14; Col. 1:28; 1 Thess. 4:16; 5:18; 1 Tim. 1:14; 2 Tim. 1:9,13; 2:1,10; 3:15; Philem. 6.

Of Christ: 2 Cor. 2:15; Phil. 3:12; Col. 2:17.

Through Christ: Rom. 5:1,11; 6:11,23; 1 Cor. 15:57; Gal. 3:14; 4:7; Eph. 2:7; Phil. 4:7,13; Heb. 13:21.

With Christ: Rom. 6:8; Gal. 2:20; Eph. 2:5; Col. 2:20; 3:1,3.

By Whom: Rom. 5:2,11; Gal. 6:14.

From Whom: Eph. 4:16.

In Whom: Eph. 1:7,11,13; 2:21,22; 3:12; Col. 1:14; 2:3,11; 1 Pet. 1:8.

By His Blood: Heb. 9:12; 10:19.

In My Name: Matt. 18:20; Mark 16:17; John 14:13,14; 16:23,24.

In the Beloved: Eph. 1:6.

In the Lord: Eph. 5:8; 6:10.

Part III is from *The Word Study Bible.*

PART IV

READING THE BIBLE IN ONE YEAR

A Complete Program

January

22   Gen. 43-44; Ps. 22; Mark 2
23   Gen. 45-46; Ps. 23; Mark 3
24   Gen. 47-48; Ps. 24; Mark 4
25   Gen. 49-50; Ps. 25; Mark 5
26   Ex. 1-2; Ps. 26; Mark 6
27   Ex. 3-4; Ps. 27; Mark 7
28   Ex. 5-6; Ps. 28; Mark 8
29   Ex. 7-8; Ps. 29; Mark 9
30   Ex. 9-10; Ps. 30; Mark 10
31   Ex. 11-12; Ps. 31; Mark 11

February

1   Ex. 13-14; Ps. 32; Mark 12
2   Ex. 15-16; Ps. 33; Mark 13
3   Ex. 17-18; Ps. 34; Mark 14
4   Ex. 19-20; Ps. 35; Mark 15
5   Ex. 21-22; Ps. 36; Mark 16
6   Ex. 23-24; Ps. 37; Luke 1
7   Ex. 25-26; Ps. 38; Luke 2
8   Ex. 27-28; Ps. 39; Luke 3
9   Ex. 29-30; Ps. 40; Luke 4
10   Ex. 31-32; Ps. 41; Luke 5
11   Ex. 33-34; Ps. 42; Luke 6
12   Ex. 35-36; Ps. 43; Luke 7
13   Ex. 37-38; Ps. 44; Luke 8
14   Ex. 39-40; Ps. 45; Luke 9
15   Lev. 1-2; Ps. 46; Luke 10

16 Lev. 3-4; Ps. 47; Luke 11
17 Lev. 5-6; Ps. 48; Luke 12
18 Lev. 7-8; Ps. 49; Luke 13
19 Lev. 9-10; Ps. 50; Luke 14
20 Lev. 11-12; Ps. 51; Luke 15
21 Lev. 13; Ps. 52; Luke 16
22 Lev. 14; Ps. 53; Luke 17
23 Lev. 15-16; Ps. 54; Luke 18
24 Lev. 17-18; Ps. 55; Luke 19
25 Lev. 19-20; Ps. 56; Luke 20
26 Lev. 21-22; Ps. 57; Luke 21
27 Lev. 23-24; Ps. 58; Luke 22
28 Lev. 25
29 Ps. 59; Luke 23

March

1 Lev. 26-27; Ps. 60; Luke 24
2 Num. 1-2; Ps. 61; John 1
3 Num. 3-4; Ps. 62; John 2-3
4 Num. 5-6; Ps. 63; John 4
5 Num. 7; Ps. 64; John 5
6 Num. 8-9; Ps. 65; John 6
7 Num. 10-11; Ps. 66; John 7
8 Num. 12-13; Ps. 67; John 8
9 Num. 14-15; Ps. 68; John 9
10 Num. 16; Ps. 69; John 10
11 Num. 17-18; Ps. 70; John 11

12 Num. 19-20; Ps. 71; John 12
13 Num. 21-22; Ps. 72; John 13
14 Num. 23-24; Ps. 73; John 14-15
15 Num. 25-26; Ps. 74; John 16
16 Num. 27-28; Ps. 75; John 17
17 Num. 29-30; Ps. 76; John 18
18 Num. 31-32; Ps. 77; John 19
19 Num. 33-34; Ps. 78; John 20
20 Num. 35-36; Ps. 79; John 21
21 Deut. 1-2; Ps. 80; Acts 1
22 Deut. 3-4; Ps. 81; Acts 2
23 Deut. 5-6; Ps. 82; Acts 3-4
24 Deut. 7-8; Ps. 83; Acts 5-6
25 Deut. 9-10; Ps. 84; Acts 7
26 Deut. 11-12; Ps. 85; Acts 8
27 Deut. 13-14; Ps. 86; Acts 9
28 Deut. 15-16; Ps. 87; Acts 10
29 Deut. 17-18; Ps. 88; Acts 11-12
30 Deut. 19-20; Ps. 89; Acts 13
31 Deut. 21-22; Ps. 90; Acts 14

April

1 Deut. 23-24; Ps. 91; Acts 15
2 Deut. 25-27; Ps. 92; Acts 16
3 Deut. 28-29; Ps. 93; Acts 17
4 Deut. 30-31; Ps. 94; Acts 18
5 Deut. 32; Ps. 95; Acts 19

6   Deut. 33-34; Ps. 96; Acts 20

7   Josh. 1-2; Ps. 97; Acts 21

8   Josh. 3-4; Ps. 98; Acts 22

9   Josh. 5-6; Ps. 99; Acts 23

10   Josh. 7-8; Ps. 100; Acts 24-25

11   Josh. 9-10; Ps. 101; Acts 26

12   Josh. 11-12; Ps. 102; Acts 27

13   Josh. 13-14; Ps. 103; Acts 28

14   Josh. 15-16; Ps. 104; Rom. 1-2

15   Josh. 17-18; Ps. 105; Rom. 3-4

16   Josh. 19-20; Ps. 106; Rom. 5-6

17   Josh. 21-22; Ps. 107; Rom. 7-8

18   Josh. 23-24; Ps. 108; Rom. 9-10

19   Judg. 1-2; Ps. 109; Rom. 11-12

20   Judg. 3-4; Ps. 110; Rom. 13-14

21   Judg. 5-6; Ps. 111; Rom. 15-16

22   Judg. 7-8; Ps. 112; 1 Cor. 1-2

23   Judg. 9; Ps. 113; 1 Cor. 3-4

24   Judg. 10-11; Ps. 114; 1 Cor. 5-6

25   Judg. 12-13; Ps. 115; 1 Cor. 7

26   Judg. 14-15; Ps. 116; 1 Cor. 8-9

27   Judg. 16-17; Ps. 117; 1 Cor. 10

28   Judg. 18-19; Ps. 118; 1 Cor. 11

29   Judg. 20-21; Ps. 119:1-88; 1 Cor. 12

30   Ruth 1-4; Ps. 119:89-176; 1 Cor. 13

May

1	1 Sam. 1-2; Ps. 120; 1 Cor. 14
2	1 Sam. 3-4; Ps. 121; 1 Cor. 15
3	1 Sam. 5-6; Ps. 122; 1 Cor. 16
4	1 Sam. 7-8; Ps. 123; 2 Cor. 1
5	1 Sam. 9-10; Ps. 124; 2 Cor. 2-3
6	1 Sam. 11-12; Ps. 125; 2 Cor. 4-5
7	1 Sam. 13-14; Ps. 126; 2 Cor. 6-7
8	1 Sam. 15-16; Ps. 127; 2 Cor. 8
9	1 Sam. 17; Ps. 128; 2 Cor. 9-10
10	1 Sam. 18-19; Ps. 129; 2 Cor. 11
11	1 Sam. 20-21; Ps. 130; 2 Cor. 12
12	1 Sam. 22-23; Ps. 131; 2 Cor. 13
13	1 Sam. 24-25; Ps. 132; Gal. 1-2
14	1 Sam. 26-27; Ps. 133; Gal. 3-4
15	1 Sam. 28-29; Ps. 134; Gal. 5-6
16	1 Sam. 30-31; Ps. 135; Eph. 1-2
17	2 Sam. 1-2; Ps. 136; Eph. 3-4
18	2 Sam. 3-4; Ps. 137; Eph. 5-6
19	2 Sam. 5-6; Ps. 138; Phil. 1-2
20	2 Sam. 7-8; Ps. 139; Phil. 3-4
21	2 Sam. 9-10; Ps. 140; Col. 1-2
22	2 Sam. 11-12; Ps. 141; Col. 3-4
23	2 Sam. 13-14; Ps. 142; 1 Thess. 1-2
24	2 Sam. 15-16; Ps. 143; 1 Thess. 3-4
25	2 Sam. 17-18; Ps. 144; 1 Thess. 5

26 2 Sam. 19; Ps. 145; 2 Thess. 1-3
27 2 Sam. 20-21; Ps. 146; 1 Tim. 1-2
28 2 Sam. 22; Ps. 147; 1 Tim. 3-4
29 2 Sam. 23-24; Ps. 148; 1 Tim. 5-6
30 1 Kings 1; Ps. 149; 2 Tim. 1-2
31 1 Kings 2-3; Ps. 150; 2 Tim. 3-4

June

1   1 Kings 4-5; Prov. 1; Titus 1-3
2   1 Kings 6-7; Prov. 2; Philem.
3   1 Kings 8; Prov. 3; Heb. 1-2
4   1 Kings 9-10; Prov. 4; Heb. 3-4
5   1 Kings 11-12; Prov. 5; Heb. 5-6
6   1 Kings 13-14; Prov. 6; Heb. 7-8
7   1 Kings 15-16; Prov. 7; Heb. 9-10
8   1 Kings 17-18; Prov. 8; Heb. 11
9   1 Kings 19-20; Prov. 9; Heb. 12
10 1 Kings 21-22; Prov. 10; Heb. 13
11 2 Kings 1-2; Prov. 11; James 1
12 2 Kings 3-4; Prov. 12; James 2-3
13 2 Kings 5-6; Prov. 13; James 4-5
14 2 Kings 7-8; Prov. 14; 1 Pet. 1
15 2 Kings 9-10; Prov. 15; 1 Pet. 2-3
16 2 Kings 11-12; Prov. 16; 1 Pet. 4-5
17 2 Kings 13-14; Prov. 17; 2 Pet. 1-3
18 2 Kings 15-16; Prov. 18; 1 John 1-2
19 2 Kings 17; Prov. 19; 1 John 3-4

20 2 Kings 18-19; Prov. 20; 1 John 5

21 2 Kings 20-21; Prov. 21; 2 John

22 2 Kings 22-23; Prov. 22; 3 John

23 2 Kings 24-25; Prov. 23; Jude

24 1 Chron. 1; Prov. 24; Rev. 1-2

25 1 Chron. 2-3; Prov. 25; Rev. 3-5

26 1 Chron. 4-5; Prov. 26; Rev. 6-7

27 1 Chron. 6-7; Prov. 27; Rev. 8-10

28 1 Chron. 8-9; Prov. 28; Rev. 11-12

29 1 Chron. 10-11; Prov. 29; Rev. 13-14

30 1 Chron. 12-13; Prov. 30; Rev. 15-17

July

1 1 Chron. 14-15; Prov. 31; Rev. 18-19

2 1 Chron. 16-17; Ps. 1; Rev. 20-22

3 1 Chron. 18-19; Ps. 2; Matt. 1-2

4 1 Chron. 20-21; Ps. 3; Matt. 3-4

5 1 Chron. 22-23; Ps. 4; Matt. 5

6 1 Chron. 24-25; Ps. 5; Matt. 6-7

7 1 Chron. 26-27; Ps. 6; Matt. 8-9

8 1 Chron. 28-29; Ps. 7; Matt. 10-11

9 2 Chron. 1-2; Ps. 8; Matt. 12

10 2 Chron. 3-4; Ps. 9; Matt. 13

11 2 Chron. 5-6; Ps. 10; Matt. 14-15

12 2 Chron. 7-8; Ps. 11; Matt. 16-17

13 2 Chron. 9-10; Ps. 12; Matt. 18

14 2 Chron. 11-12; Ps. 13; Matt. 19-20

15 2 Chron. 13-14; Ps. 14; Matt. 21
16 2 Chron. 15-16; Ps. 15; Matt. 22
17 2 Chron. 17-18; Ps. 16; Matt. 23
18 2 Chron. 19-20; Ps. 17; Matt. 24
19 2 Chron. 21-22; Ps. 18; Matt. 25
20 2 Chron. 23-24; Ps. 19; Matt. 26
21 2 Chron. 25-26; Ps. 20; Matt. 27
22 2 Chron. 27-28; Ps. 21; Matt. 28
23 2 Chron. 29-30; Ps. 22; Mark 1
24 2 Chron. 31-32; Ps. 23; Mark 2
25 2 Chron. 33-34; Ps. 24; Mark 3
26 2 Chron. 35-36; Ps. 25; Mark 4
27 Ezra 1-2; Ps. 26; Mark 5
28 Ezra 3-4; Ps. 27; Mark 6
29 Ezra 5-6; Ps. 28; Mark 7
30 Ezra 7-8; Ps. 29; Mark 8
31 Ezra 9-10; Ps. 30; Mark 9

August

1 Neh. 1-2; Ps. 31; Mark 10
2 Neh. 3-4; Ps. 32; Mark 11
3 Neh. 5-6; Ps. 33; Mark 12
4 Neh. 7; Ps. 34; Mark 13
5 Neh. 8-9; Ps. 35; Mark 14
6 Neh. 10-11; Ps. 36; Mark 15
7 Neh. 12-13; Ps. 37; Mark 16
8 Esth. 1-2; Ps. 38; Luke 1

9   Esth. 3-4; Ps. 39; Luke 2

10 Esth. 5-6; Ps. 40; Luke 3

11 Esth. 7-8; Ps. 41; Luke 4

12 Esth. 9-10; Ps. 42; Luke 5

13 Job 1-2; Ps. 43; Luke 6

14 Job 3-4; Ps. 44; Luke 7

15 Job 5-6; Ps. 45; Luke 8

16 Job 7-8; Ps. 46; Luke 9

17 Job 9-10; Ps. 47; Luke 10

18 Job 11-12; Ps. 48; Luke 11

19 Job 13-14; Ps. 49; Luke 12

20 Job 15-16; Ps. 50; Luke 13

21 Job 17-18; Ps. 51; Luke 14

22 Job 19-20; Ps. 52; Luke 15

23 Job 21-22; Ps. 53; Luke 16

24 Job 23-25; Ps. 54; Luke 17

25 Job 26-28; Ps. 55; Luke 18

26 Job 29-30; Ps. 56; Luke 19

27 Job 31-32; Ps. 57; Luke 20

28 Job 33-34; Ps. 58; Luke 21

29 Job 35-36; Ps. 59; Luke 22

30 Job 37-38; Ps. 60; Luke 23

31 Job 39-40; Ps. 61; Luke 24

September

1   Job 41-42; Ps. 62; John 1

2   Eccl. 1-2; Ps. 63; John 2-3

3   Eccl. 3-4; Ps. 64; John 4
4   Eccl. 5-6; Ps. 65; John 5
5   Eccl. 7-8; Ps. 66; John 6
6   Eccl. 9-10; Ps. 67; John 7
7   Eccl. 11-12; Ps. 68; John 8
8   Song of Sol. 1-2; Ps. 69; John 9
9   Song of Sol. 3-4; Ps. 70; John 10
10   Song of Sol. 5-6; Ps. 71; John 11
11   Song of Sol. 7-8; Ps. 72; John 12
12   Isaiah 1-2; Ps. 73; John 13
13   Isaiah 3-5; Ps. 74; John 14-15
14   Isaiah 6-8; Ps. 75; John 16
15   Isaiah 9-10; Ps. 76; John 17
16   Isaiah 11-13; Ps. 77; John 18
17   Isaiah 14-15; Ps. 78; John 19
18   Isaiah 16-17; Ps. 79; John 20
19   Isaiah 18-19; Ps. 80; John 21
20   Isaiah 20-22; Ps. 81; Acts 1
21   Isaiah 23-24; Ps. 82; Acts 2
22   Isaiah 25-26; Ps. 83; Acts 3-4
23   Isaiah 27-28; Ps. 84; Acts 5-6
24   Isaiah 29-30; Ps. 85; Acts 7
25   Isaiah 31-32; Ps. 86; Acts 8
26   Isaiah 33-34; Ps. 87; Acts 9
27   Isaiah 35-36; Ps. 88; Acts 10
28   Isaiah 37-38; Ps. 89; Acts 11-12
29   Isaiah 39-40; Ps. 90; Acts 13

30   Isaiah 41-42; Ps. 91; Acts 14

October

1   Isaiah 43-44; Ps. 92; Acts 15

2   Isaiah 45-46; Ps. 93; Acts 16

3   Isaiah 47-48; Ps. 94; Acts 17

4   Isaiah 49-50; Ps. 95; Acts 18

5   Isaiah 51-52; Ps. 96; Acts 19

6   Isaiah 53-54; Ps. 97; Acts 20

7   Isaiah 55-56; Ps. 98; Acts 21

8   Isaiah 57-58; Ps. 99; Acts 22

9   Isaiah 59-60; Ps. 100; Acts 23

10   Isaiah 61-62; Ps. 101; Acts 24-25

11   Isaiah 63-64; Ps. 102; Acts 26

12   Isaiah 65-66; Ps. 103; Acts 27

13   Jer. 1-2; Ps. 104; Acts 28

14   Jer. 3-4; Ps. 105; Rom. 1-2

15   Jer. 5-6; Ps. 106; Rom. 3-4

16   Jer. 7-8; Ps. 107; Rom. 5-6

17   Jer. 9-10; Ps. 108; Rom. 7-8

18   Jer. 11-12; Ps. 109; Rom. 9-10

19   Jer. 13-14; Ps. 110; Rom. 11-12

20   Jer. 15-16; Ps. 111; Rom. 13-14

21   Jer. 17-18; Ps. 112; Rom. 15-16

22   Jer. 19-20; Ps. 113; 1 Cor. 1-2

23   Jer. 21-22; Ps. 114; 1 Cor. 3-4

24   Jer. 23-24; Ps. 115; 1 Cor. 5-6

25 Jer. 25-26; Ps. 116; 1 Cor. 7

26 Jer. 27-28; Ps. 117; 1 Cor. 8-9

27 Jer. 29-30; Ps. 118; 1 Cor. 10

28 Jer. 31-32; Ps. 119:1-64; 1 Cor. 11

29 Jer. 33-34; Ps. 119:65-120; 1 Cor. 12

30 Jer. 35-36; Ps. 119:121-176; 1 Cor. 13

31 Jer. 37-38; Ps. 120; 1 Cor. 14

November

1 Jer. 39-40; Ps. 121; 1 Cor. 15

2 Jer. 41-42; Ps. 122; 1 Cor. 16

3 Jer. 43-44; Ps. 123; 2 Cor. 1

4 Jer. 45-46; Ps. 124; 2 Cor. 2-3

5 Jer. 47-48; Ps. 125; 2 Cor. 4-5

6 Jer. 49-50; Ps. 126; 2 Cor. 6-7

7 Jer. 51-52; Ps. 127; 2 Cor. 8

8 Lam. 1-2; Ps. 128; 2 Cor. 9-10

9 Lam. 3; Ps. 129; 2 Cor. 11

10 Lam. 4-5; Ps. 130; 2 Cor. 12

11 Ezek. 1-2; Ps. 131; 2 Cor. 13

12 Ezek. 3-4; Ps. 132; Gal. 1-2

13 Ezek. 5-6; Ps. 133; Gal. 3-4

14 Ezek. 7-8; Ps. 134; Gal. 5-6

15 Ezek. 9-10; Ps. 135; Eph. 1-2

16 Ezek. 11-12; Ps. 136; Eph. 3-4

17 Ezek. 13-14; Ps. 137; Eph. 5-6

18 Ezek. 15-16; Ps. 138; Phil. 1-2

19 Ezek. 17-18; Ps. 139; Phil. 3-4
20 Ezek. 19-20; Ps. 140; Col. 1-2
21 Ezek. 21-22; Ps. 141; Col. 3-4
22 Ezek. 23-24; Ps. 142; 1 Thess. 1-2
23 Ezek. 25-26; Ps. 143; 1 Thess. 3-4
24 Ezek. 27-28; Ps. 144; 1 Thess. 5
25 Ezek. 29-30; Ps. 145; 2 Thess. 1-3
26 Ezek. 31-32; Ps. 146; 1 Tim. 1-2
27 Ezek. 33-34; Ps. 147; 1 Tim. 3-4
28 Ezek. 35-36; Ps. 148; 1 Tim. 5-6
29 Ezek. 37-38; Ps. 149; 2 Tim. 1-2
30 Ezek. 39-40; Ps. 150; 2 Tim. 3-4

December

1 Ezek. 41-42; Prov. 1; Titus 1-3
2 Ezek. 43-44; Prov. 2; Philem.
3 Ezek. 45-46; Prov. 3; Heb. 1-2
4 Ezek. 47-48; Prov. 4; Heb. 3-4
5 Dan. 1-2; Prov. 5; Heb. 5-6
6 Dan. 3-4; Prov. 6; Heb. 7-8
7 Dan. 5-6; Prov. 7; Heb. 9-10
8 Dan. 7-8; Prov. 8; Heb. 11
9 Dan. 9-10; Prov. 9; Heb. 12
10 Dan. 11-12; Prov. 10; Heb. 13
11 Hos. 1-3; Prov. 11; James 1-3
12 Hos. 4-6; Prov. 12; James 4-5
13 Hos. 7-8; Prov. 13; 1 Pet. 1

14 Hos. 9-11; Prov. 14; 1 Pet. 2-3
15 Hos. 12-14; Prov. 15; 1 Pet. 4-5
16 Joel 1-3; Prov. 16; 2 Pet. 1-3
17 Amos 1-3; Prov. 17; 1 John 1-2
18 Amos 4-6; Prov. 18; 1 John 3-4
19 Amos 7-9; Prov. 19; 1 John 5
20 Obad.; Prov. 20; 2 John
21 Jonah 1-4; Prov. 21; 3 John
22 Mic. 1-4; Prov. 22; Jude
23 Mic. 5-7; Prov. 23; Rev. 1-2
24 Nah. 1-3; Prov. 24; Rev. 3-5
25 Hab. 1-3; Prov. 24; Rev. 6-7
26 Zeph. 1-3; Prov. 26; Rev. 8-10
27 Hag. 1-2; Prov. 27; Rev. 11-12
28 Zech. 1-4; Prov. 28; Rev. 13-14
29 Zech. 5-9; Prov. 29; Rev. 15-17
30 Zech. 10-14; Prov. 30; Rev. 18-19
31 Mal. 1-4; Prov. 31; Rev. 20-22

REFERENCES

The Amplified Bible (AMP). Old Testament section copyright © 1965, 1987 by Zondervan Corporation. New Testament section copyright © 1958, 1987 by the Lockman Foundation. Used by permission.

The Bible. A New Translation (Moffatt). Copyright © 1950, 1952, 1953, 1954 by James A. R. Moffatt. Harper & Row Publishers, Inc., New York, New York.

The Epistles of Paul by W. J. Conybeare. Baker Book House, Grand Rapids, Michigan.

The Holy Bible: New International Version® (NIV). Copyright © 1973, 1978, 1984 by International Bible Society. Used by permission of Zondervan Publishing House. All rights reserved.

The Living Bible (TLB). Copyright © 1971. Used by permission of Tyndale House Publishers, Inc., Wheaton, Illinois 60189. All rights reserved.

New American Standard Bible (NAS). Copyright © by the Lockman Foundation 1960, 1962, 1963, 1968, 1971, 1972, 1973, 1975, 1977. Used by permission.

The New English Bible (NEB). Copyright © the Delegates of the Oxford University Press and the Syndics of the Cambridge University Press 1961, 1970. Reprinted by permission.

The New King James Version (NKJV). Copyright © 1979, 1980, 1982 by Thomas Nelson, Inc., Publishers.

The New Testament: An American Translation by Edgar J. Goodspeed, copyright © 1923, 1948 by the University of Chicago, The University of Chicago Press.

Additional copies of

The Spirit-Filled Believer's
Topical Bible

are available from your local bookstore

or from:

Harrison House
P. O. Box 35035
Tulsa, Oklahoma 74135

The Harrison House Vision

Proclaiming the truth and the power

Of the Gospel of Jesus Christ

With excellence;

Challenging Christians to

Live victoriously,

Grow spiritually,

Know God intimately.